CONTEMPORARY CHINA INSTITUTE PUBLICATIONS

CENTRE AND PROVINCE IN THE PEOPLE'S REPUBLIC OF CHINA
SICHUAN AND GUIZHOU, 1955–1965

Publications in the series include:

Mao Tse-tung in the Scales of History (1977) *edited by Dick Wilson*

Shanghai: Revolution and Development in an Asian Metropolis (1980) *edited by Christopher Howe*

Mao Zedong and the Political Economy of the Border Region. A Translation of Mao's *Economic and Financial Problems* (1980) *edited and translated by Andrew Watson*

The Politics of Marriage in Contemporary China (1981) *by Elisabeth Croll*

Food Grain Procurement and Consumption in China (1984) *by Kenneth R. Walker*

Class and Social Stratification in Post-Revolution China (1984) *edited by James L. Watson*

Warlord Soldiers. Chinese Common Soldiers, 1911–1937 (1985) *by Diana Lary*

CENTRE AND PROVINCE
IN THE
PEOPLE'S REPUBLIC OF CHINA

SICHUAN AND GUIZHOU, 1955–1965

DAVID S. G. GOODMAN

Department of Politics
University of Newcastle upon Tyne

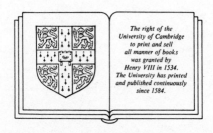

The right of the
University of Cambridge
to print and sell
all manner of books
was granted by
Henry VIII in 1534.
The University has printed
and published continuously
since 1584.

CAMBRIDGE UNIVERSITY PRESS

Cambridge
London   New York   New Rochelle
Melbourne   Sydney

Published by the Press Syndicate of the University of Cambridge
The Pitt Building, Trumpington Street, Cambridge CB2 1RP
32 East 57th Street, New York, NY 10022, USA
10 Stamford Road, Oakleigh, Melbourne 3166, Australia

First published 1986

Printed in Great Britain at the University Press, Cambridge

British Library cataloguing in publication data
Goodman, David S. G.
Centre and province in the People's Republic of China:
Sichuan and Guizhou, 1955–1965.
(Contemporary China Institute publications)
1. China, southwest – Politics and government
I. Title   II. Series
951′.305   DS793.S6465

Library of Congress cataloguing-in-publication data
Goodman, David S. G.
Centre and province in the People's Republic of China.
(Contemporary China Institute publications)
Bibliography.
Includes index.
1. Szechwan Province (China) – Politics and government.
2. Kweichow Province (China) – Politics and government.
I. Title.   II. Series.
DS93.S8G66 1986   951′.34   86–8245

ISBN 0 521 32530 7

CONTENTS

LIST OF TABLES

PREFACE

Every visitor to the People's Republic of China, however short their stay, must at some time have been informed quite solemnly by their Chinese hosts that 'China is a large country.' Dutifully received, the visitor then, of necessity, proceeds to obtain only the merest glimpse of the size and variety indicated by that truism. Space is clearly of more than passing significance to decision-makers in the People's Republic. Social scientists in general, and political scientists in particular, who ignore its implications, do so to their loss. It is not just that distance and diversity create administrative problems of policy implementation for the Chinese Communist Party. Decision-making itself is subject to both ideological imperatives and environmental constraints, though the balance between the two may have varied considerably since 1949. The consequences of China's size and diversity, and their particular relevance in the decision-making process, have been matters of debate within the leadership. Moreover, China's size and diversity have over time created sub-systems within the political whole. For the most part China's provinces are not simply recent administrative divisions created at the convenience of the Chinese Communist Party. In general, their existence has resulted from traditional patterns of human interaction. Each is thus not only to some extent a microcosm of the national whole, but also of interest in its own right.

The theme of this book is the interaction between centre and province in the decision-making process. However, its primary concern is with the mechanisms of that process rather than with the results. Thus, it is not so much concerned to describe or evaluate how the Chinese Communist Party has attempted to solve problems such as those of integration and the spatial distribution of resources (though these are obviously worthy of attention) as with the nature of provincial involvement in decision-making. Interest in that particular focus was first stimulated by the enigma of a People's

vii

Preface

Republic that was described as both a Communist Party state in which decision-making was highly centralized, and as a large and diffuse political system in which the possibility of provincial bases of power (suggested not least by the role of provincial leaders in national politics) could not be excluded. Years later that contradiction is more apparent than real, but the spatial dimensions of decision-making remain as fascinating as ever.

Research for this study was undertaken whilst a Research Fellow at the Contemporary China Institute, School of Oriental and African Studies, London University (1971–4); and a Lecturer in the Department of Politics, University of Newcastle upon Tyne (after 1974). I would like to thank both institutions for their invaluable financial support and general assistance over the years. Moreover, since the bulk of research has been library-based, my thanks must also go to the library of the School of Oriental and African Studies; the East Asian Library, Hoover Institution, Stanford University; the library of the Center for Chinese Studies, University of California, Berkeley; the library of the Harvard–Yenching Institute, Harvard University; and the Beijing University library; and their librarians, for their help and assistance.

More personally, I would like to acknowledge all those who in their various ways have given advice and encouragement, suggested material, and provided stimulating conversation. In particular, thanks are due to John Gardner, who from the first encouraged my interest in the provincial politics of the People's Republic of China: Professor Christopher Howe, who first suggested Sichuan as a subject for detailed investigation; Mrs Rule, who as always provided invaluable secretarial assistance; Professor Stuart Schram; Dorothy J. Solinger; Edwin A. Winckler; and Rod Wye.

University of Newcastle upon Tyne   DAVID S. G. GOODMAN

ABBREVIATIONS

APC	Agricultural Producers Co-operative
CB	*Current Background*
CCP	Chinese Communist Party
CDRB	*Chengdu ribao* (Chengdu Daily)
CQ	*The China Quarterly*
CQRB	*Chongqing ribao* (Chongqing Daily)
GLF	Great Leap Forward
GMRB	*Guangming ribao* (Guangming Daily)
GPCR	Great Proletarian Cultural Revolution
GZRB	*Guizhou ribao* (Guizhou Daily)
HSC	Higher Stage Collective
HQ	*Hongqi* (Red Flag)
JPRS	Joint Publications Research Services
LSC	Lower Stage Co-operative
NCNA	New China News Agency
NPC	National People's Congress
PC	Rural People's Commune
PLA	People's Liberation Army
PPC	Provincial People's Congress
PRC	People's Republic of China
RMRB	*Renmin ribao* (People's Daily)
SCMP	*Survey of the China Mainland Press*
SCRB	*Sichuan ribao* (Sichuan Daily)
SW5	*Selected Works of Mao Tsetung*, vol. 5
YCL	Young Communist League (of the CCP)
XHBYK	*Xinhua banyuekan* (New China semi-monthly)
XHRB	*Xinhua ribao* (New China Daily, Chongqing)
XQRB	*Xinqian ribao* (New Guizhou Daily)
ZNHYS	*Zhongguo nongye hezuohua yundong shiliao* (Historical Materials on China's Agricultural Co-operativization Movement)

GLOSSARY OF CHINESE
TERMS USED IN THE TEXT

da minzhu	extended/external democracy; see p. 46
da she	large cooperative (1956); see p. 73
	large collective (1958); see p. 144
jin	unit of weight: equivalent to ½ kilogramme or approx. 1.1 pounds
li	unit of distance: equivalent to ½ kilometre or approx. just under ⅓ mile
lian she	federated cooperative; see p. 144
mou	unit of area: roughly equivalent to 0.17 of an acre or 0.07 of an hectare
shengchan dui	production brigade/team; see p. 137
si qing	the 'four clean-ups': part of the Socialist Education Movement; see p. 126
tu si	system of appointing native hereditary headmen during Yuan, Ming and Qing dynasties; see p. 35
xiafang	the downward transfer of personnel
xian (hsien)	county
xiang (hsiang)	village
xiao minzhu	limited/internal democracy; see p. 46
yuan	unit of currency: a PRC dollar
yi da, er gong	'large and communal': a description of People's Communes when first established during 1958; see p. 139
zhou	prefecture: a district between county and province in the administrative hierarchy
zhuan qu	special district: an area between county and province in the administrative hierarchy

Glossary of Chinese terms

Note on transliteration

In general the *pinyin* system of romanization for Chinese has been employed throughout this book. However, where reference is made to publications and quotations which use other methods of transliteration, then the original has been cited.

INTRODUCTION

Decision-making in the PRC (People's Republic of China) and indeed generally in communist party states, is all too easily characterized as a narrowly centralized activity. Politics is often portrayed as being the preserve not simply of the CCP (Chinese Communist Party) nor even of its cadres, but largely of the political bureau and its immediate environment located in Peking. However, there is a spatial dimension to politics in most political systems, even where there is a high degree of centralization, and the PRC is no exception. The re-establishment of the province as the immediate sub-central level of the political system in 1954 added a provincial dimension to national politics which persists to this day. What follows examines the evolution of the provincial role in national politics during the decade before the Cultural Revolution, and in particular its consequences and causes.

The PRC, like many other political systems – notably not only communist party states but also those with government-led economic modernization or which cover an extensive territory – has been, and continues to be, faced by the problem of reconciling competing needs for control and flexibility in its economic development and political management. Overcentralization may cause inefficiencies, not the least of which is the formulation of national policies and plans, both economic and political, which may be inapplicable or inappropriate to all local conditions. On the other hand, too much local autonomy may threaten the unity of the political system, or more likely, mean a constant drift away from the aims and goal-oriented policies of central government.

The leaders of the CCP attempted to resolve those problems during 1957–8 by decentralizing certain previously centralized economic management functions.[1] That decision was taken as a result of a relatively widespread debate during the previous two years about the strategy and tactics to be adopted generally for the

I

development of a specifically Chinese 'road to socialism'. It was a debate which was most clearly visible at the 8th party congress of the CCP held during September 1956.[2] The debates and decisions of these years have been crucial to the emergence of post-Mao China, not least since its legitimacy is to no small extent based on the rejection of the Soviet Model, which occurred at that time. Moreover, as became clear in (and at the time of) the 'Resolution on Party History' adopted by the CCP during June 1981, the 8th party congress of the CCP is currently regarded highly in retrospect.[3] The implication is quite clearly that the form and content of the debate of the mid-fifties represents the legitimate limits for contemporary politics.

Even before 1949 the CCP had long recognized the need for local flexibility in the implementation of its policies within the areas of China it controlled. To 'do the best according to local conditions' was a significant administrative principle which emerged, at least partially, as a result of the CCP's guerrilla heritage. After 1949 that principle was retained to some extent even during the period of Soviet influence in internal developments, when centralized decision-making might be considered at its height. However, a constant theme for almost all the participants in the debates of the mid-fifties was that the Soviet Model had been too centralized and there was a need to encourage greater local flexibility and initiative.[4]

The solution eventually agreed and adopted by the CCP in 1957 was to emphasize the role of the intermediate level – that of the province[5] – within the political and administrative hierarchy. In general, that tactic is not uncommon and is intended to provide both the flexibility necessary at a level of decentralization within the political and administrative hierarchy, and yet to ensure that control is exercised in line with central government's vision (and indeed in turn to be held responsible by central government). For those reasons the chosen level of decentralization must be close enough administratively and politically to the centre to ensure efficient communication. Moreover, it must also be large enough as an administrtive unit to have at its disposal resources sufficient to allow flexible responses to both central directives and subordinate demands.[6]

However, there is a danger that such a tactic could easily prove counter-productive if the attempt to co-ordinate central control and local flexibility at an intermediate level in the political and administrative hierarchy rests on an area defined by the '*circulation*' of men,

2

goods and ideas over time.[7] In that case, the territory subordinate to the intermediate level is likely to be identifiable as a unit in non-political, as well as political, terms. Its boundaries result from the patterns of human interaction and are likely to enclose, in no small measure, a local economy, a communications network and political culture. In general terms, China's provinces are just such administrative (and otherwise functional) units.[8]

There is then the possibility of a contradiction between the imperatives of administrative efficiency on the one hand, and those of political control and direction, on the other. As has often been noted in other contexts, political institutions whose intended function is to ensure integration may also encourage conflict.[9] Indeed, it is reasonable to argue that within certain limits political conflict (or perhaps, more accurately, its mediation) is necessary to efficient integration. In any case, where the area subordinate to the intermediate level has for historical, geographical and economic reasons, its own identity – as is the case with China's provinces – then decentralization may become a risky business for central government. Local flexibility may not become a desire for total independence – that will depend on the dominant 'state idea'.[10] However, it is possible that local flexibility may become an excuse for resistance to central *diktat*, or a vehicle for the articulation of a partial local interest. The problem of reconciling competing national and local interests thus overlays the need for both central control and local flexibility.

At the same time that the CCP has demonstrated its awareness of the need for local flexibility, it has also shown itself keenly aware of the possible problems inherent in the exercise of any degree of local autonomy. It was for this reason that when decentralization was introduced during 1957–8 the role of the CCP (as a highly centralized hierarchy) at the heart of the new system of administration was emphasized. Where previosuly enterprises and units within a central ministry had operated as its branch agencies in a direct line of command, now a system of 'dual subordination' or 'dual rule' was introduced. Each unit was supervised both by its superior and in its own hierarchy and by the relevant party committee at the same level within the political system. In addition, decentralization was accompanied by a rectification campaign directed specifically at provincial leaders. It was designed to ensure their continued loyalty to the centre and the CCP (as opposed to the locality) and conformity to the CCPs new line.[11]

Behind the CCPs general concern is a more specific interpretation of Chinese conditions. The balance of power between the capital and the provinces has been a recurrent problem for Chinese politicians, administrators and historians throughout China's history. There has been a wide acceptance that the unity of the Chinese polity was inherently unstable: that both the variety of social interaction and historical experience resulted in essentially centrifugal tendencies. Possibly with the most recent evidence of the warlord era fresh in the mind, that attitude has persisted even towards the PRC since 1949. Thus, the centralized political system established immediately after 1949 and particularly the CCP's ability to permeate and control society, has been described as one of its most remarkable and significant achievements.[12]

Though the CCP may have been (and indeed continues to be) aware not only of the need for both control and flexibility, but also of the problems inherent in decentralization and localization, the consequences of the measures adopted in 1957–8 are far from clear. Commentators outside China have disagreed as to whether political power remained centralized or became provincialized. It is a debate which has been fuelled by developments within the PRC. At the start of the GPCR (Great Proletarian Cultural Revolution) during 1966–8, almost every provincial and Regional[13] leader was criticized for having been engaged in 'localism'. Often accused of having established 'independent kingdoms' in the provinces, leading cadres of the party, state administration and sometimes the PLA (People's Liberation Army) were said to have promoted a particular interest – either their own or the locality's – against the more universal policy of the CCP.

Events between the mid-1950s and the GPCR have led some to suggest that the decentralization of 1957–8 resulted in the provinces, and in some cases the Regions, becoming at least as important as the centre in the political process. Thus, Donnithorne, for example, has argued that the decentralization measures were both cause and effect of the strong centrifugal forces seen as being traditionally inherent in Chinese politics which are said to have contributed to a devolution of political power in the PRC after an initial period of intensive centralization.[14] In her opinion, decentralization during 1957–8 simply recognized and reinforced the emerging relationship between centre and province. China's traditions and political culture had led to a situation where 'highly centralized control was impossible', and

4

there was a drift of power from the centre to the provinces.[15] Moreover, the party at the centre was relatively powerless to check such a trend because: 'Once a provincial party secretary becomes de facto responsible for the government of a province, he necessarily becomes identified with the provincial administration, with its particular interests and problems.'[16] Indeed, in this context Chang has suggested that provincial leaders specifically campaigned for decentralization during the two years before its implementation.[17]

Barnett, from another perspective, has indicated that the regional party bureaux of the central committee were established during the early 1960s precisely in order to curb the increased political power of the provinces.[18] That is a view shared to some extent by Donnithorne.[19] However, the functions of the party regions operational during the early 1960s are far from clear, let alone their political significance. For example, Whitson's analysis of military politics leads him to conclude that the regions were in fact bases of power for each of the Field Armies of the PLA. These were the major army groupings which existed during the last phases of the civil war. In identifying these six large factions with their origins in the military, and their interaction, he claims that decentralization during 1957–8 supplemented their emerging powers by providing control of economic resources.[20]

Certainly, provincial leaders as a group were afforded increased status during the late 1950s. After 1954, when the province was re-established as the immediate sub-central level of the political and administrtive hierarchy, provincial leaders became increasingly involved in national politics. A dramatic example of that trend occurred at the unique second session of the 8th party congress of the CCP, held in May 1958. Twenty-five new members were appointed to the central committee and three to the politburo (full and alternate members in both cases). Of the 25 new central committee members, 16 were provincial leaders, as were two of the three additions to the politburo.

During the GPCR the differential impact – as between centre and province – of the attack on the provincial system, and in particular 'those in authority taking the capitalist road', also seems to suggest that the provinces are of more than passing significance to the political process. Although it was the position of those who 'rebelled' during 1966–8 that the whole of the political and administrative system had to be reorganized, that did not appear to result. The weight of the attack, in both an institutional and associational sense, was felt more strongly at the provincial level than at the centre. In the provinces the system of provincial party committees and people's councils was replaced completely by the 'new proletarian organ of power', the revolutionary committee, during 1967–8. Yet the departments and ministries under the State Council remained relatively inviolate. Similarly, of the 366 ministers, vice ministers and their equivalents under the State Council who were active in April 1966, 180 (49.2%) were still active by April 1968. However, only 34 (13.8%) of the 247 provincial party secretaries and 23 (8.7%) of the 266 provincial governors, vice governors, or their equivalents of April 1966 were still politically active two years later.[21]

Against that background the criticisms levelled at provincial leaders during the GPCR that they had established 'independent kingdoms' seem rather less unlikely than appears at first sight. To some extent it is thus the less remarkable that such accusations have also been used, sometimes without supporting evidence, as proof positive by those who wish to argue that political power was decentralized after 1957.[22] On the other hand, the strength of the arguments and evidence that political power was provincialized may yet be more apparent than real. Notwithstanding arguments about the senses in which political traditions manifest themselves, it would also seem reasonable to suggest that the conditions which had shaped any relationship between centre and province before 1949 might have changed dramatically after that time.

The decentralization measures of 1957–8, the increased national importance of provincial leaders, the differential impact of the GPCR on centre and province, and the accusations of 'localism' levelled at provincial leaders, all could indeed indicate provincialized political power. However, they could also be interpreted as manifestations of a political system in which power remained centralized. The decentralization measures of 1957–8 can be seen solely as a decentralization of economic management functions, with no necessary results for the distribution of political power, which is after all how they were presented at the time they were introduced. It can be argued that provincial leaders were brought increasingly into national politics for reasons of central control just as much as of provincial representation.

The differential impact of the GPCR on centre and province could be explained by Zhou Enlai's presumed concern to protect the central machinery of the state administration because it was considered more important than the provincial; or by a recognition that the operational node of centralized party control was in fact the provincial party committee, where, as a result of the 1957–8 decentralization measures and the introduction of the principle of 'dual rule' into the political and administrative hierarchy, co-ordination of activities in any given territory was maximized.[23]

Finally, there is no necessary territorial base to the accusations of 'independent kingdomism'. Many of those leading cadres attacked during the GPCR were criticized for such behaviour, regardless of whether they were provincial or local leaders in any sense. The term was in fact employed as a synonym for a generalized particularism in that context. Such particularism, if it existed outside the rhetoric of the GPCR, could be interpreted as provincialism, if only because those accused were provincial leaders. Equally, it could be seen as a form of factionalism within centralized bureaucratic politics.

THE DIMENSIONS OF PROVINCIAL POWER

The consequences of the decentralization measures of 1957–8 is an obvious place to start an examination of the balance of power between centre and province. However, the choice between a starkly centralized political system and one just as absolutely decentralized clearly involves a false dichotomy. The particularism of province and faction need not be mutually exclusive phenomena in Chinese politics. Nor for that matter do they exhaust the possible explanations of the interaction between centre and province in the Chinese decision-making process. Political power is not an undifferentiated commodity, and it is rarely as concentrated in communist party states as totalitarian models would seem to suggest. For example, there clearly are acceptable (to the centre) provincial variations in the implementation of national policy. In general, the principle of 'do the best according to local conditions' means that the centre lays down the broad outline of a policy, and the provinces adopt specific provincial measures for its implementation. Clearly, that process allows considerable potential for deviation from central policy. A province might claim to be adapting a central policy to local conditions when in fact its provincial implementation is intended to achieve some other goal. That was, of course, a frequent criticism of local leaders during the GPCR.[24] Moreover, in a situation where the

7

provincial party committee monitors its own implementation of national policy on behalf of the centre, then information is (very definitely) power. Mao Zedong at times actively encouraged local initiative. But he also recognized the potential threat to central authority (regardless of its undesirability from his viewpoint) for – in his words – 'carrying out decisions is also a form of power'.[25] The point at issue then is not whether there is a provincial contribution in national politics, but the forms it takes, and the factors which determine its dimensions.

One limiting factor is that the vision of a decentralized political system can be overstated. Whatever the validity post-1949 of the argument that there have been centrifugal forces at work throughout China's history, provincial political powers are hardly likely to be utilized in the cause of absolute autonomy within a communist party state. Indeed, Mao once again had perhaps the clearest notion of the extent (both in theory and in practice) of provincial autonomy under the PRC. In criticizing the over-centralization and bureaucratization of both the traditional Chinese imperial system of government and the Soviet Union, he said: 'Conditions are completely different now. We want the whole country to be united *and* each province to be independent; a relative unity and a relative independence.'[26] That essentially relative nature of provincial autonomy is easily ignored, especially when it is being argued that political power became decentralized in and after 1958.

Another limiting factor is that of necessity there are differences among provinces which affect their willingness and ability to comply with central directives. In terms of a province's ability to comply with central directives, it is quite clear that because of provincial circumstances not every province is required by the centre to act in the same way at the same time. Not only are provinces encouraged to 'do the best according to local conditions', but certain provinces may be exempted (at least temporarily) from implementing national policy. Thus during the early 1950s the centre did not require land reform in national minority areas. Indeed, the decentralization measures of 1957–8 fully recognized differing provincial abilities in the devolution of central powers. For example, unlike other provinces, Yunnan, Guizhou and Ningxia were not given control of their coal mines, because it was said that they were 'economically backward areas'.[27] Similarly, disregarding once again for the moment arguments about the pattern of Chinese history, there seems to be no reason to suppose

8

that each province desires the same degree of dependency on the centre. Moreover, even if the influence of political traditions were to be considered relevant after 1949 – and that would require a demonstration that the same conditions which had created those traditions in the past still applied under the PRC – that would not provide evidence to suggest that the provinces shared common traditions in relation to the centre.

There is then no need to assume either a necessary conflict (or lack of it) between centre and province, or that in the relationship between centre and province every province acts in an identical manner. On the contrary, there is more than likely to be more than one relationship between centre and province. Admittedly, there may be common characteristics of each province's relations with the centre but it is just as likely that there are important differences, and it is the determinants of these similarities and differences which need to be identified. In other words, any assessment of the relationships between centre and province, and of the dimensions of the provincial contribution in national politics must be built up, in the first instance, through a series of studies from a provincial as opposed to a national perspective. Surprisingly few accounts of Chinese politics from a provincial perspective, particularly for the period of the 1950s and early 1960s, have been published.[28]

This study examines the provinces of Sichuan and Guizhou within the Southwest Region in order to illustrate the provincial dimension of politics. The provincial perspective on Chinese politics is important not least because of what it reveals about the national decision-making process. The analysis presented here confirms a specific model of decision making in the PRC. That model is based not on consensus (whether ideologically determined or otherwise) but on coalition building.

The cleavages which divide China's decision makers are so varied and numerous that on single issues or programmatically reaching a decision (particularly a binding decision) may be difficult. The groups within the leadership which result from these cleavages may be based on policy orientation, self-interest, personal relationships, or even happenstance. Moreover, individual decision makers themselves undoubtedly act out of mixed motives. Consequently, it is frequently easier for the Chinese leadership to reach a negative decision – that is to agree what it does not want – than it is to make a positive decision. That was certainly the case during 1956–7 when the Soviet model had been rejected for China's future and an alternative 'Chinese Road to Socialism' was being sought. It would also appear to have been the case at, and after, the time of the 3rd plenum of the 11th central committee of the CCP when the politics of the Cultural Revolution were decisively rejected. Furthermore, a leadership divided many times by issues of principle, personal relationships, self-interest and power is more likely to maintain the status quo than to radically change the direction of policy. Thus, to take but one well-known example, despite all the evidence available to decision makers during the winter of 1958–9 the policy initiatives of 1958 could be diffused only gradually. As a result decisions are reached incrementally, through lobbying and by the creation of alliances amongst decision makers. Such alliances include those between provincial and central leaders. The process can be short-circuited but it requires a Mao or some similarly disproportionate influence. Even then success for an initiative is not guaranteed, for as Mao's case demonstrates, disproportionate influence creates polarization and the opposition may combine to act negatively.

Unlike other interpretations here it is suggested that national policy making in the PRC is almost always an incremental process.[29] Guidelines are drafted generally and policy then implemented on an experimental basis. Central directives frequently only specify the general aims of a campaign and leave the specific arrangements to each province. Particularly when there is no need for immediate action, provinces establish 'experimental points'. These are chosen in order to provide information about the effect of policy implementation and will be established in different areas with varying characteristics dependent on the nature of the campaign. The results of such experiments are then incorporated in a programme for the extension of the campaign. Sometimes there will be further experimentation and refinement, and cadres from the newly-targeted areas are prepared for the implementation of policy. As the campaign is widened it is usual to find some of the experimental areas adopted as 'models' for emulation (both nationally and provincially).

The choice of 'experimental points' and 'models' is clearly crucial to the emergence of policy. Different desiderata will lead to different choices. It is a process which demands manipulation. The period and mechanism of experimentation provides an access to influence not only the implementation but also the formulation of national policy.

Clearly, experimental areas could be (and are) selected in order to produce desired results consistent with previously determined policy preferences, which are then advocated and adopted nationally as 'models' in a campaign.[30] In the process initiatives are promoted and implemented experimentally by some of the decision makers in order to lobby others. To that end, alliances develop between provincial and central leaders. The former provide the opportunities for such initiatives. The latter provide the necessary clout to encourage and protect their policy preferences. In short, policy initiatives are given a trial run in order to lead and demonstrate success by example.

In a similar fashion, provincial leaders may react to central initiatives and suggestions before the formal national adoption of a policy or the pronouncement of a central directive. The decision-making process frequently starts with a policy issue being placed on the national political agenda in some way. For example, the pace and level of collectivization were highlighted during the spring of 1955; rectification was agreed to in principle without any further details as to method or timing at the 8th party congress during the autumn of 1956. Reactions in the first case culminated in the 'High Tide' of agricultural cooperativization; in the second they climaxed in the 'Hundred Flowers' of May 1957. Alternatively, national decision makers may engage in kite-flying in order to raise an issue on to the agenda. Mao's promotion of the commune during the spring of 1958 is an excellent example. In either case provincial leaders once again provide the opportunity for empirical evidence to be placed before decision makers.

The questions that are faced here relate not to whether there is a group dynamic to Chinese decision making but rather to its basis. In general, the provincial role in national politics neither results from nor is determined by provincial conditions alone. The case presented here is not that each province is an inviolable power base in Chinese politics. Political traditions, socio-economic conditions, and administrative arrangements (such as the decentralization measures of 1957–8) all significantly influence the exercise of provincial political power. However, the involvement of the provinces in national politics, and particularly the central decision-making process, results primarily from the incremental nature of that process: the specific role played by any one province from its factionalized nature.

A FRAMEWORK FOR ANALYSIS

There are essentially three strands to the argument that there was a shift in the balance of power between centre and province during the decade before the GPCR. The first is that China's political traditions, and particularly its reputed centrifugal tendencies, reasserted themselves. The second is that provincial variations in the formulation and implementation of national policy did more than simply reflect local conditions and became a vehicle for the articulation of provincial interests. The third is that the decentralization measures of 1957–8 recognized and reflected the demands for greater provincial autonomy for which provincial leaders had campaigned. In order to define the dimensions of the provincial role in national politics discussion of those three possibilities informs the structure of this book.

A significant problem in pursuing those lines of investigation is that it is easy to use concepts or a conceptual framework which do not take sufficient account of either Chinese reality or the problems of analysing Chinese politics. For example, the relative nature of provincial autonomy has already been emphasized. Again, the lack of direct access to the PRC, and all the problems inherent in considering a 'closed' political system, mean that the use of terms and perspectives related to behavioural analysis must be questionable at best. Yet, as has already been indicated, the pattern of Chinese history has been described as if it were a provincial political culture (specifically, of course, tending to independence). That may be a useful shorthand. However, the validity of such arguments rests on an examination of each province's traditions and whether the conditions which had shaped these traditions remain relevant. More problematical still is any discussion of interest in this context. The observation of competing national and local interests is difficult enough in a relatively 'open' political system. However, with respect to the PRC it is too often a perplexing activity. Nor only may there be no necessary conflict of interests, but the actors themselves may see events in a different perspective from that of the outside observer. For example, a provincial party first secretary could conceivably act in his province's long-term interests by supporting a central policy which is unfavourable to the province in the short-term. There is no independent assessment of provincial or national interests and it is the leading cadres in the formal political system at these levels alone who can be seen to articulate interests. Any discussion of interests thus becomes a circular argument.

Indeed, when scrutinized more closely the concept of province itself is extremely vague. It is in fact the provincial leadership which is under examination, and it is their behaviour (as expressed mainly through or in the provincial media) which is the focus of analysis rather than concepts of 'province' and 'interest'. Where the latter must remain hypothetical, the former is real and observable.

As several prominent social scientists have emphasized, the role of the 'political middleman' is an essential part of the relationship between centre and locality in a political system.[31] Leading provincial cadres in the PRC would appear to be 'political middlemen' par excellence. They are appointed by the centre and dependent on it for their political future. However, the provincial leader who does not also satisfy local requirements will find it difficult to implement national policy. In a very real sense they are both national and provincial politicians. They may be seen as both the representative of the province to the centre, and the agents of the centre in the province. The problem for analysis lies in distinguishing between these two roles, and trying to assess which was of greater importance.

In sum, then, a major portion of the analysis presented here considers the relative autonomy of Sichuan and Guizhou through the behaviour of their formal political leaderships. Essentially that is a two part process. The first is an examination of the behaviour of the two provinces' leaders in the formulation and implementation of policy in order to identify apparent local variations from national policy. The second is the attempt to determine whether such apparent local variations can be explained more by reference to provincial conditions or national politics.

In attempting such an examination there are several further problems of a practical and analytical nature which must be borne in mind. A first is that it should be reiterated that the PRC is not an 'open' political system. There is little direct evidence (documentary or otherwise) from the decision-making process. Of necessity almost any evidence that can be produced is circumstantial and inferential. In this particular case the source material for both Sichuan and Guizhou during the decade investigated here is far from ideal. There is an exceptionally long run (by comparison with other provinces) of the Sichuan provincial party newspaper available stretching from 1952 well into the 1960s. Unfortunately, the same is not true for

Guizhou. Almost no copies of the party newspaper are available for the period after 1961, and there is a gap during the 'High Tide' of 1955–6. However, the lack of issues of the provincial party newspaper does not mean that there is no information available. Provincial newspapers provide much specific detail about local conditions. But almost every major speech by a provincial leader at a national or provincial meeting is available for both provinces elsewhere, as well as most of the provincial plans and budgets, and reports of major provincial party and government meetings. In particular, there are transcripts and translations of national and provincial broadcasts, as well as news agency reports (Chinese and otherwise) all available outside China. Where gaps remain, there are sources from the Cultural Revolution which can be informative if used with care; and secondary source material (particularly that from China) so that analysis although difficult is not impossible. Of course a lack of documentary evidence means that it is somewhat tendentious to make negative statements about behaviour. If a less salient problem elsewhere, that is so throughout contemporary Chinese studies. In the final analysis it is the author's judgement which is on the line.

Similarly, it is somewhat unsatisfactory to treat a province's leadership as though it were an undifferentiated whole. Clearly, it is conceivable that there are differences among provincial leaders just as there are at the national level. Moreover, the equation of provincial leadership with activities within the province and as reported through (for the most part) the provincial media, may also mask political differences. None the less, that set of equations is both useful and necessary. It is a justifiable rule of thumb since divergence would either be a matter for discipline or publicity, or it would not be politically significant.

The assumption of a single perspective for each province (in the absence of evidence to the contrary) comes about because it is primarily political rhetoric which is being examined. At issue generally is not what actually happened (though that is clearly not irrelevant) but what politicians said in their statements about these events. Essentially the distinction here between self-stated perception on the one hand and performance on the other matches that between politics and economics. That is not to decry economic analysis, particularly of the relationship between centre and province. However, the relationship between economics and politics in the provincial dimension of national decision making is far from clear, as the previous discussion on 'interest' indicates. Moreover, the economic relationship between centre and province has been extensively investigated elsewhere, particularly in the works of Donnithorne, Lardy and Walker.[32] The primary focus here is provincial participation in decision making not the end result of that process. That discussion is worth emphasizing at this point because it has several consequences for the analysis which follows. Thus, it might seem strange (especially to economists) that even though there are now so much more in the way of economic data available about the years under examination than there were at the time, this study persists in referring to the contemporary record. At first sight this discordance appears particularly acute with respect to the years of the Great Leap Forward. However, in terms of the approach adopted here it is the contemporary record, as the public statements of provincial leaders, which is of greater import. The emphasis on the contemporary and the public also explains partially the reticence for referring to sources from the Cultural Revolution – particularly those alleging 'independent kingdomism' – and the limits placed on their use. Finally, the distinction between political and economic analysis is important because there are clearly are occasions when what is said on the political stage is at odds with policy implementation. The most significant example of this in the account which follows was the treatment of the '1956–1967 Outline for National Agricultural Development' (the Twelve Year Plan) between April 1956 and October 1957. The Twelve Year Plan was politically out of favour throughout that period, but none the less its implementation continued.[33] It is clearly not usual for policy to be implemented for so long in that way without political comment. However, the incremental nature of the decision making process outlined earlier entails that policy formulation and policy implementation are not perfectly synchronized.

A final set of problems concern the identification and assessment of provincial variations. Two examples of policies central to the account which follows in Part I may aid clarification both conceptually (the nature of variation) and empirically (for all provinces and not just Sichuan and Guizhou). The first is the collectivization of agriculture as a result of the 'High Tide' of 1955–6. Table 1 indicates the extent to which each province had managed to establish higher stage collectives by June 1956. Rapid collectivization had not been official policy twelve months beforehand. However, during that year lower stage cooperativization (the establishment of the 'semi-socialist' form)

The second is the attempt to bring forward the completion of the First Five Year Plan. Also as a result of the success of the 'High Tide', Mao had launched this policy initiative in late November 1955. It lasted until April 1956 along with other of Mao's initiatives of the time which were then checked.[34] Towards the end of 1955 several provinces responded to Mao's initiative by announcing they would complete the Five Year Plan (originally scheduled to end with 1957) during 1956. Though never a formal central directive, the attempt to complete the plan in four years became effective national policy on 31 December 1955 with the publication of an editorial in *People's Daily* – 'Strive for the overall fulfilment and overfulfilment of the Five Year Plan ahead of schedule.' Table 2 lists provinces according to their reaction during November 1955 to April 1956. Some provinces announced before the end of 1955 that they would complete their First Five Year Plans a year ahead of schedule, and some only after the year's end. Others did not announce an early completion but did pledge themselves to increases in production.

Acknowledgement of provincial variation in the formulation and implementation of policy depends upon both the time-scale in which they are viewed, and the level of conformity (and detail) established or required. For example, the two cases illustrated in Tables 1 and 2 provide evidence both for variation and conformity. At the most general level of analysis all provinces confirmed to national policy in that they did collectivize, and most attempted to meet the rallying call of the editorial of 31 December 1955 between that date and April 1956. However, from the point of view of examining the provincial dimension of politics it is the relative degree of non-conformity which is more interesting. Thus, in the case of collectivization it is those provinces whose percentage of peasant households in higher stage collectives by June 1956 was well below average (Table 1) which demand attention. Sichuan's performance is particularly enigmatic since a year earlier it had been a national pace-setter for higher stage collectivization. In the example of the early completion of the First Five Year Plan the most interesting cases are those provinces who were clearly in advance of national policy formulation. Of secondary interest, but more tendentiously given the nature of the evidence, are those provinces that after December 1955 did not announce they too would attempt to complete the Five Year Plan during 1956, though they may have promised increases in production.

However, the examples of agricultural collectivization and the attempt to complete the First Five Year Plan in 1956 indicate that there are two dimensions to provincial variations in the formulation and implementation of policy. There are variations amongst provinces; and there are variations from national policy. Given the nature of the decision-making process that distinction is not simply a reflection of the difference between policy formulation and policy implementation for the two clearly overlap. Consequently, not all provincial variations can be regarded as examples of purposive non-conformity, let alone provincial resistance to central authority. In particular, just as it is possible to oversimplify the concept of province in the relationship between centre and province, so too is it possible to oversimplify the concept of centre. Divisions at the centre also mean that there cannot be a simple single relationship between centre and province. Provincial leaders may appear to have resisted or complied with the centre's wishes when, in fact, they were responsive to only part of the centre.

SICHUAN AND GUIZHOU

Sichuan and Guizhou are neighbouring provinces in the southwest region. Sichuan is an obvious subject for any examination of provincial autonomy in the PRC. It is a large and wealthy province with a reputation for being remote and independent. Guizhou provides a useful yardstick and a marked contrast. Like Sichuan, Guizhou also has a reputation for being remote. However, it also has the reputation of being incredibly poor and backward. So much so, in fact, that during the Great Leap Forward the whole province was publicized as a national model of Mao's principle of the advantage to being 'poor and blank'.[35]

The contrast between Sichuan and Guizhou, and their very different patterns of interaction with national politics, is a major theme throughout this book. Sichuan is a high-profile province in national politics and its leading cadres are major political figures on the national stage. Indeed, the province's party first secretary for most of the period before the GPCR, Li Jingquan (provincial first secretary 1952–65, and regional first secretary 1960–7) became a member of the party's politburo. It is frequently a trend-setter for new policy initiatives during this period, as indeed it has been since the mid-1970s.[36] Guizhou, on the other hand, has a much lower profile in national politics and often seems isolated from mainstream developments. Far from being a trend-setter, it frequently appears a political backwater, reliant too often upon some visiting dignitary for its information about national policy changes. Their respective provincial conditions undoubtedly help shape those relationships between centre and province.

Sichuan was a well-integrated political entity long before 1949, Guizhou was not. In general, providing for the material requirements of Sichuan's population was not a daunting, or usually particularly difficult task. In Guizhou, on the other hand, such problems were too often insurmountable. Unsurprisingly, Guizhou's leaders were largely preoccupied with local problems. Moreover, the two provinces appear to have adopted different positions in contemporary political debates. The opportunities when provinces could exercise their relative autonomy – largely through either influencing the central decision-making process or by resisting central policy – were clearly restricted. None the less, on such occasions Sichuan appears to have pursued the more radical tendencies in Chinese politics, Guizhou to have been more conservative. Though there is considerable evidence that Guizhou's attitudes at those instances were shaped by local conditions, the same cannot be said of Sichuan. Sichuan's role as a radical trend-setter reflects not the province's conditions, but rather the close political relationship between its leadership and Mao Zedong, who sometimes used the province as a test-bed for his ideas and initiatives.

There are then at least two variants of the relationship between centre and province in the decision-making process which result from the contrast between Sichuan and Guizhou. The latter indicates that a poor and less integrated province will have less room for political manoeuvre in national politics, but that provincial policies will result more from provincial conditions. The second variant is of a wealthy and well-integrated province which has considerable room for political manoeuvre in national decision-making, but whose policies follow less from provincial circumstances.

As already indicated, three hypotheses about the factors influencing the role of the province in national politics have structured what follows. One is the possibility that the decentralization measures of 1957–8 had resulted in greater provincial autonomy. To examine that possibility, this examination of Sichuan and Guizhou is divided into two parts, with the decentralization measures themselves as the chronological divide. In general, it is concluded that the decentralization of 1957–8 did not result in any greater provincial autonomy for either Sichuan or Guizhou. Indeed it is argued that both had considerable relative autonomy even before 1958, and perhaps more importantly less room for manoeuvre in national politics after that time. Guizhou, in particular, was much more constrained after 1958, especially as a result of the activities of the Southwest bureau of the CCP's central committee. These activities are examined in Chapter 8, where it is also suggested that Sichuan's decreased manoeuvrability in national politics is to some extent offset by its increased influence in the Southwest region through its control of the regional bureau.

In addition, part of the hypothesis that 1957–8 marked a turning point in relations between centre and province is the possibility that provincial leaders had campaigned for decentralization during the national discussions of 1955–7 about the future shape of China's development strategy. Chapter 4 considers that possibility generally, as well as both provinces' reactions to the national debate. It concludes that there is little evidence to support such an argument, and that though neither Sichuan nor Guizhou campaigned for decentralization (indeed the former specifically requested greater central involvement in the province) Sichuan none the less supported Mao's position in that debate.

A second hypothesis about the factors influencing the role of the province in national politics is that there are provincial traditions which might be of continued relevance. Chapter 1 outlines the political traditions of Sichuan and Guizhou, and provides a survey of the conditions which determined those traditions before 1949. Though both had reputations for being remote and separate, the contrast between their traditions was considerable. Guizhou had been for the most part little more than an unintegrated – either in itself or with China – colony acting as a buffer state against Southeast Asia. In so far as it had a tradition of autonomy it was not expressed at the provincial level. However, Sichuan did have a tradition of separatism, but only when the central polity disintegrated. For the rest of the time its tradition was one of co-operation and close interaction with the rest of China.

Comparison between the traditions outlined in Chapter 1 and conditions in Sichuan and Guizhou described in later chapters covering 1955–7, 1958–61, and 1961–5 suggest that though the conditions which had encouraged Sichuan's separation no longer existed after 1949, other traditions of both provinces were still relevant. In particular, Sichuan's role as the Southwest region's political and economic centre had not been inconsiderable before 1958, however it was later deliberately enlarged. In Guizhou's case, though its leadership attempted (and with no small measure of success) to combat the problems of political control and a weak economic base between 1949 and 1957, thereafter it reverted to its traditional status as an internal colony.[37]

Finally, there is the possibility that provincial interests came to dominate the policy-making process. The exercise to identify and interpret provincial variations in the formulation and implementation of policy proceeds on a broad front in Chapter 2 (for 1955–7), Chapter 5 (1958–61), and Chapter 6 (1961–5). Detailed discussion of the provinces under the PRC starts in 1955 rather than 1954 (when the provinces were re-instated as the immediate sub-central level of administration) because it was only in 1955 that Xikang was incorporated partially into Sichuan. There have been no changes in the external provinces of Sichuan or Guizhou since 1955. It should be emphasizd that in those chapters (and indeed throughout) the intention is not to provide a comprehensive account of Sichuan and Guizhou from 1955 to 1965. On the contrary, there are two specific concerns. The first, as already indicated, is to highlight the main preoccupations of their leaders during each period in order to assess the continued relevance of provincial traditions. The second, and more important, is the attempt to identify provincial variations from national policy. Thus in considering the provincial leaderships' attitudes and reactions to national politics it is the particular which is of interest.

In addition, Chapters 3 and 7 examine rural social policies (as opposed to policies on agricultural production) in detail from the provincial perspective for both the period before and the period after decentralization. The rural sector is an almost ideal area for detailed examination of provincial involvement in the national policy process precisely because the decentralization measures of 1957–8 were more concerned with industrial and commercial affairs. If the decentralization of 1957–8 did in fact have wider political repercussions, then these should also be apparent in the rural sector, as well as being more readily distinguishable from the specified measures themselves. Obviously, such a choice is facilitated by the coincidence of the 'High Tide' of agricultural co-operativization before decentralization

(Chapter 3) and the establishment and development of the rural people's communes thereafter (Chapter 7).

In fact, those two chapters confirm a similar picture of the decision-making process on either side of the 1957–8 divide. In both instances provincial leaders were allowed considerable flexibility in formulation and implementation of policy. Moreover, both chapters highlight the role played by Sichuan and its leadership in supporting Mao's initiatives and policy preferences. More generally, it is possible to identify five basic types of provincial variation in the national policy process. Sometimes, provinces were explicitly exempted from certain aspects of policy implementation. There were occasions when provinces were encouraged to experiment with policy. There were provincial variations which resulted from central policy debate when provinces were either reacting to, or being encouraged by, central leaders. On occasion, provincial leaders could delay implementation of a central directive. Lastly, there were a very few instances when central policies were not implemented. Though the forms of these variations may have reflected local conditions, there is little to suggest that they were caused by the exercise of provincial political power. Only one instance of variation appears as an anti-centre act. Rather variation was either permitted, encouraged, or resulted from the central decision-making process. The decision-making process did not shift from centre to province: it expanded to incorporate provincial leaders.

PART I

BEFORE DECENTRALIZATION

1

POLITICAL TRADITIONS AND THE CONSOLIDATION OF RULE

The contrast between the reputations of Sichuan and Guizhou is an understandable one. Traditionally, forced and directed labour forces were sent to work in Guizhou, whereas exiled magistrates positively preferred Sichuan. The latter, for the most part, and particularly on the Chengdu plain, was an area of relatively high standard of living and cultural attainment. Guizhou was considerably less hospitable. It provided not only a hostile environment, but all too frequently a hostile population.

This chapter, in outlining the political traditions and the conditions which shaped them in Sichuan and Guizhou, also serves as an introduction to those two provinces. In addition, it also presents an introduction to Sichuan and Guizhou during the decade before the Cultural Revolution, by surveying the CCP's consolidation of rule when it attempted to meet the conditions which confronted it immediately after 1949. As remarkable as the contrast between Sichuan and Guizhou is the relative success of the CCP between 1949 and 1954. The Southwest was a region which had seen relatively little CCP influence before 1949, and indeed had been the Nationalist base during the Sino-Japanese War. None the less in both Sichuan and Guizhou the CCP was able to develop its organization and become relatively efficient and effective within a very short space of time. As will become apparent, not all problems were capable of immediate solution. However, the soluble were taken in hand and steps implemented to resolve longer term difficulties.

Regardless of traditions, the problem of a united provincial resistance to the CCP was remote indeed. During the Republican period, Sichuan's unity had been on paper only, and Guizhou did not really exist in political and administrative terms outside Guiyang. When political traditions are taken into account, the contrast between Sichuan and Guizhou is once again sharp, but neither suggests the potential for necessary conflict with Beijing. Guizhou's traditions suggest a tendency for internal disunity and dependence on the region, particularly Sichuan. In the event, those traditions proved an excellent indicator of Guizhou's politics before the GPCR. Though not to the same extent, Sichuan's traditions also help explain aspects of its politics during that period. In particular, it came increasingly to act as the political and economic centre of the Southwest. However, in Sichuan's case it is its inter-relationship with national politics which is emphasized, not its isolation.

SICHUAN'S POLITICAL TRADITIONS

Throughout the modern period of Chinese history, Sichuan has been noted for its wealth, its remoteness, and its independence. Writing in 1872, Baron Richthofen described the province in glowing terms:

There are few regions in China, that if equal areas are compared, can rival with the plain of Chengtu-fu as regards wealth and prosperity, density of population and productive power, fertility of climate and perfection of natural irrigation; and there is no other where, at the present time, refinement and civilization are so generally diffused among the population.[1]

Archibald Little, a British adventurer stationed in Shanghai in the late nineteenth century, was so attracted by Sichuan's wealth, that at great personal cost he set out to force the British and Chinese governments' hands, by sailing up the Yangtze to Chongqing in order to open up the province as a British market. He estimated that in 1888, '... the all round external trade of this province ... [was] ... £27 million, or nearly twice as much as the whole import and export trade of Great Britain with China combined'.[2] By comparison, Great Britain's exports in 1888 were worth £297,885,000. In more recent times the wealth of Sichuan's agricultural produce has been recognized explicitly by the national and provincial governments. In

August 1957 in his work report to the 5th session of the 1st Provincial People's Congress, Governor Li Dazhang, stressed not only the phenomenal output of provincial agriculture, but also that 'it was a public duty' for Sichuan to supply other less fortunate areas with their food grains and other agricultural necessities.[3]

Sichuan's remoteness from the rest of China is also renowned. To quote Archibald Little again,

Even Europeans, who had made their home in China, lived on in ignorance of the Great West. Engaged for the most part in business on the eastern sea-board, they had no contact or concern with this distant region, and if a rare traveller or missionary alluded to it occasionally, the passing interest left little beyond a misty impression of a kind of Rasselas' Happy Valley, shut in by almost impassable mountains, which it would take longer to reach than to make a trip to Europe.[4]

More recently, in March 1968, both Jiang Qing and Zhou Enlai referred to Sichuan's remoteness in speeches to Sichuanese Red Guards. Jiang Qing is reported as having said: 'You people come from a faraway land, a very remote region to us.'[5]

Coupled with this remoteness from the rest of China, Sichuan has a reputation for independence and lack of responsiveness to central control. Zhou Enlai was with Jiang Qing at the meeting with Sichuanese Red Guards, and in part of his conversation he alluded to this, when he said: 'An old saying has it that Szechuan always was the scene of turmoil before other provinces, and that order was always restored in that area later than the rest of the country.'[6] In 1921, during the birth of Sichuanese militarism, the isolationist elements even went so far as to issue a 'Declaration of Independence', even though the concept of a unified Sichuan was only as real as that of a united China.[7] All these aspects of Sichuan's reputation were recognized by the Qing. Whereas most provinces were administered by a Governor, with a Governor-General over regional groups of two or three provinces, Sichuan was one of only three provinces considered as a region on its own, with its administration headed by a Governor-General, because of the importance of its wealth and the danger of its remoteness.[8]

On the other hand Sichuan's wealth, remoteness and independence should not be considered as unbounded. Certain limitations must be put on the picture of Sichuan as a separate and self sufficient State within a state that is emerging. Despite her incredible wealth in certain respects, Sichuan suffered from chronic economic deficiencies. Of these the two most important were a lack of cotton and an almost non-existent transport system. According to Alexander Hosie, who was Britain's Consul-General in Chongqing in the late nineteenth century, 'Cotton will not flourish in Ssu-chuan, and the greater part of her surplus wealth is consumed in the purchase of raw cotton, native cotton, and, what is of importance to British commerce, foreign cotton and woolen goods.'[9] The difficulties of communication with and within Sichuan were extremely apparent. For example, there was not a single wheeled vehicle in Chongqing before 1927.[10] As Cressey pointed out in the thirties,

Szechwan has probably been more hampered by inadequate transportation than by any other single factor. The movement of agricultural and mineral products together with other commerce requires an abnormally large number of people, for means of travel are slow and inefficient. This is true throughout China, but is especially pronounced in Szechwan. Animals are rare, carts unknown, railroads but dreams, canals impossible, and the rivers too swift.[11]

In the nineteenth century, trade and travel were restricted to the river system, based on the Yangtze, the Jialing, Tou, Min and Yalong, which served as the main axes of communication.[12] This situation persisted into the Republican period despite the fact that Sichuan's leaders were aware, as Robert Kapp puts it that 'internal communications were monumentally backward in the 1920s and 1930s'.[13] Away from the river system travel was by foot or sedan chair. The major land routes were unsuitable for wheeled vehicles, and the only railway in the whole of the province was a short narrow-gauge coal line just north of Chongqing.[14] As a result of these deficiencies, Sichuan can only be considered wealthy up to a point, as Hosie recognized in 1922. 'Szechwan, unlike many other provinces of the country, is almost but not quite self contained.'[15]

Although Sichuan was considered to be remote, it was still certainly part of Chinese culture and an integral part of the Empire. Reporting from Sichuan in 1948, Barnett wrote: 'The majority of the people in Szechwan share with other Chinese the common cultural heritage – with its deep philosophical, historical, and linguistic roots – that has kept China together as a nation despite regional differentiation.'[16] The Sichuanese dialect is not unlike Mandarin – the major difference is that Sichuanese has shorter tones[17] – thus facilitating communication. As a land of opportunity, Sichuan was a magnet for immigrants from other parts of China from the third century on,[18] although significantly, these immigrants kept their emotional ties with the rest of China. To quote Hosie again, '... it is rare indeed to find anyone who will tell you that he is a native of Szechwan. As a rule he claims to the province of his immigrant ancestors.'[19] Furthermore, Sichuan was also a place of exile for recalcitrant magistrates, along with Guangzhou and Gansu, although given the high standard of living most preferred Sichuan. Finally, because of her agricultural output, Sichuan was one of the key economic areas whose control was vital to the control of China.[20]

The concept of Sichuan's independence must also have conditions placed upon it. In the first place, although the term *zizhi* is often translated as 'autonomous' in English,[21] this is not the same as independence. There is a definite distinction in Chinese between *zi zhi*, meaning self-government, and *zijue*, meaning self-determination. In English, autonomy may imply both. Moreover, in Chinese the term *zizhi* refers to a very limited autonomy for it implies subordination to an external authority. When 'autonomy' is used to translate *zizhi*, its meaning is clearly not one of absolute independence. Thus a completely different emphasis should be given to statements such as that of Allen, the US Consul-General in Chongqing, in commenting on the post-1921 Independence movement, when he reported: 'The Szechwanese appear determined not to go back into any national government that does not provide for a maximum of provincial autonomy.'[22] The impression of a separate Sichuan in the early Republican period must thus be modified.

This is directly connected to the second limitation. The existence of a separate Sichuan would require its political legitimacy to be vested in the Sichuanese political system without reference to the rest of China. However, this is clearly not the case. The 1921 Declaration of Independence stated that 'While a legal unified government of the Republic of China has yet to be established, Szechwan province is entirely self-governing.'[23] Whilst this may be dismissed as merely a form of words, it clearly shows that the political legitimacy of the Sichuan government lay in the national system as a whole. This is in fact an example of the concept of *pian an* or 'partial peace', first applied to Liu Bei's establishment of the Kingdom of Shu in the Three Kingdoms' period. In times of imperial disorder, which were recognized as the manifestations of improper rule, correct rule could be applied to a temporarily separated part of the Empire on the periphery (though not in the Chinese 'core-area' itself). However, this was seen as a purely transient expedient, for it was incumbent on the rulers of the partial area to extend the area of 'correct' rule to recover the whole Empire. In other words, the dominant 'State-idea', to borrow a term from political geography, for Sichuan's leaders was not Sichuan, but China.[24]

Finally, when talking about Sichuan's separateness and independence in the Republican period, it must be remembered that Sichuan was not united – *provincial* independence was a remote possibility indeed. At the height of Sichuanese militarism from 1927–34, the province was divided into five Garrison Areas, and to quote Kapp: 'Within their garrison areas, the Szechwanese Army Commanders were independent of higher authority, and independent of each other.'[25] Each had its own administration, its own currency, and raised its own taxes, and unlike in other provinces no single warlord ever came to dominate the province.[26]

The key to understanding these aspects of Sichuan's reputation is undoubtedly its geography. Bounded on three sides of a diamond by high mountains, and in the South-east by the Yangtze, it has natural boundaries which have proved a barrier to communications in either direction.[27] These boundaries have traditionally been used to describe the administrative area of Sichuan and in consequence have led to the creation of a clearly-defined geo-political entity.[28] Sichuan's geography is such that within these borders is an area of extremely fertile land with an ideal climate for year-round agricultural production.'[29] Since the third century, Sichuan has been China's main grain producer – the 'Storehouse of Heaven' of the '*Shi ji*' (Records of the Historian), and in addition, in the modern period, the main producer of salt, sugar, and silk.[30]

Both these factors have combined to produce Sichuan's historical role in Chinese politics. This role may be seen in four interrelated parts.[31] In the first place, Sichuan has been a kind of 'world apart', a separate and almost self-sufficient state cut off from outside political developments. During periods of weakened central authority, independent rulers have governed the province. Thus, for example, during the Three Kingdoms Period Liu Bei established the Kingdom of Shu; at the end of the Tang dynasty, Wang Qian, the military governor of the province, crowned himself Emperor of Shu; and at the end of the Ming, Zhang Xianzhong similarly became King of the Great Western Country.

Secondly, Sichuan has traditionally been a refuge from disorder in the rest of China, especially in times of Imperial weakness. This occurred, for example, twice during the Tang. On the first occasion in the eighth century, the 'Xuan zong' Emperor fled from Changan to Shu during the Anlushan rebellion; as did the 'Xi zong' Emperor during the Huang Chao uprising. In more recent times, Sichuan was also, of course, the refuge of the Republican government during the Japanese War.

Thirdly, Sichuan was important as a supply base and staging post for military expeditions. Its productive wealth and geographical position were invaluable assets in the incorporation of Yunnan, Guizhou, and Tibet, carried out from the Han onwards.[32] Because of its wealth and position, Sichuan is also of strategic importance for the lower Yangtze region, and the South and West periphery of China, although it has never been used as a military base for northern expeditions. Although Sichuan was often used as a springboard for conquest, it never produced movements or leaders that extended over the entire country, or who became national military or political figures.

Finally, Sichuan has traditionally been the economic and cultural centre of the Southwest. The wealth of the province, which made it attractive to immigrants, also made it a focal point for the Southwest region, which apart from Sichuan was pitifully poor. In 1884, Hosie described Guizhou and Yunnan as '... half depopulated by internecine struggles, only partly cultivated and partly developed ...'[33] and extremely dependent on Sichuan for economic necessities, in particular salt[34] and cotton manufactures,[35] despite Sichuan's own shortage of the raw material. Hardly surprisingly, Sichuan also had a political role to play with regards to these other provinces. As already indicated, the integration of Guizhou and Yunnan into the Chinese Empire was carried out from Sichuan. As the economic situation deteriorated in the late nineteenth century, this influence probably grew. For example, Hosie, when planning his trips to Yunnan and Guizhou in 1882, had to apply for permission to the Governor-General of Sichuan, rather than to the Governor-General of Yunnan and Guizhou.[36]

Associated with this predominance is Sichuan's reputation for cultural refinement and technical achievement. For example, salt has been produced from wells at Ziliuqing since the Minor Han dynasty (when Liu Bei ruled as King of Shu), and since the Qin in Jianwei.[37] Sichuan has the oldest large-scale irrigation system in the Toujiang

Weir, originally started by Li Ping in the third century BC;[38] whilst wood-block printing started in Sichuan long before it was in use in Western Europe.[39] Although Sichuan produced no military leaders of national standing, she did produce poets, of whom the most important were probably Li Bai and Du Fu (in the Tang), and Su Dongpo (during the Song). The pre-eminence was epitomized by the cities of Chengdu, which Hosie described as ' ... without exception ... the finest city I have seen in China',[40] and Chongqing, which he called ' ... the commercial metropolis of ... Western China'.[41] Whilst the former was well known for its cultural life, the latter was the economic centre.

That these traditions were actively known by Sichuan's provincial leadership before 1949 becomes clear from Kapp's study of Sichuanese militarism from 1911 to 1938.[42] Here he traces the development of warlordism in Sichuan and concludes that the main theme throughout the period was the rise of provincial separatism and the search for a new political legitimacy to justify it. The separatist movement, grounded on Sichuan's wealth and remoteness, started from the province's first major conflict with the Central government over the building of the Chengdu–Hankou railway, and developed to its peak under the leadership of Liu Xiang between 1927 and 1934. However, even in this period, separatism could only go so far. The two aspects of the theme were, in fact, opposed, and eventually centralism reasserted itself with the fulfilment of another of Sichuan's traditional roles – as a haven for the Emperor.

The notion of Sichuan's traditional political relationship with the centre that emerges is thus one of a high degree of provincial autonomy tempered by historical circumstances and ultimate central authority. This autonomy could develop into separatism, but the basic determinant of this relationship was not the strengths or weaknesses of the province, but those of the centre. When the centre was strong, in terms of policies and organization, then provincial separatism was a non-starter. Even when provincial separatism may be said to be at its height this was still only seen as a temporary expedient. Moreover, it did not always unite the province. In the light of comments which suggest that warlordism during the Republic is related to post-1949 'provincialism'[43] it should be emphasized that warlordism in Sichuan did not result in a movement for provincial separatism which united the province. As Kapp points out, each of the five garrison area commanders in Sichuan was more concerned with his own personal army and territory rather than with the welfare of Sichuan,[44] and even within these areas their control was limited.[45]

GUIZHOU'S POLITICAL TRADITIONS

Although Guizhou shares Sichuan's reputation for remoteness, in every other respect both its reputation and political traditions are almost the complete antithesis. Perhaps it is partially in contrast with neighbouring Sichuan that conditions in Guizhou are, and have been, considered so bleak, however, the province's reputation would certainly seem to belie its name. Often referred to as 'the mountain country'[46] – Alexander Hosie, in extraordinarily lyrical vein christened the province 'China's Switzerland'[47] – Guizhou has had an unwavering reputation for abject poverty, cultural and economic backwardness, and internal fragmentation. Such a bleak reputation is neatly encapsulated in the traditional Guizhou proverb, repeated by every travelogue, commentator and politician throughout the nineteenth and twentieth centuries up to and including the period since 1949 –

> There are not three *li* of level ground
> There are not three sunny days in a row
> There are not three coins in the people's pockets.[48]

Speaking at the 8th National Congress of the CCP in September 1956, Zhou Lin, the first provincial party secretary of Guizhou, stated that 'Before Liberation Guizhou was a poor and backward area and all the nationalities lived a frightful existence';[49] and by all accounts it would be hard to disagree with that assessment. As has already been noted, Alexander Hosie described the province (in 1884) as dangerous, barely cultivated, and economically backward.[50] Richthofen, after a visit in the 1870s, wrote scathingly about conditions there. For example,

The climate is said to be very unhealthy. The country has little running water, but much which is stagnant, and only those who are born there can withstand the effects of the malaria which it creates. To this circumstance is ascribed the fact that the population of Kweichau has always been thin. The climate has deteriorated since the commencement of the troubles, because it constantly happens that corpses of the killed are putrifying in the fields. The drinking water of wells is considered particularly unhealthy.[51]

Moreover, he pointed out that 'Even the opium' – a common cash crop in economically depressed areas – 'grown there is of inferior quality to that of Szechwan.' Even Zhou Lin's comment seems something of an understatement when compared to that of his director of propaganda. Echoing Richthofen, Wang Xiaochuan wrote in 1958

Before Liberation people called this a poor mountain area. At that time there was not enough food for everyone. The people wore rags and used straw for bedding and their shabbiness was indescribable. There was no industry at all. The province was economically and culturally backward. It was difficult to find anyone literate except in a few county towns. Malaria was alarmingly prevalent and continued all-year round. As a result people referred to the province as 'a land devoid of cultivation, and a region of disease'.[52]

The major determinants of Guizhou's poverty and lack of internal unity were its geography and political situation, notably as a border area of the Chinese Empire with a substantial population of non-Han peoples. Apart from the lowland and relatively 'fertile crescent' stretching from Zunyi in the north through Guiyang to Anshun in the southwest of the province, Guizhou is almost completely covered by mountains.[53] Even in the west, where the Yunnan–Guizhou plateau extends into the province there are extremes in relief (as there are elsewhere in the province resulting from karst formations) caused by the erosion of the basalt and limestone sub-stratum which in turn result from the heavy and frequent rainfall.[54] As a result, agricultural production was extremely low and internal communications were near-impossible.

Cressey considered Guizhou to be the poorest agricultural province in the whole of China,[55] and that is no surprise. Only 4% of the total land area was under cultivation (as opposed to 15% in Sichuan),[56] and during the nineteenth and twentieth centuries two-thirds of that was given over to opium cultivation.[57] In general it was hard to raise either cash or arable crops on the mountainsides. Although attempts at colonialization (notably from Hunan, Jiangxi and Sichuan) occurred under the Ming and Qing, the immigrants faced insurmountable difficulties –

... poverty-stricken peasant immigrants rented reclaimed barren mountains and eked out a bare subsistence ... After reclaiming and planting for two to three years, the land was washed away by rain, so they were forced to migrate elsewhere.[58]

Even before the dislocations of the twentieth century there had traditionally been shortages of grain, cloth and salt, with peasants 'always living on the edge of starvation';[59] and during the Nationalist domination of the southwest, Guizhou remained a constant and considerable drain on the exchequer.[60]

Internal communications were similarly and adversely affected by the terrain. Most of the province's rivers were, and remain, unnavigable, as a result of the mountainous terrain through which they pass. There were few roads, or even paths, or wheeled vehicles before the twentieth century, and both freight and messages had to be carried. Of his visit to the province in 1882, Hosie observed: 'During the whole of my time in Kuei-Chow I never once saw a cart, the entire trade – such as it is – being conducted on the backs of bipeds and quadrupeds.'[61] Even during the twentieth century there was no telegraph or railway in the province, presumably because of the high investment cost, and any transport within or across the province was difficult. A major cause was Guizhou's mountains which also made the province very remote from the rest of China. Moreover, because of the terrain and rain-sodden climate Guizhou was as hard to hold as it was to cross and this too created problems.

Guizhou's poverty, though great for physical reasons, was worsened by internal conflict, particularly in the nineteenth and twentieth centuries, and particularly between the indigenous non-Han and the Chinese immigrants. Although Guizhou was formally incorporated into the Chinese Empire under the Ming, it was never really fully integrated.[62] Before 1949, it was to all extents and purposes treated as a border area – a series of buffer states between China and 'the barbarians' where rule was indirect rather than direct. As throughout the southwest, the essence of indirect rule was the *tu si* system which persisted until at least 1945.[63] Local village chiefs, heads of localized tribes and ethnic groups and their like were appointed in the non-Han areas as the local agents of the central government, rather than the district magistrates to be found elsewhere in China. The aim of the *tu si* system was the protection of the Han heartland. Theoretically, neighbouring non-Hans stood between central China and any outside invader; whilst localized indirect rule would keep pacific border areas where direct rule would have been difficult at best. Approximately 70% of Guizhou was administered in that way, although only about 40% of the province's total population were not Chinese.[64] In practice the existence of the *tu*

35

si system in Guizhou was only marginally successful. It strengthened local non-Han feelings of identity (and autonomy) to such an extent that friction between the Chinese and other ethnic groups, and amongst the non-Han, often erupted into violence. In addition to the Miao, the largest single non-Han 'national minority' in Guizhou, there are also substantial populations of Puyi, Tong, Hui, and Shui. These minority groups were often hostile not only to the Chinese, but also to each other.[65]

The roots of that conflict lay not only in the attempts to incorporate Guizhou into the empire, but also to a large extent in the unsuccessful measures employed to colonize the province. As may be imagined, unlike Sichuan, Guizhou was not a totally inviting prospect for potential immigrants and most were directed rather than willing volunteers.[66] Originally the Jiangkou prefecture had been established during the Han when it was described as '... having few domestic animals ... neither silk worms nor mulberry trees ... the poorest prefecture'. During the Sui and Tang it was 'a very backward region to which convicted officials were exiled', and under the Song and Yuan its economic development was said to be very slow. Even when Zunyi and the fertile areas were incorporated into Guizhou, after the 1720s (during the Qing dynasty), the bulk of immigrants were 'poverty-stricken peasants'. The results of Chinese attempts at immigration were to drive the non-Chinese into the mountains off what little fertile ground existed.[67] However, the Chinese colony, for reasons of size, climate, and terrain, were not in a position to hold their area for long against counter attack.

Conflict between Chinese and non-Chinese worsened after the second half of the eighteenth century. Under the 'Qian long' and 'Jia qing' emperors (1736–1821) determined attempts were made to subjugate the minorities of Guizhou. The minorities replied with force and huge numbers were destroyed at Huang Bing (Miao) and during the Bangjiang revolt of 1797 (Puyi).[68] Despite these defeats resistance, particularly among the Miao, continued and became an integral part of folklore and culture. Thus, in the early 1950s, Fei Xiaotong found that the Miao 'Song of Revolt' was still known to all –

> The Han oppress us one day
> And we reply the same day,

which was reported as having been said by a rebel Miao leader to his Chinese torturer and interrogator.[69] Miao resistance broke out into open revolt after 1848, at first under the leadership of Zhang Xinmei. Although that revolt had connections with the Taiping, it continued long after, and sporadic Miao–Han violence erupted throughout the Republican period.

In addition to the internal disorder resulting from conflict between the minorities and the Chinese, social banditry became a feature of Guizhou life from the middle of the nineteenth century onwards. Occasioned no doubt by Guizhou's grinding poverty and using the anti-Miao feeling as a pretext, the province became '... infested by lawless bands roving through the country, and robbing and killing the peaceable inhabitants'.[70] Social banditry and conflict between the Chinese and the minority ethnic groups not only led to wholesale emigration from Guizhou between 1848 and 1870,[71] but also to the disruption of the province's never-strong economy. Thus, for example, although Guizhou had previously exported minerals such as copper and mercury (for which it was a major national export earner) production and distribution ceased completely in the first half of the nineteenth century.[72] The effects of both social banditry and ethnic minority disorder were well summarized by Richthofen in a statement that can well serve as the province's epitaph before 1949: 'So long as this state of affairs lasts, Kwei-chau will continue to be the least productive, the least populous, and the least important among the eighteen provinces of China.'[73]

To all extents and purposes, therefore, Guizhou as a political entity existed traditionally as no more than an administrative fiction. For the Chinese it was a hostile land populated by hostile peoples, well outside the mainstream of Chinese culture due to its geographic isolation and poverty. Developments after the 1911 revolution and during the Republican period did little to alter that picture. Social banditry was replaced by numerous petty warlords, none of whom attempted or succeeded in uniting the province. For a while, parts of the province came under the control of Cai Ao's Protection Army from Yunnan, and although the provincial assembly declared its independence in 1916, any attempt at unity (albeit together with Yunnan) died with Cai in the same year.[74] Similarly, as Zhu De wrote when the Red Army passed through Guizhou, poverty persisted:

Corn, with bits of cabbage, chief food of people. Peasants too poor to eat rice; sell it to pay rent and interest. Rice seized by militarists as 'war rice tax' ... Peasants call landlords 'rent gentry' and themselves 'dry men' – men sucked dry of everything ... Three kinds of salt: white for the rich; brown for middle classes; black salt residue for toiling masses. Even black salt so expensive peasants place small chunk in bowl and rub cabbage on it when eating ... Poor hovels with black rotten thatch roofs everywhere. Small doors of cornstalks and bamboo ... People digging rotten rice from ground under landlord's old granary.[75]

Even when the Nationalist government moved to Chongqing in 1937, little was done to improve the economy and transport system outside Guiyang.[76]

It is thus hard to conceive of Guizhou asserting its independence after 1957 as a result of either its imperial or republican traditions. In so far as Guizhou could be said to have political traditions qua province, a dubious process at best, then those might be described as dependence on the region (or more accurately neighbouring provinces) and non-integration. Sichuan's role as a supply base for Guizhou has already been noted.[77] In addition, such river transport as was possible was on rivers between Guizhou and Sichuan.[78] Other than being dependent generally on Sichuan, Guizhou had also been dependent on Yunnan militarily. Cai Ao's attempted conquest of Guizhou from Yunnan was an extension of the *status quo ante* where under the empire Guizhou and Yunnan shared a Governor-General located in Kunming. Guizhou's tradition of non-integration existed at two levels. The province was neither integrated in itself, nor was it integrated into the nation. In essence it was traditionally a border area. Certainly there were centrifugal forces at work within the province and strong feelings of localized autonomy, which had an institutional expression in the *tu si* system. However, it would be hard to argue that those were evidence of a tradition of provincial separation, or indeed even that there was (unlike Sichuan) a clear 'sub-State idea' of the province.

SICHUAN AND GUIZHOU, 1949–54: POLITICAL CONTROL AND ADMINISTRATION

During the first five years of the PRC local government was organized on a regional basis, both following the PLA's pattern of military conquest and for reasons of political control. Beneath the regional administrative committees was an almost bewildering array of provinces, sub-bureaux and offices.[79] From 1949 to 1952 both Sichuan and Guizhou were subject to the Southwest Military and

Administrative Committee, and from 1952 to 1954 (when the system of regional government was abolished) the Southwest Administrative Committee. However, in line with their political traditions and major administrative problems Sichuan and Guizhou existed in different forms at sub-regional level. In Guizhou, where integration was as important a problem as control, a provincial government was established. However, in Sichuan where control was all-important (not least because of the importance of the province's food grains to the rest of the country) the province was divided into four Administrative Offices until 1952 when it was re-united.[80] In addition, Xikang, whose eastern part was not incorporated into Sichuan until mid-1955, was a separate province.[81]

Although Sichuan and Guizhou after 1949 presented the CCP with very different problems, as southwestern provinces they none the less shared several difficulties which were capable of common solution. In general these resulted from the fact that the southwest was the area of the country which was taken last by the new regime, had least experience of the Communist movement before 1949, and contained a higher proportion of national minorities. Sichuan and Guizhou were among the very last provinces to be conquered by the PLA, Guiyang not falling until 15 November 1949, Chongqing 30 November, and Chengdu 27 December. The Nationalist troops had in fact been driven back into the southwest by a pincer movement from the north by He Long and the First Field Army, and from the west by Liu Bocheng and the Second Field Army.[82] As a result, although all armed resistance was classified as 'counter-revolutionary activity' there were undoubtedly more 'bandits' in the southwest than elsewhere.[83] For those who did not surrender the problem was solved generally with force,[84] and by late 1951 it was claimed that armed resistance had ceased[85] with a 'total of 118,708 bandit troops exterminated in Sichuan and Guizhou'.[86] A second result of the PLA's drive to the southwest was that the region was left with some two million government dependents, including not only disbanded Nationalist troops, but also former civil servants and communist soldiers. As Deng Xiaoping, the first party secretary, stressed in his report to the Southwest Military and Administrative Committee, considerable disorder might ensue if they were not fed and suitably dispersed.[87] That problem too was resolved through regional action, although more gradually, through a policy of providing jobs and homes together.

A second major problem in both Sichuan and Guizhou was the lack of adequate cadres in general, and of CCP members in particualr. The CCP had little influence before 1949 in either Sichuan or Guizhou, and in 1952 only 7% of all villages had a party organization.[88] It seems likely that the problem of government dependents was at least partially solved by enlisting them as administrative cadres (a practice by no means unique although perhaps more acute in the Southwest),[89] and after October 1952 a determined campaign was launched to recruit new CCP members and establish party branches in all basic level units.[90] From an organizational viewpoint at least this policy was relatively successful in both Sichuan and Guizhou. In Chongqing alone 3,000 new members were admitted in November 1952,[91] where only 300 had been in the previous two years,[92] and in 1954 8,000 joined the party branch.[93] In Guizhou, 11,000 new members had been admitted by November 1952.[94] Moreover, the occupational background of these new members boded well for the CCP's administrative control, since 35% were employed in government offices.[95] Although the work of party expansion was reported to have run into problems in early 1954,[96] none the less it was reported that during 1954 in Sichuan 100,000 new members had been recruited in the rural areas alone and that party branches had been established in 96% of the villages;[97] and in Guizhou that 42,410 new members had joined the CCP.[98] On the other hand, as the CCP repeatedly found, a large and sudden recruitment may adversely influence the quality of party leadership, and this would appear to have happened in and after 1952 to some extent.[99] Furthermore despite rapid expansion the CCP in both Sichuan and Guizhou remained comparatively small. By mid-1956 the Sichuan CCP was the smallest (proportionate to the population) of all the provincial parties, and the Guizhou CCP was not much larger.[100] None the less, despite the lack of experience (unlike other areas) and the weakness of party organization, land reform was completed surprisingly swiftly and efficiently in Sichuan and Guizhou, which in itself helped to strengthen the CCP's control. Apart from the temporarily exempted national minority areas, land reform was completed in Sichuan by May 1952,[101] and by September 1952 in Guizhou.[102]

Finally, there was the problem of the minority nationalities. According to the 1953 census approximately 3% of Sichuan, 25% of Guizhou and most of Xikang were national minority peoples. In

Sichuan the two largest groups were the Yi and the Tibetans, and the minorities are almost exclusively in the west of the province; in Guizhou, as has already been indicated there are Miao, Puyi, Tong, Hui and Shui; and most of Xikang was Tibetan.[103] For the CCP in all three provinces the problem of the national minorities was that their customs and attitudes were considered to be both feudal and antagonistic to the Chinese government. Before 1956 CCP policy towards the national minorities throughout the southwest attempted to reduce their antagonism by establishing self-governing areas and measures of positive discrimination. The abolition of feudalism and the implementation of policies such as land reform, to which the CCP had an ideological commitment, were to be left until later, and the national minority areas were explicitly exempted.[104] Thus in the Tibetan areas alone the *ula* servitude system was abolished, serfdom was allowed to remain, and emphasis was instead placed on the establishment of the two autonomous *zhou* of Ganzi (in 1950) and Apa (in 1953), both in post-1955 Sichuan.[105] In addition, there were specifically designated *zhou*-level national minority areas in Guizhou for the Miao and Puyi, and for the Yi in Sichuan, as well as other smaller order later-to-become-autonomous areas.[106]

Apart from the need to restore economic and political stability, Sichuan's specific problems after 1949 concerned economic and transport development for both national and provincial reasons. Its agricultural output, so important not only to the region but also to the national economy,[107] had dropped drastically by 1949 compared to the pre-war years,[108] and had to be restored at the very least to that level. In particular, it was important that there were large increases in the production of both cotton (for the province and the region) and food grain (for the nation).[109] The policy of actively encouraging cotton production met with some success and Sichuan's cotton output rose from 15,000 tons in 1949 to 41,300 tons in 1952,[110] although imports were still needed from Shaanxi and Hubei.[111] Food grain output increased considerably so that, as Li Jingquan, the First secretary of Sichuan, reported in 1955, during 1954 'the people of 18 provinces and municipalities ate Sichuan's grain'.[112]

Before 1949, Sichuan's industry was not highly developed and what industry had entered the province with the Nationalists had left with them[113] or been destroyed during the Civil War.[114] After 1949 a determined effort was made to modernize existing industries and start new enterprises both in order to exploit Sichuan's plentiful natural resources and to supply capital goods. Chongqing and Chengdu were designated as the two main industrial centres: the former concentrating on iron, steel, coal, machine building, the chemical industry and textiles; and the latter on iron and steel, textiles and food products; with industrial development of the salt industry at Zigong, the paper industry at Yibin, the sugar processing at Neijiang.[115]

Finally, the new leadership saw a need to develop Sichuan's transport system, both in order to open up the more isolated areas of the province and to make its resources more widely available to the national economy.[116] Before 1949, even though the rivers were the main lines of communication, all-year-round navigation was only possible on the Yangtze below Yibin, and the Jialing below Hechuan; there were a few short and unconnected roads which had not been maintained in good repair; and the only railway was a coal transporting line between Datiankou and Paimiaozi.[117] Starting in 1950, river transport was extended through improved navigation, port expansion and new steamship lines; existing roads were improved, and new highways and local roads built; and railway construction (for both internal and external communication) undertaken.[118] The most publicized transport development was the Chongqing–Chengdu railway. Construction having started in June 1950,[119] the 329 mile railway was opened on 1 July 1952.[120] The line was important for political as well as economic reasons. Its construction had been discussed unsuccessfully for forty years, and it had been the clash of imperial and provincial interests over the railway that had led to the outbreak of the 1911 revolution in Sichuan.

Guizhou's specific preoccupations during the five years after 1949 were much more basic than those of Sichuan, and almost exclusively centred on the problems of survival and internal integration. Problems which were equally as acute but of less importance – such as the need to develop an industrial base, since in 1949 Guizhou's value of industrial output was only 2.2% of the total value of industrial and agricultural output[121] – were in general not addressed until after 1954. As a result great emphasis was placed on increasing agricultural production, particularly in the first instance of food grains, and creating an internal communications system.

Although the suppression of banditry and the subsequent re-establishment (or perhaps more accurately, creation) of political stability cannot but have had a beneficial effect on Guizhou's agricultural output, its increases were remarkable. Before 1949 Guizhou had been historically a grain importer, not producing enough food for its own population. Yet, according to Zhou Lin, the first secretary, 'In 1953, for the first time in the history of the province, the harvest of grain was enough to meet the demands of the local population.'[122] Moreover, in 1954 Guizhou became a grain exporter, providing 285,500 tons of grain for export to other provinces between July 1954 and August 1955.[123] Despite a drought in 1951 and severe flooding in 1952, rice output increased by almost 12% between 1949 and 1952, wheat by 55%, corn by 23%, and rape by 49%, the last leaving Guizhou second only to Sichuan in the provincial production league tables.[124] Those increases were the results of several measures. The area of reclaimed land – that is 'reclaimed' with respect to the area of general traditionally cultivated land – was increased. Whereas in 1950 only 8% of arable land was reclaimed, by 1955 this figure had reached 35%.[125] Greater use was made of irrigated land where this proved feasible,[126] and loans to peasants for agricultural improvement were heavily publicized.[127] Finally, free tools, fertilizer and light agricultural machinery worth 5,000 million *yuan* were distributed during 1953.[128]

The creation of a transport system was crucial not only to Guizhou's development, but also at first to its survival, since quantities of various basic commodities (such as food and cotton) had to be imported from Sichuan. To this end great emphasis was placed on the development of local roads to connect with the province's major north-south and east-west highways. By late 1952 it was reported that 68 of Guizhou's 81 *xian* were now within reach of highways;[129] and the length of paved road had increased from 2,469 kms (in 1950) to 4,027 kms (in 1952). Moreover, by 1952 some 1,700 kms of river were open to traffic where none had been in 1950. However, presumably because of the high costs involved no railway construction was undertaken before 1954.[130]

Although the province placed little emphasis on industrial production during this period all its indices of output (e.g. for coal, electric power etc.) showed substantial increases,[131] largely because of its almost nonexistent base in 1949. Moreover, the province did assume control of all the enterprises previously controlled by the Guizhou Enterprise Corporation, which included a cement factory, a tyre factory and a few mines.[132] However, it is a measure of the province's problems of integration that it took until 1952 before

2

1955–7: THE END OF
THE SOVIET MODEL

The period from the 2nd session of the 1st National People's Congress (NPC) in July 1955, when the First Five Year Plan (1952–7) was officially published, to the 3rd plenum of the 8th Central Committee of the CCP in September–October 1957, when the first decentralization measures were approved, was relatively dramatic even by the standards of the PRC.[1] During the second half of 1955 agricultural co-operativization proceeded so quickly – in its 'high tide' – that by the end of 1956 China's industry and agriculture were fully socialized, well ahead of the targets outlined in the First Five Year Plan. At least partially as a result, the Chinese leadership, and Mao in particular, considered that the Communist Party regime was firmly established and began to consider how the country should be governed in the future, and how the economy should develop. Associated with this change in perspective was the drive in the first half of 1956 to complete the Five Year Plan a year ahead of time. However, that attempt proved more than somewhat problematical and had been relinquished by May. Thereafter, a far-ranging debate on the pattern for China's future developed within the leadership. To oversimplify greatly, debate polarized between, on the one hand, the more gradualist approach of a group which centred on Chen Yun and the economic planners, and on the other, a more adventurous section of the leadership whose leader must be supposed to have been Mao, but which also included some of his later opponents of the GPCR such as Peng Zhen. The debate was played out to a large extent in public with both national and provincial leaders making their views relatively well known at the 3rd session of the 1st National Party Congress in June 1956 and at the 1st session of the 8th NPC in September of the same year.

By the end of 1956 a compromise appeared to have been reached within the leadership. A second Five Year Plan had been drafted and a rectification of the CCP agreed for the future. Rectification was deemed necessary for a number of reasons. The party's tasks were considered to have changed since its control was now consolidated. Administrative problems had become apparent during both the 'high tide' of co-operativization and the economic setbacks of early 1956. Finally, in the wake of the 20th Congress of the Communist Party of the Soviet Union and events in Poland and Hungary during 1956, rectification was designed to avoid both the bureaucratic abuses of Stalin's rule and the problems between party and people which had arisen in Eastern Europe. However, the rectification campaign was planned for 1958 and agreement had not yet been reached on whether it should be executed as 'limited democracy' (*xiao minzhu*) or 'extended democracy' (*da minzhu*). Sometimes referred to as internal and external democracy respectively, these two concepts were at the centre of the debate about rectification during the mid-fifties. Simply defined, 'limited democracy' entailed that the CCP would itself carry out its own rectification, whereas 'extended democracy' implied that the party would be rectified with the active participation of non-party members. Mao forced the issue in early 1957, in particular in his speech 'On the correct handling of contradictions among the people', delivered to a Supreme State Conference in February. Mao eventually secured agreement within the leadership for rectification of the party from without but the exercise misfired badly. During the 'Hundred Flowers' of May the party was bitterly criticized by both non-party intellectuals and the former bourgeoisie, the very groups whose support Mao was trying to enlist through that exercise. Unsurprisingly, rectification rapidly turned into an 'Anti-Rightists' movement.

Mao's strategy was salvaged from the ruins of the 'Hundred Flowers' experiment by the severity of the economic problems facing the country.[2] At the 3rd plenum in September–October 1957, the much-needed compromise within the leadership united those, on the one hand, such as Liu Shaoqi and Peng Zhen, who wanted the party to maintain its previously strong position of control (including over its own affairs), and, on the other, those who together with Mao were prepared to attempt fast economic growth. The results were the Great Leap Forward, the abandonment of the Soviet model of management and economic development, and a back seat for the gradualist economic planners.

This and the following two chapters concern the actions and attitudes of provincial leaders in Sichuan and Guizhou during

1955–7. In particular, they focus on the concerns of provincial leaders, and how they reacted to both national politics and central directives from their provincial perspective. Chapter 3 deals with the implementation of agricultural collectivization in Sichuan and Guizhou; and Chapter 4 with provincial attitudes to decentralization and the wider debate of which it was a part.

This chapter highlights the major preoccupations of Sichuan and Guizhou during 1955–7. At the same time it identifies provincial variations from national norms and central directives in the policy process. What is clear from all three chapters is that provincial leaders were almost positively encouraged to exercise a high degree of relative autonomy well before decentralization was introduced. On the contrary, as the evidence here compared to later chapters would seem to suggest, it appears likely that they had greater degrees of freedom before 1958 than after. The principle of a necessary degree of local flexibility enshrined in the slogan of 'Do the best according to local conditions', was very much in evidence during those years. Under a system of 'vertical rule' (such as was in force before 1958) provincial leaders were the main channel for the two-way flow of information between centre and province. The consequent freedom was clearly limited – party organizations parallel government and military hierarchies, and visiting delegations and periodic inspections from Beijing all provide alternative channels for information on activities within a province. None the less, the system of 'dual rule' (which was implemented along with decentralization) may well, and does seem to impose even greater restraints. Provincial participation in the policy process is considered further in the next chapter.

More particularly, what is also clear from all three chapters is the contrast between Sichuan and Guizhou in terms of the relationship between centre and province. Guizhou's internal problems and disorders led it not to resistance but to a definite back seat in national politics. It followed national policy and national trends over agricultural collectivization. However, that process was not trouble-free, and together with other difficulties led to a delay in policy implementation on other issues. On the other, Sichuan was increasingly in the fore of developments in national politics during this period. Moreover, it is hard not to identify the positions it took in national politics and the attitudes its leaders expressed increasingly with the political stance of Mao Zedong. The emerging alliance (however informal) between Li Jingquan and Mao appears most vivid in discussions of the post-1956 rectification campaign and Sichuan's attempts at collectivization.

SICHUAN

The major preoccupations of Sichuan's leaders during this period were the implementation of agricultural collectivization and the provincial first five year plan, the provincial supply crisis of 1956–7, and a growing concern with administrative problems. In retrospect, there can be little doubt that the provincial supply crisis resulted, to a large extent, from the attempt to implement both agricultural collectivization and the provincial first five year plan as quickly as possible. Moreover, all three in turn highlighted the administrative problems which became the province's major concern during 1957 and led to the provincial form of the national rectification movement.

The five year plan

The implementation of the provincial first five year plan is of particular interest because it is an indicator of the extent to which, on the one hand, those circumstances which had shaped Sichuan's propensity to independence no longer applied, and on the other, the provincial leadership's attitudes were a reaction to national politics. Of course, it could easily be argued that the newly established communist party regime did represent strong central government and that therefore Sichuan's autonomy was restrained. However, the priorities of the plan itself are the best evidence that Sichuan's economic development during these years was shaped by national rather than provincial considerations.

Although the provincial five year plan had been mentioned beforehand, as for example by Li Jingquan in his speech to the second session of the 1st PPC in 1954,[3] it was not officially announced until November 1955.[4] Far from emphasizing the development of Sichuan's industry, which barely existed, emphasis was placed on the importance of her agricultural production to the national economy. The plan's ordered priorities were for the increased output of grain, cotton, and other agricultural products. Only five of the 694 above-norm products of the national plan were located in Sichuan. Where industry was mentioned it was almost totally in terms of agriculture-based or agriculture-supporting industry, and even then the plan envisaged investment capital being generated in the province. Communications and transport too were to be developed, only in this instance with central financial aid, in order to facilitate the supply of the province's agricultural production to the rest of the country. Moreover, these themes were repeated in the media throughout 1955–7.

Although the targets set by the plan were bound to result in an unbalanced provincial economy, they were largely over-fulfilled. For example, by 1957 Sichuan's total grain output had reached 44,500 instead of the 41,836 million *jin* p.a. planned target, and grain was exported to 21 provinces. Li Dazhang, in his report to the PPC pointed out: '... the peasants of our province have made an important contribution to aid the disaster-stricken areas and the industrial and mining cities. During the period of the first five year plan our province has supplied 149 mn *jin* of grain to the outside areas.'[5] Moreover, the 1957 Budget proposed a 5% increase in the agricultural levy over the previous year 'to make good the quota deficiencies of calamity-stricken areas'.[6] Raw cotton output similarly increased to 1.41 mn *jin* p.a. by 1957,[7] as opposed to the planned target of 1.281 mn *jin* p.a: an increase which was needed to meet not only Sichuan's deficit, but also those of Yunnan and Guizhou, both of whom were heavily dependent on Sichuan.[8]

However, the implementation of the plan was not without its difficulties (as will become apparent in the next two sections) and minor failures. Such problems also emphasize the extent to which Sichuan's leaders were reacting to national politics. In the first place, there is the simple point that many of the problems of the provincial supply crisis resulted from its unbalanced growth strategy. Secondly, although the plan's targets were eventually met by the end of 1957, there were minor failures in the plan's implementation after 1955. Those failures resulted from Sichuan's reaction to national politics – the desire to accelerate the pace of development – and contributed to its economic and administrative problems during 1956–7.

In late 1955, a few but by no means all provinces, notably Shanxi, Jiangxi and Shandong, had unilaterally (that is without central approval but presumably with Mao's later blessing) brought forward the achievement of their five year plan targets from 1957 to 1956.[9] Sichuan not only revised its 1956 plan,[10] but as early as November 1955 it also increased its targets for 1957 and explicitly indicated that the new targets were higher than those provided in the State Plan.

For example, grain output for 1957 was now set at 46,200 mn *jin* p.a., 'a target which we will try to surpass'.[11] Although it was claimed that the original provincial five year grain target had been completed in 1956,[12] the targets revised in 1955–6 were rarely mentioned after April 1956,[13] and as a comparison between the figures previously quoted for the 1957 grain output and the revised target shows, it seems likely that the higher targets were not met. Moreover, although the original plan had envisaged that investment for provincial industry would be supplied by the province, the 1957 Budget explicitly recognized a deficit of almost 3 million *yuan*, 'an amount which will be made up through a loan from the central government'.[14]

The provincial supply crisis of 1956–7

During the second half of 1956 and the beginning of 1957 Sichuan's leaders explicitly admitted that in general supply did not meet demand.[15] There were two main aspects of the crisis. In the first place, despite improvements in the province's transport and distribution system,[16] there was still in 1956, as Li Dazhang put it, 'a contradiction between the amount of material resources and the province's transport capacity'.[17] Stockpiling occurred, not only within Sichuan of goods waiting to be transferred between the towns and villages, but also on the provincial borders, notably in Baoji and Yichang, of the raw materials, machinery, and manufactures which were vital to her developing economy.[18] Within the province, shortages and stockpiling became commonplace. For example, in October the Zigong Department of Salt Administration complained bitterly about 'the critical situation in edible salt distribution', for whilst the salt was piling up in Zigong (after a drive for increased production) there were shortages around the province.[19]

Given the importance of Sichuan's agricultural output to the rest of the country, the realization of the defects in freight transport led to a rush of emergency measures. Construction of the Bao-Cheng railway, connecting the Chengdu-Chongqing railway with Shaanxi and the north of China was accelerated and opened in early September 1956, over a year ahead of its scheduled date.[20] On 22 September the first fully loaded 'rice train' from Sichuan arrived in Baoji,[21] and in the first half of the month the line was used to import more than 3,100 tons of 'cotton cloth, consumer goods and industrial equipment'.[22] More spectacularly, given both the difficulties of the 5,000 km journey from Shanghai and the size of China's navy at the time,[23] two warships of the East China Fleet, 'full of all kinds of steel products necessary to construction, and everyday commodities', travelled up the Yangtze to Chongqing, arriving in the afternoon of 27 September.[24]

Within the province, measures were also taken to alleviate the situation. In industry, enterprises which had hoarded material resources (in response to shortages) were encouraged to make their surplus stock available in a series of mutually helpful re-allocation meetings.[25] An attempt was made to make the transport system more efficient, both by the provision and more efficient utilization of vehicles. A two-shift system was introduced and routes were adjusted so that vehicles should not return empty after delivery.[26] Finally, a campaign was started to use 'the popular forms of transport – oxen, pack-horses, carts – as one way of making up the deficiencies and solving the problems of transport capacity';[27] and surplus labour was encouraged to participate in short-distance transportation.[28]

The second aspect of the crisis was that there were shortages of certain agricultural products which were necessary not only as subsidiary foodstuffs, but also as the raw materials for light industry. Some shortages were of items whose production had traditionally created problems, and the immediate solution was to try to raise output by technical improvements. Thus in the cotton industry, the cultivated acreage was increased, cotton planting forwarded by 15–20 days,[29] and more spindles brought into operation. None the less, the raw cotton production plan for 1956 was not met,[30] and the output of cotton cloth still only met 40% of demand.[31] Even more serious were the shortages of those agricultural products whose outputs was traditionally high. Almost all economic crops failed to meet production targets,[32] and sideline production actually decreased.[33]

One reason for the shortages, as both Governor Li Dazhang (in his Government Work Reports of 1956 and 1957) and Li Jingquan (in his speech to the 8th National Party Congress) recognized was that state prices for agricultural produce in the province were too low. On the open market prices for agricultural products were generally 10–20% over the state's, although in Nanchong they reached 40–60% higher.[34] As a result peasants were reluctant to participate in the state procurement campaigns[35] and they consequently did not meet their targets.[36] Originally Sichuan's agricultural prices had been set lower than the national average, and industrial prices higher, in line with the policy of encouraging provincial industry.[37] The immediate solution was to raise the state-sale prices of agricultural products.[38] The price for oil-bearing crops was raised 25% in October 1956,[39] and the grain price by 6%.[40]

However, the major reason for those shortages would seem to be that at the time of co-operativization, grain production was emphasized to the virtual exclusion of all else. Speaking at the 4th session of the 1st PPC, Li Dazhang stated that:

The most important reason (for these deficiencies) was that whilst producing cotton and grain, they (the agricultural producer cooperatives) did not do a good job of arranging for the production of economic crops and sideline production.[41]

During 1955–6, when production of economic crops and from sideline industry decreased, grain output increased by 10%[42] – an increase equivalent to twice the average annual net increase for the previous three years, and a quarter of the national net increase in 1956.[43] The situation was serious because many peasants, particularly those outside the Chengdu plain, did not depend on grain for their income. The result, as one survey of Jiangjian *xian* showed, was that 'Although grain output has increased a lot, the decline in sideline industry income has meant that income from agriculture has not increased at all.'[44] To combat this tendency the Provincial People's Council laid down new regulations for sideline and economic crop production.[45] However, such problems were also blamed on cadres' weakness, and provided positive argument for administrative reorganization and rectification.

'Better troops and simpler administration'

Throughout 1956 Sichuan's leaders and media frequently criticized the over-bureaucratization of both the administrative system and cadres' leadership-style, to which they attributed many of the problems which had become apparent during 1956, such as the overemphasis on grain production during collectivization. Cadres were urged to 'Leave the office' and 'Go down to the front line of production'.[46] The 1st Provincial Party Congress, meeting in July, devoted itself exclusively to problems of leadership style, and emphasized the importance of ideological education and the 'mass line'[47] as did Li Jingquan in his speech to the 8th National Party Congress.[48] In the fourth section of his Government Work Report for 1956, Li Dazhang provided a clear statement of the leadership's concern about bureaucratization.[49]

We must see that at present a kind of bureaucratic tendency has become apparent in leadership organs throughout the province. This tendency departs from reality and the masses, and is harmful to the cause of socialist construction. Where is this tendency manifested? Where there are many leadership cadres satisfied with sitting in their offices, studying documents and deciding problems, and not paying attention to going down deep amongst the masses so as to understand the problems at lower levels, and not carrying out effective investigation and research. Whenever problems arise, enough attention isn't paid to conferring with lower levels, and many just ignore the opinions of the masses. As a result, when drawing up plans and deciding tasks and targets, they often have no idea of numbers, they simply act subjectively as the fancy takes them, or rely on statistics from written reports whose inaccurate figures they follow. They therefore aren't starting out from reality, with the result that unnecessary things, some of which surpass the realm of possibility, are given priority and made urgent.[50]

Li also went on to criticize those cadres who revelled in giving orders, and whose level of ideological education was low; 'red-tapism'; and the creation of complex bureaucratic organization for its own sake.[51]

In its concern with problems of administrative growth and its advocacy of rectification towards the end of 1956 Sichuan's leadership was by no means unusual. However, the measures which it took to combat 'bureaucratism' are particularly relevant on two counts. The first is that Sichuan's leaders would seem to have followed Mao's policy preferences towards rectification during 1956–7. Rectification had been discussed at the 8th National Party Congress in September 1956 but scheduled for 1958. However, in Sichuan a rectification campaign started in late 1956. In his report to the November PPC, Li Dazhang had outlined four measures to combat 'bureaucratism'. Cadres were to be organized for political study; the administration was to be slimmed down with unnecessary units abolished and surplus cadres transferred to strengthen basic-level organizations; the 'supervisory function of the masses' was to be strengthened; and the 'mass line' was to be emphasized as the leadership principle for cadres.[52] Under the slogan of 'Diligently construct the nation, promote a plain and simple working style', a rectification movement was launched along the lines of Li Dazhang's suggestions by the 2nd plenum of the provincial party committee, held from 3 to 8 December 1956.[53]

Moreover, Sichuan's leaders would appear to have taken a pro-Mao stance in the national-level debate on rectification which came to a head in April/May 1957. MacFarquhar lists four indicators of provincial leaders' attitudes during May 1957 to Mao's directive on rectification of late April, derived from 'the publicity they chose to have given to their activities connected with the campaign'.[54] Provincial leaders can be said to have been favourably disposed to Mao's policy if it was 'unequivocally stated that the first secretary would take command' of rectification; a special leadership group established to oversee the campaign; the 'Three Evils' that rectification was designed to combat – namely 'bureaucratism, sectarianism, and subjectivism' – were listed in that correct order in provincial publicity; and if the provincial first party secretary was involved in manual labour. Contrary to his assertion, based on incomplete data, that Sichuan disapproved of Mao's line on rectification, the opposite would appear to be the case.[55] The provincial attitude to rectification was not only decided before Mao's directive of 27 April, but was also pro-Mao according to all four of MacFarquhar's indicators, as was its response to that directive. The provincial party committee had launched the rectification campaign in Sichuan at its 4th plenum held 13–16 April. A 'small group' was established from within the provincial secretariat to direct the campaign; and the 'Three evils' of 'bureaucratism, sectarianism, and subjectivism', were listed in the correct order in the plenum's communiqué.[56] Throughout the rectification campaign it was led by the provincial first secretary, Li Jingquan; starting in December 1956 at the 2nd plenum of the provincial party committee when he had first advocated rectification as such,[57] right through to October 1957.[58] Finally, not only Li Jingquan, but all the provincial leadership, engaged in manual labour on several occasions.[59]

Finally, it would seem possible that with respect to rectification, Sichuan's leaders shared Mao's view on 'extended democracy' (*da minzhu*), and the importance of 'airing one's views', and 'big blooming and contending' (*da ming da fang*). Thus, articles on rectification repeatedly stressed the need for *da ming da fang*[60] and that it was 'an all-people' rectification,[61] even after the debacle of the 'Hundred Flowers'. Later still, Li Dazhang criticized those who had deliberately mis-interpreted the term *da minzhu* in too broad and permissive a sense.[62]

The second, is that in the rationalization of the administrative system designed to combat the growth in bureaucracy, it would seem that Sichuan began to experiment with the implementation of 'dual rule'. In that it was presumably not unusual, since the 8th National Party Congress in September 1956, had called for the strengthening of 'dual rule'.[63] Greater co-ordination at each level, under party leadership, in order to cut down on waste and unnecessary bureaucratic procedures, was a major proposal of the 1st provincial party congress in July 1956;[64] and Li Dazhang in his 1956 Government Work Report criticized the overemphasis on perpendicular channels of communication within each hierarchy and the lack of coordination between them, which led to 'contradictions and dislocations in administrative work'.[65] Early in 1957, Special Commissioners' Offices were created to that end in order to co-ordinate economic planning at provincial level,[66] although the exact extent of their powers and the practice are unknown. Certainly, in this connection, it is interesting to note that according to Li Jingquan it had been the provincial party committee which had overseen the rectification campaign '... in all this province's provincial-level organs, including units of the centre stationed in the province'.[67]

GUIZHOU

The major preoccupations of Guizhou's leadership, as reported through the media, during 1955–7 were the implementation of agricultural collectivization and severe problems with both agricultural production and the province's national minorities. Although the latter partially resulted from the centre's changed policy on the integration of national minorities after 1955, to a large extent Guizhou seems more introspective and less part of national politics than Sichuan. At first sight Guizhou's apparent slow response to central directives and national politics, as for example in the implementation of the provincial five year plan during 1956–7 or the rectification movement of 1957–8, might appear to signify provincial resistance. However, such slow responses are perhaps more reasonably explained by the scale of the problems facing Guizhou's leadership from within the province at the time. Certainly, although three of the province's leaders were removed from office in 1957–8, they all went as a result of the problems with national minorities in the province,[68] and there was no major reorganization of the provincial party leadership as occurred elsewhere.[69] Guizhou's apparent deviations from national norms are thus explained as a result of its lack of internal integration and the CCP's problems of control at provincial-level. Despite advances economically and politically from 1949 to 1955, Guizhou by 1957 was hardly beginning to relinquish its status as an internal colony.

Economic problems

Particularly by comparison with Sichuan, the implementation of the provincial five year plan in Guizhou was very low-key indeed, not to say disappointing. The provincial plan was announced at the 5th representative conference of the Guizhou CCP in September 1955[70] and, as became apparent to a fuller extent later,[71] was almost exclusively concerned with increasing agricultural production. Few of the plan's targets were ever specifically put into figures, even retrospectively, although in 1958 it was stated that the 'First Five Year Plan had been fulfilled ahead of schedule'.[72] As was made explicit at the time, resources for non-agricultural development in the Southwest were to be concentrated on Sichuan, which was to be developed as the centre of the regional economy.[73] It was intended that any provincial industrial development should be generated by increased agricultural production, and Guizhou was clearly economically dependent on Sichuan throughout the period. Otherwise, the only non-agricultural area of intended development was local transport, which was seen as the basis of growth for an integrated provincial economy.[74]

At first sight Guizhou's economic development under the five year plan would appear to have been more than moderately successful. Although historically not a province self-sufficient in grain, during 1954–5 it not only supplied its own needs (for the second consecutive year) but had also exported 80.7 mn *jin* to other provinces.[75] Moreover, it was stated that in 1956 the province's grain output had passed the 1957 target by 14%.[76] Similarly, where before 1949 twelve of the province's *xian* had not been approachable by any kind of wheeled traffic,[77] and 28 inaccessible to motor vehicles, all were by the end of 1957.[78] 3,000 kms of new local roads had been built, 944 kms of trunk roads, and river navigation improved.[79] New long-distance coach routes ran within the province,[80] and it was reported that every country, region and village was accessible by post and telegraph.[81]

However, Guizhou's remarkable economic development had been bought at a cost and occurred under conditions which effectively limited growth to the period before 1956. Continued growth had been predicated on increased agricultural production, that had been achieved up to 1955 by a variety of measures including the extension of the arable acreage, improved agricultural techniques, the extension of the irrigated acreage, and the distribution of free agricultural implements. Similar measures were implemented after 1955 in order to increase agricultural output still further but the attempt failed. 'Thus, for example, despite the distribution of almost 134 mn *yuan* of agricultural fertilizer and implements,[82] the extension of irrigated and arable acreages, and output, slowed.[83] Apart from the fact that the Guizhou leadership's expectation of still greater increases in the rate of increase of agricultural production were unrealistic, there were two connected factors limiting further growth. The first was the weather, which (although fine in 1953 and 1954) led to floods in the province every summer during 1955,[84] 1956[85] and 1957.[86] Zhou Lin argued in his speech to the 8th Party Congress in 1956, that because of the nature of mountain farming in Guizhou there was a need for large-scale flood control and water conservancy projects.[87] However, Guizhou's budget had already been stretched by earlier agricultural construction projects in order to achieve the initial successes, and money was the second limiting factor. Guizhou was heavily dependent on aid from the central government. 46.3% of its 1956 income was from central sources[88] and 40.4% in 1957.[89] Moreover even without the need for a disaster fund, its planned expenditure on agricultural construction projects was nowhere met by its income from agricultural production, which was approximately 60 mn *yuan* as against 40 mn *yuan* in both years.

In order to combat the flood danger, the leadership devoted the first halves of both 1956 and 1957 to campaigns aimed at developing small-scale flood control and water conservancy projects;[90] although at the same time they did not abandon the idea of collecting 'a bumper harvest'.[91] The concern with economic problems may at least partially explain why Guizhou did not attempt to forward the completion of its first five year plan during the first half of 1956. Thus, at that time only one plan target was said to have been completed a year ahead of schedule,[92] and it was not until August 1957 that the leadership announced the 'early' fulfilment of five year plan targets for '13 of the 20 major products outlined in the plan'.[93] Similarly in 1957, when preparation work was followed by even more serious floods, lasting two months,[94] the rectification campaign was only mentioned as such for the first time in June,[95] much later than in the rest of the country. Moreover, the leadership's concern with increasing agricultural production would also seem to have had effects on the non-agricultural sectors of the economy. According to the final budgets for both 1956 and 1957, some planned new projects were not started and others were not completed. In addition, both the transport and provincial industry plans were not fulfilled.[96] Given both the underdeveloped nature of Guizhou's economy (and in particular the importance of transport and local industry) and the tight financial situation, it seems reasonable to assume that funds were diverted into the agricultural sector.

National minorities, rectification and the 'Anti-Rightists Movement'

Guizhou's problems with its national minorities came about largely as a direct result of the change in national policy which occurred at the end of 1955. Before that date, as has already been indicated, the CCP's policy toward national minorities had been extremely conciliatory. However, following the 'high tide' of co-operativization, the decision was taken to speed up the process of democratic reform and socialization in national minority areas. On 29 December 1955 the State Council issued a directive to the effect that 'national minority democratic coalition governments', such as existed in the Miao areas of Guizhou, had to become either 'autonomous' (i.e. national minority) area governments or ordinary administrative units by the end of 1956.[97] Guizhou's response was to establish the Qiandongnan Miao-Tong Autonomous *zhou* (June 1956); the Qiannan Puyi-Miao Autonomous *zhou* (August 1956); and the Sandu Shui Autonomous *xian* (January 1957).[98]

However, it was the socialization of agriculture in national minority areas (to be considered in more detail in Ch. 3)[99] which led to friction, resentment and resistance. When collectivization was eventually completed in March 1957 it was stated that there had been problems in the national minority areas.[100] Moreover, in the 'Anti-Rightists Movement' which started three months later, it became apparent that collectivization had done little to aid racial harmony in Guizhou. National minority 'rightists' were said to have derided collectivization and preferred private ownership,[101] and it would seem likely that the resurgence of armed 'counter-revolutionary activities' in Guizhou's rural areas during 1956-7[102] resulted from their antagonism. These problems too would seem to have contributed to the delayed start of the rectification campaign in Guizhou. Although rectification might have been more necessary here than in Sichuan, there were more immediate problems in the first half of 1957.

The rectification campaign and the 'Anti-Rightists Movement' were barely distinguishable in Guizhou, and were almost always referred to together by provincial leaders.[103] Although rectification had been mentioned once or twice at the beginning of 1957 by the provincial media,[104] and Zhou Lin had been interviewed in the national press during May on the importance of participating in manual labour,[105] in fact, for reasons already suggested, rectification started late in Guizhou. By way of comparison, whereas the *Sichuan Daily* reported Mao's 'On the correct handling of contradictions among the people' extensively on 16 April, it was not publicized at all in the *Guizhou Daily* until 19 June 1957. In fact the time difference may have been even greater for where Mao's speech was referred to as a study document in Sichuan during mid-April,[106] it was not reported as having been used as a discussion document in Guizhou until August.[107] On the other hand, though it started later than elsewhere it also went on longer, for Zhou Lin in his 1958 Government Work Report referred to both the rectification campaign and the 'Anti-Rightists Movement' lasting from August 1957 until September 1958.[108] Certainly, the latter was still claiming victims well into 1958.[109]

Although the joint campaign did result in measures for the implementation of 'Better Troops and Simpler Administration',[110] its main thrust was elsewhere, particularly during 1957. Emphasizing the importance and difficulties of Guizhou's internal integration, the rectification campaign/'Anti-Rightists Movement' was directed straight at the province's minority nationalities. The removal of the Miao Vice-Governor Ou Baichuan in November 1957 has already been mentioned. On 2 December 1957, Zhou Lin emphasized the reasons for Ou Baichuan's dismissal by delivering a blistering attack on 'local nationalism'. Although he criticized 'great Han chauvinism'

3

AGRICULTURAL
CO-OPERATIVIZATION

The role of provincial leaders in general in the national decision-making process, and of Sichuan's leaders in particular, is amply demonstrated by the 'High Tide' of agricultural co-operativization. Without the participation of the provincial leaders, the 'High Tide' is unlikely to have occurred in the form it did, if at all. Certainly, provincial leaders can influence national policy in a number of ways, both formal and informal. As both Chang[1] and Lieberthal[2] have indicated, provincial leaders came to play a significant role in the formulation of policy at national level after the beginning of 1955. In particular, not only were they invited to attend 'enlarged meetings' of the Politburo and Central Committee, but they also had their own national-level forum for debate and discussion – the regular meetings of first secretaries of provinces, municipalities and autonomous regions.[3] Indeed, it was at one such meeting that the 'High Tide' was in effect launched.

However, as indicated in the Introduction, provincial leaders can also influence national policy through their implementation of central directives. In particular the selection of areas for experimentation, and of models for emulation is crucial to the emergence of policy. 'Experimental points' are established to provide information about the effect of policy and the problems encountered. Thus during 1956 in the trial period of Higher Stage Collectivization, both Sichuan and Guizhou experimented. In Sichuan 'experimental plots' were established in the province's 'mountain areas, foothill regions, and plainlands';[4] in Guizhou, on the other hand, the emphasis (though not exclusively) was on experimental collectives in the mountain (and problem) areas.[5] In Guizhou, whereas the Chinese tend to inhabit the few plains and lowlands the national minorities are concentrated in the mountain regions. As has been suggested earlier, the two major problems facing Guizhou's leadership concerned the national minorities and agricultural growth. In general, provincial leaders could and did use the period of experimentation to influence the formulation as well as the implementation of national policy.[6] The selection of experimental areas could have been made in order to produce the results desired, which are then incorporated into national policy as the basis for a campaign. Or specific ideas could simply be put into practice in one area to try and influence others or the formulation of policy generally. Certainly, this would appear to have been the case with communization in 1958.[7] In this case this is what would appear to have happened in Sichuan during the 'High Tide'. This chapter explains Sichuan's apparent aberrant behaviour at that time as an abortive attempt to influence the decision-making process. Moreover, provincial leaders can also influence national policy through their control of the pace of implementation.[8] The example of those provincial leaders who forwarded the implementation of the First Five Year Plan during 1955–6 has already been discussed.

THE 'HIGH TIDE' OF AGRICULTURAL CO-OPERATIVIZATION

The creation of Agricultural Producer Cooperatives (APCs) in China's countryside was conceived originally as a two-stage process exending over a number of years.[9] First, Lower Stage Co-operatives (LSCs, or just 'co-operatives') were to be established, on the basis of the already existent permanent or seasonal Mutual Aid Teams. Later, Higher Stage Collectives (HSCs, or simply 'collectives') were to be created through the amalgamation of co-operatives. The essential differences between the two forms of APC were size and ownership. HSCs were not only to be larger but also to be based on collective ownership. To simplify, in the LSCs peasants retained ownership of their draught animals, land, tools, implements, etc., all of which were rented or sold to the co-operative. In return they received remuneration in proportion to their original share in the co-operative in addition to their work. In the collective, agricultural property in general was pooled, although each household was allocated a private plot and retained ownership of some domestic livestock and small agricultural tools, and peasants were paid according to their work alone. However, the socialization of agriculture during 1955–6 was an excellent example of provincial leaders' ability to influence national policy. Agricultural co-operativization only started in earnest nationally in the summer of 1955, yet by the summer of 1956 higher stage collectivization was near completion. In that process, as both Chang[10] and Schurmann[11] have suggested, there is more than a hint of an alliance between Mao and provincial leaders.

The acceleration in agricultural co-operativization came after July 1955. Before that date, co-operativization had been carried out gradually but unspectacularly. Moreover, in March 1955 a policy of consolidation, and to a certain extent retrenchment, had been executed in line with a State Council directive which stated that:

> In order to ensure the healthy and normal development of the co-operativization movement, the pace ... should be slowed down a bit. Before spring farming, development of new agricultural producer co-operatives should be stopped and efforts concentrated on recognizing existing agricultural producer co-operatives.[12]

Caution in co-operativization was also implicit in the first five year plan outlined by Li Fuchun on 5 and 6 July to the National People's Congress. According to the plan, approximately one-third of peasant households were to be in lower stage co-operatives by the end of 1957.[13] However, Mao's speech 'On the question of agricultural cooperation' delivered to a work conference of provincial and municipal party secretaries on 31 July[14] proved a decisive turning point. Mao not only criticized the cautious attitude of March,[15] but called for the establishment of 1.3 million APCs by October 1956,[16] set the target of 50% of peasant households to be in APCs by the spring of 1958, and advocated the completion of co-operativization by 1960.[17] All of which represented a considerble increase on Li Fuchun's target published only four days earlier. Somewhat in parenthesis, but not totally so, it is perhaps worth underlining the more general significance of the work conference held on 31 July 1955. This would appear to have been the first occasion after 1949 on which Mao used his position and prestige to bypass a decision made by the leadership *in toto*, but with which he seems to have disagreed, by appealing to others over his colleague's heads – a technique he was to use to effect later and more frequently. Moreover, that work conference would also appear to have been the first important occasion on which provincial leaders (however passively at first) were drawn into the national decision-making process.

Provincial leaders' reactions were dramatic and led to a series of revisions in the schedule for the implementation of co-operativization which occurred from Mao's speech to the end of the year. In August and September each province organized study groups on Mao's speech and conducted investigations of their own provinces. As a result they each issued new targets which brought forward Mao's target of 1.3 million APCs to the spring of 1956. Furthermore, 18 of the 19 provinces which publicized revised targets for 1957 aimed at 50% of peasant households to be in APCs by that date.[18] Those revisions led to the 6th plenum of the 7th Central Committee in October, which again set new targets. Areas which had already 30–40% of peasant households in APCs by the summer of 1955 were to achieve 70–80% completion by the spring of 1957, whilst other areas were expected to complete co-operativization by the spring of 1958.[19] However, following the plenum the provinces issued new targets that were equivalent to the basic completion of co-operativization by the spring of 1957, and all of the 21 provinces which issued targets for mid-November 1955 aimed at a minimum 30% completion by that date.[20] Finally, in late November, the provinces issued further revised targets which called for 'advanced areas' to complete co-operativization by the end of 1955, and other areas by the end of 1956.[21]

By the end of 1955, 60% of peasant households had been co-operativized,[22] that is they had joined at least lower stage co-operatives. With the 'basic' completion of co–operativization by the end of January 1956,[23] attention at both national and provincial levels turned to the creation of higher stage collectives.[24] As with, and part of, the acceleration in the implementation of the first five year plan, enthusiasm for collectivization continued throughout the first few months of 1956. Despite Deng Zihui's criticisms of the co-operativization movement in May,[25] the momentum was barely checked and collectivization was completed nationally well before the end of the year.

By the summer of 1956, 91.7% of all peasant households in China were in APCs. Of those 62.2% were in collectives and 29.1% were in co–operatives. Furthermore, 23 out of the 27 provinces for which figures are available had more than 40% of peasant households in HSCs.[26] These figures should be compared to those for the summer of 1955 to obtain some idea of the speed of transformation. Then only 14.2% of peasant households were co-operativized, 14.16% in lower stage co–operatives and 0.03% in higher stage collectives.[27]

Table 3 *Agricultural co-operativization in Guizhou, 1955-7*

Date[2]	% of peasant households in all APCs[1]	Number of APCs	% of peasant households in HSCs[1]	Number of HSCs	% of peasant households in LSCs[1]	Number of LSCs
1954		519[3]				
1955						
March		6,000[4]				
June	5.5	6,625	–	–	5.5[5]	6,625[5]
mid-August		16,000[6]				
August		17,000[7]				
September	30.0[8]	31,000+[8]				
December	31.0[9]	35,600[9]				
1956						
January	77.7[10]	57,222[10]				
June	93.6	34,579	51.6[11]	5,827[11]	42.0[12]	28,752[12]
November	96.1[13]		83.0[13]		13.1	
December	94.2[14]					
1957						
March			85.7[14]			
April			87.5[15]			

[1]. Agricultural Producer Cooperative (APC) is a generic term for both Higher Stage Collective (HSC) and Lower Stage Cooprtive (LSC). No collectives were established in Guizhou before January 1956.

[2]. All dates are end month unless otherwise indicated.

[3]. *Guangming ribao* (GMRB) 5 August 1954, Report on PPC.

[4]. NCNA Guiyang 21 March 1955, 'Guizhou Provincial People's Council holds meeting on ploughing and production', in SCMP 1037, p. 45.

[5]. Shi Jingtang et al. (ed.) *Zhongguo nongye hezuohua yundong shiliao* (ZNHYS) Sanlian shudian, Beijing, Vol. 2, p. 1011.

[6]. NCNA Guiyang 26 August 1955, 'Guizhou turns from a grain deficit into a grain surplus area', in SCMP 1121, p. 30.

[7]. NCNA Guiyang 1 September 1955, in SCMP 1125, p. 9.

[8]. NCNA Guiyang 28 September 1955, 'Fifth Representative Conference of CCP held in Guizhou', in SCMP 1142, p. 17.

[9]. NCNA Guiyang 29 December 1955, in SCMP 1210, p. 32.

[10]. XQRB 2 February 1956, p. 1 'Our province has basically realized Lower Stage Co-operativization'.

[11]. ZNHYS, op.cit., p. 1019.

[12]. ibid., p. 1012.

[13]. GZRB 8 February 1957, p. 1. 'What is at present the most important rural contra-diction?'

[14]. GZRB 15 August 1957, p. 2, in the 1956 final budget.

[14]. GZRB 20 August 1957, p. 1, 'Our province's economic departments have completed and surpassed most of the plan in the first half of the year'.

Table 4 *Agricultural co-operativization in Sichuan, 1955–7*

Date[1]	% of peasant households in all APCs	Number of APCs	% of peasant households in HSCs	Number of HSCs	% of peasant households in LSCs	Number of LSCs
1952		604[2]				
1954		866[3]				
1955						
March	6.17[4]	25,000[5]				
June	7.8[6]	30,314	0.67[7]	278[7]	7.4[8]	30,036[8]
August		28,800[9]				
October	17.4[10]	57,400[10]				
November	37.8[11]	134,700[11]				
December	44.0[12]	154,574[12]	4.0[13]		40.0	
1956						
January	70.0[14]	210,000[14]				
February			4.0[15]	1,861[15]		
April	77.8[16]					
June	76.7	195,143	7.4[17]	3,969[17]	69.3[18]	191,174[18]
July			14.0[15]	6,500[15]		
August			17.26[19]			
mid-Sept.			21.6[15]	13,294[15]		
September	89.87[20]		30.46[21]		59.41	
October			41.13[19]			
November			83.0[13]			
December	94.38[22]					
1957						
June	95.1[23]	194,000[23]	88.3[23]	175,000[23]	6.8	19,000

APC = Agricultural Producer Co-operative
HSC = Higher Stage Collective
LSC = Lower Stage Co-operative

[1]. Dates are end of month, unless otherwise indicated.
[2]. GMRB 10 August 1952, Li Jingquan's report to PPC, August 1952.
[3]. SCRB 19 January 1955, Li Jingquan's report to PPC, December 1954.
[4]. NCNA Chengdu, 8 March 1955, 'Plan of setting up co-operatives in Sichuan basically fulfilled'.
[5]. SCRB 6 March 1955, p. 1, 'Plan of 25,000 APCs before spring farming completed'.
[6]. NCNA Chengdu, 14 June 1955 in SCMP 1071, p. 27.
[7]. Shi Jingtang et al. (ed.) *Zhongguo nongye hezuohua yundong shiliao* (ZNHYS) Sanlian Shudian, Beijing, 1959, Vol. 2, p. 1018.
[8]. ibid., p. 1011.
[9]. NCNA Chengdu, 24 August 1955, in SCMP 1120, p. 26.

THE 'HIGH TIDE' IN GUIZHOU AND SICHUAN

The implementation of agricultural co-operativization in Sichuan and Guizhou, their response to national politics, and their parts in the 'High Tide' provide an interesting contrast. Both developed similarly to the end of 1955. However, during 1956 their experiences were very different. Guizhou, despite (or rather because of) its problems with national minorities and agricultural production, did not depart significantly from national norms. Sichuan, on the other hand, as Walker has indicated,[28] appears to have been extremely slow in implementing higher stage collectivization. Selected available data on agricultural co-operativization in Guizhou have been provided in Table 3, and for Sichuan in Table 4.

Broadly speaking, both Guizhou and Sichuan followed national trends throughout 1955. The two provinces' targets for co-operativization set during 1955 have been listed in Table 5. In the spring those APCs already established were consolidated, as a result of the change in national policy. However, this did not lead to a reduction in the

Notes to Table 4 (*cont.*)

10. NCNA Chengdu, 20 November 1955, in SCMP 1180, p. 14.
11. CQRB 2 December 1955, Yan Xiufeng's report on the provincial five year plan to the PPC, November 1955.
12. NCNA Chengdu, 13 December 1955, in SCMP 1195, p. 5.
13. SCRB 2 January 1957, p. 1, 'Natural village Higher Stage collectivization basically realized'.
14. NCNA 21 January 1956 report, datelined Sichuan 19 January 1956, reprinted in ZNHYS, op.cit., p. 888.
15. SCRB 3 October 1956, p. 1, 'More than 13,000 higher stage collectives in the province'.
16. XHBYK 15, 1956 (General No. 89) p. 39, Li Dazhang, 'The Conditions of Sichuan's Agricultural Cooperativization Movement'.
17. ZNHYS op. cit., p. 1019.
18. ibid., p. 1012.
19. SCRB 6 December 1956, p. 2, 'Why it's generally inappropriate at present to run *da she*'.
20. SCRB 23 November 1956, p. 2, Li Dazhang's Government Work Report to the PPC.
21. SCRB 29 October 1956, p. 1, 'The whole country's higher stage agricultural co-operativization movement continues to develop'.
22. SCRB 31 August 1957, p. 3, 'The province's agricultural co-operatives have shown their excellence'.
23. SCRB 20 August 1957, p. 1, 'Provincial People's Congress preparatory meeting continues discussion on retaliating from every angle at rightist elements'.

Table 5 *The raising of co-operativization targets in Sichuan and Guizhou,
1955*

Date	Sichuan target	Guizhou target
Date 1954	17,000 APCs to be created by Spring 1955 and a further 15,000 APCs by Autumn 1955, so that 10% of peasant households would be in APCs[1]	5,000 APCs to be created by Spring 1955.[2]
1955		
March		6,000 APCs to be consolidated[3]
May	25,000 APCs to be consolidated[4]	
August	100,000 new APCs to be established by Spring 1956 so that 27% of peasant households would be in APCs[5]	31,000 new APCs planned for Spring 1956 so that 30% of all peasant households would be in APCs. A further 60,000 planned for 1957 to make a total of 55% of peasant households.[6]
October	129,000 APCs planned for Spring 1956[7]	
November	77,000 new APCs to be created during December–May making a total of 134,000, so that 40% of peasant households would be in APCs by May[8]	
Late November	According to the provincial five year plan, 100,000 new APCs were to be created in the Autumn–Winter of 1956 so that a total of 76% of peasant households would be in APCs[9]	
December	Completion of Co-operativization by end 1956[10]	By Summer 1956, 29,000 additional APCs to be built so that a target of 75% of peasant households would be in APCs by the Autumn Harvest of 1956.[11]

---

[1]. SCRB 19 January 1955, Li Jingquan's report to PPC, December 1954.
[2]. *Guangming ribao* (GMRB) 5 August 1954, report of 1st PPC.

numbers of APC, such as occurred in other provinces, notably Zhejiang.[29] On the contrary, in both provinces there was a continued rise, though small, in the numbers of APCs to the end of June. After Mao's speech both Guizhou and Sichuan responded by creating agricultural co-operatives at a faster rate than intended and by raising their targets for the future. Although slightly slower in agricultural co-operativization than the national average, both provinces performed well when compared to other southern and 'later liberated' provinces'; for in general the northern and 'early liberated' areas were in the forefront of the movement to advance co-operativization. Comparative data have been provided in Table 6. Guangdong has been chosen as a representative of similar southern 'later-liberated' provinces. Certainly, in January 1956, both provinces claimed to have 'achieved the semi-socialist transformation of agriculture' (i.e. the establishment of LSCs) by the end of 1955,[30] although according to contemporary accounts it seems more likely that this was 'basically' (i.e. more than 70%) achieved during January 1956 itself.

During 1956, as Table 6 indicates, the paths of the two provinces diverged. On the one hand, Guizhou maintained the momentum of its co–operativization campaign and completed higher stage collectivization by at least November. Although collectivization was slower than the national norm at mid-year, it performed rather well by comparison with Guangdong. Sichuan, on the other, appears to have had problems or to have been reluctant to collectivize in the first half of 1956. However, it should be pointed out that collectivization in Sichuan had reached national standards by November.

Guizhou's normal implementation of agricultural co-operativization might seem somewhat surprising given the province's concerns

Notes to Table 5 *(cont.)*

3. NCNA Guiyang, 21 March 1955, in SCMP 1037, 'Guizhou Provincial People's Council holds meeting on ploughing and production', p. 45.
4. SCRB 6 May 1955, p. 1, Editorial, 'Advance and do a good job of consolidating cooperatives'.
5. NCNA Chengdu, 25 August 1955, in SCMP 1120, p. 26.
6. CB 373, 20 January 1956, *Agricultural Cooperativization in Communist China*, p. 15. The sources cited in CB 373 are from the national-level media.
7. ibid., p. 20.
8. NCNA Chengdu, 28 November 1955 in SCMP 1185, p. 11.
9. CQRB 2 December 1955.
10. CB 373, op.cit., p. 23.
11. NCNA Guiyang 29 December 1955, in SCMP 1210, p. 32.

Table 6 *Comparative rates of co-operativization in China*

	% of peasant households in Agricultural Producer Co-operatives							
	Lower Stage Co-operatives				Higher Stage Collectives			
	in:				in:			
Date	China	Guangdong	Sichuan	Guizhou	China	Guangdong	Sichuan	Guizhou
1955								
June	14.2	6.6	7.4	5.5	0.3	–	0.67	–
September		7.0		30.0		–		–
November		40.0	37.8			–		–
December	59.3		40.0	31.0	4.0		4.0	–
1956								
January	49.6	80.7	66.0	77.7	30.7	–	4.0	–
February					51.0		4.0	
March	34.0	48.5			54.9	44.3		
June	28.7	47.7	69.3	42.0	63.2	44.1	7.4	51.6
July	29.0	50.0			63.4	45.0		
November	13.1	6.6		13.1	83.0	88.9	83.0	83.0

Sources: For data on China as a whole and Guangdong, K. R. Walker 'Collectivization in retrospect: The "Socialist High Tide" of Autumn 1955–Spring 1956' in CQ 26, p. 35–6; and on Guizhou and Sichuan, Tables 5 and 6.

Note: Dates are end month.

with agricultural production and the national minorities. As has already been indicated, those concerns had led to a delayed response to other aspects of national politics during 1956 and 1957. However, to a large extent, co-operativization offered Guizhou's leaders possible solutions to these two problems. In agriculture Guizhou's leaders were concerned with increased production (particularly of grain), flood control and water conservancy. All three were heavily emphasized as major reasons for co-operativization when the province accelerated its creation of APCs during the late summer of 1955.[31] Again, during the first half of 1956, when attention turned to higher stage collectivization, that campaign was explicitly linked with anti-flood preparatory work and the need for water conservancy projects.[32] As elsewhere, much was made of the benefits of co-operativization. For example, peasant incomes were said to have risen,[33] and the provincial wheat harvest to have increased by 23.57%.[34] By implication collectivization would bring even greater gains. Thus, an investigation during late 1956 of six of the earlier established collectives (presumably designed to attract the few remaining dissenters and minority nationalities) indicated that grain production had increased 12.2%, individual grain consumption by 5.5%, individual income by 8.9%, and sideline production by 40.3%. Moreover, collectivization had led to successful flood control and water conservancy projects.[35]

As has been indicated, a second concern for Guizhou's leaders during the mid-1950s was that the province was barely integrated, either economically or politically. In particular, there was a substantial proportion of minority nationalities whose allegiance to the new regime was dubious at best, and over whom control was difficult. In line with national policy, agricultural co-operativization presented Guizhou's leaders with the opportunity to attempt the greater integration of the minority nationalities. At first, agricultural co-operativization in national minority areas was handled very carefully. 'Respect was paid to the customs and habits of the national minorities', and their co-operativization was envisaged as being gradual and a slower process than in the Chinese areas,[36] as had generally been the case beforehand. However, in December 1955, the 6th representative conference of the Guizhou CCP, decided that as far as agricultural co-operativization was concerned, the national minority areas were no different to the rest of the province. Indeed, co-operativization in those areas was criticized as unnecessarily backward and cadres instructed to accelerate the process.[37]

Although co-operativization may have seemed like the solution for some of Guizhou's problems to its leaders, there can be little doubt that implementation was not without its problems. Not least, as has already been indicated, the response of the minority nationalities was not altogether favourable. In June 1956, an investigation of co-operativization in national minority areas found that 'there had been inadequate consideration of the special characteristics of minority peoples and that this had led to major problems'. However, the solutions suggested by the investigation did not exempt the minorities from the APCs but merely attempted to mollify them by allowing livestock and land for special use 'according to old customs',[38] such as bull-fighting amongst the Miao. Moreover, as occurred elsewhere co-operativization led to an over-emphasis on grain production, and highlighted administrative problems and deficiencies in cadres' work-style.[39]

COLLECTIVIZATION IN SICHUAN

The official view

As Table 6 indicates clearly, collectivization in Sichuan during the first half of 1956 did not follow the national trend. Understanding that phenomenon is complicated not least because no all-province figures for higher stage collectivization between December 1955 and June 1956 were published at that time. All the figures shown for collectivization during that period in Table 4 were published in or after June 1956. Moreover, the apparent lack of collectivization before June 1956 would appear to be contradicted by a 1958 source which stated that 170,000 higher stage collectives were established in Sichuan at that time.[40]

The official contemporary account of co-operativization during the first half of 1956 was provided by Li Dazhang in his speech to the 3rd session of the NPC during June 1956: 'Compared to the rest of the country, our province's agricultural co–operativization movement is clearly backward, and especially deficient in the development of higher stage collectives.' Although accepting that lower stage co-operativization had been achieved during the winter 1955–6, he claimed that only 1,861 collectives had been established, and there was no mention of 170,000. Moreover, he continued that none the less 'It can be seen from the specific conditions of our province and from all our regulations on agricultural co–operativization, that the advance and speed of the movement in our province remains comparatively suitable.'[41]

Li gave three reasons for the province's 'backwardness'. He heavily criticized the working style and bureaucratic procedures of cadres, in much the same terms he was to employ later in the year when advocating rectificaion.[42] In particular, he criticized dictatorial and hasty cadres, who had drafted management and production plans 'not in touch with reality' and had created large co-operatives that did not 'just have 100 or 200 households, but more than a thousand or several thousands'. Moreover, he pointed out that for three or four months of the year the main emphasis in rural work was to ensure increased agricultural production, rather than to establish co-operatives. As Li stressed, that was particularly important since it was only by increased production that the superiority of co-operatives could be made manifest and peasants encouraged to participate. Finally, Li pointed out that the northwest of Sichuan had suffered from torrential rain, unprecedented in the province for 60 or 70 years. Mianyang, Daxian, and Leshan had been flooded; crops had been destroyed; 108 people killed; and almost six million *jin* of grain lost.

Following Li Dazhang's speech, collectivization was certainly implemented in Sichuan. The campaign started officially in June.[43] The province's agricultural work department specially trained cadres on the implementation of the campaign.[44] Experimental collectives were established in each *xiang*, and each area drew up a schedule for implementation before the following spring.[45] Measures to combat Sichuan's 'problems' were outlined in descriptions of the models put forward for emulation when the campaign was widened throughout the province in October and November. The model Special Districts (*zhuanqu*) were Neijiang, which had 98% of peasant households in collectives by October;[46] Yibin, with 95% by September; and Wanxian, which had 93.4% of peasants households in APCs of which 44.37% were in collectives by September.[47] These models stressed the need for increased agricultural production, particularly of economic crops and sideline industry, in order that the incomes of co-operative members should rise and more peasants be encouraged to enter.[48] Emphasis was also placed on improving cadres' work-style in accordance with the 'mass line', and to the size of HSCs. Co-operatives which had already been established with several hundred or even thousand households were encouraged to dissolve and reform into several smaller co-operatives if their size had proved 'disadvantageous to production'.[49] In line with a central directive of September,[50] guidelines were laid down for the size of future collectives. Those in mountain areas were to have approximately 100 households; in the foothills, 200; and on the plains, 300.[51]

The 'large co-operative'

Size was the major concern in the implementation of collectivization after June 1956, and it is size which probably holds the clue to events during the first half of the year. The 'large co-operative' (*da she*) is the most interesting aspect of co-operativization in Sichuan, not only because it can help to explain the apparent slowness of collectivization and the contradiction in the reported statistics on collectivization during the first half of 1956, but also because of the possible association of the term with that used in the period immediately before communization.[52] From the outset it should be stressed that Sichuan's *da she* were not just over-large co-operatives, such as occurred elsewhere in China. Whilst criticism nationally was raised against APCs of several hundred households,[53] in Sichuan Li Dazhang talked about co-operatives with several thousands.[54] The nature of Sichuan's *da she* is revealed in criticisms levelled against them in the autumn of 1956. According to a speaker at the PPC, *da she* had been established in 1955 in order to make a more rational use of land and water. Furthermore, small co-operatives were not able to undertake large scale operations, particularly involving capital construction. In general there were economies of scale to be gained from larger units. Compared to the smaller co-operatives' two-level management system, of production brigades and a management committee, the *da she* established a four-level organization consisting of a management committee, area teams, production brigades, and production teams.[55] However, unlike the *da she* established in Sichuan during 1958 there does not seem to have been any intention for those earlier 'large co-operatives' to have been anything more than organizations concerned with agricultural production.[56]

Although the concept of *da she* may have been attractive in theory, it is clear that in practice there were problems. As was suggested earlier, a major problem in co-operativization was the administrative ability of local cadres. In setting up *da she* this problem was further aggravated by the size of the co-operative. A larger proportion of co-operative members, previously without leadership experience, were placed in management roles in order to run the complex four-level organization. As a result the strength of the productive labour force was reduced, the bureaucracy grew, and production declined. A comparison of a *da she* with a smaller co-operative revealed that where the *da she* had one cadre for every 2.5 households, the smaller co-operative had one for every four, and whilst the smaller APC's grain production had increased 14% in a year, that of the *da she* had fallen by 8%[57] Moreover such co-operatives were not just established in the densely populated and easily accessible areas of the province, but also in the less populated and remote mountain areas. In these regions the problem was further exacerbated because cadres often had to travel 30 or 40 *li* to cross the co-operative and direct leadership was impossible.[58]

In general, *da she* were found to be too large to be manageable, although the major contributing factor was said to be the co-operative cadres' bureaucratic work-style and lack of experience rather than bad theory, and the possibility of re-establishing them in the future was not excluded. For example, an investigation of the 27 *da she* in Daxian stressed that, 'At present, co-operative cadres are not able or willing to run *da she*.' The investigation found that the co-operatives' financial affairs were chaotic, that the work force was badly organized, that management and leadership were ineffective, and that 21 of the co-operatives had 'cadres who are incapable of leading production'.[59]

Both the tendency to establish *da she* before the summer of 1956, and the movement to emphasize smaller collectives and dissolve and reform existing *da she* after that date, appear to have been generally widespread throughout the province. The most spectacular example of the *da she* was in Neijiang *xian*. In April, 89% of its peasant households had been co-operativized into 24 APCs.[60] Although not specifically referred to as *da she* at the time, it is clear that they must have been. No precise figures are available for the number of peasant households in this *xian*, although an assessment of the size of these *da she* can be achieved by using estimates for the average *xian*. There were 13,417,290 peasant households in Sichuan in mid-1956,[61] distributed throughout 193 *xian*, giving an average of 69,520 households per *xian*. If Neijiang were the average *xian* this would mean that its average APC would have approximately 2,578 households. Since Neijiang *xian* is in one of the most densely populated areas of Sichuan,[62] these APCs may in fact have been even larger. However, it is clear that these had been reorganized by October, when collectivization was achieved in the whole of Neijiang Special District.[63] 5,728 HSCs were established, and if it were assumed that those APCs established in Neijiang *xian* by April had not been reorganized, then this would imply (again working on average estimates) that whilst the average size of APCs in that one *xian* was more than twelve times the provincial average, those in the rest of the special district were less than half the size.[64] A second example may be taken from Yibin. In this case, the problem was not just too many peasant households in each APC, but also the area and terrain that each covered. The *xian* is located in a mountainous region, yet each APC was based originally on the amalgamation of several *xiang* with several hundred households. These were found to be unmanageable and dissolved, being replaced by smaller HSCs in November.[65] The extent to which *da she* had been established in the province may be judged by the seriousness of the campaign against their continued existence, and the fact that it lasted at least six months, from the time of Li Dazhang's speech to the NPC until December 1956.[66]

It would seem that the process of first establishing and later dismembering *da she* was the major reason for the slow pace of collectivization in Sichuan. *Da she* were still not seen as a problem in April 1956, when Neijiang *xian*'s 24 *da she* were established. Assuming the decision against them was taken in May or June, slightly before Li Dazhang's speech to the NPC, this would mean that a large part of the previous half year's co-operativization had to be undone and re-started. If it is assumed that those *da she* formed before June 1956 and later reorganized were after that date no longer recognized as part of the co-operativization movement in Sichuan, and consequently not included in the published statistics, then the contradiction between the contemporary statistics and those reported in 1958 (when the national political climate was very different) becomes more understandable. Certainly, derecognition would be consistent with the contemporary reported figures on co-operativization for June 1956.

A case of provincial deviance?

Li Dazhang's attempt to justify the speed of collectivization in Sichuan according to local conditions is somewhat unconvincing. Most of the difficulties he outlined were common to the whole of China in this period and not peculiar to Sichuan. As Schurmann has pointed out, the rectification movement among rural cadres in the period preceding the Great Leap Forward was necessitated by the experience of cadres' deficiencies during co-operativization.[67] Whilst as Mao stated in July 1955, increased agricultural production was necessary in order to provide favourable conditions to encourage peasants to join co-operatives voluntarily.[68] If *da she* had been confined to the heavily populated areas of the Chengdu Basin and plains in central Sichuan then it might be possible to accept that this form of co-operative had been established in line with the principle of 'doing the best according to local conditions'. However, *da she* were also created in the sparsely populated mountain areas of western Sichuan, where management problems were multiplied by distance.

Furthermore, given the extent to which *da she* were established, it is inconceivable that these could be passed off as the deviant creations of local cadres, without the knowledge of the provincial leadership. The only explanation of a truly 'local' nature that Li Dazhang offered was the problem of natural disasters. However, here he only mentioned the flood in north western Sichuan, which had only occurred in June and so could not have possibly affected the course of co-operativization beforehand. Generally, due to its natural conditions and long-established irrigation system, Sichuan is not prone to natural disasters,[69] and there is no record of any other incidents during co-operativization. Finally, it should be pointed out that although Sichuan was not regarded as an 'advanced area' before 1956, it certainly could not be regarded as 'backward'. As previously indicated, land reform had been speedily implemented in Sichuan despite the lack of experience. In addition, by the summer of 1955, more than half the HSCs in China were in Sichuan,[70] and Sichuan had the fourth most highly organized agricultural sector after the earlier-liberated provinces of Heilongjiang, Jilin, and Shanxi.[71]

The slowness of collectivization in Sichuan, and the phenomenon of *da she* superficially appear to indicate resistance by provincial leaders to central policy. However, if this were the case, it would be necessary to explain why Sichuan's leaders were not removed for their 'conservatism' during co-operativization, as happened elsewhere at the end of 1957 and beginning of 1958.[72] One plausible explanation might be that the maintenance of Sichuan's agricultural production, and in particular its continued exports of grain, were considered to be of greater national importance than its speedy co-operativization.

However, it seems more likely that Sichuan's co-operativization was in fact a positive reaction to national politics, and in particular to Mao's policy preferences. In the first place, the pace of co-operativization was set by the provinces and only later adopted by the centre. Even though Sichuan was considerably slower in implementing co-operativization during the 'High Tide' than any other province, it still managed to complete collectivization by the end of 1956: the target set by the Twelve Year Plan of January 1956 for 'advanced areas',[73] and still considerably faster than Mao's speech of 31 July 1955 had envisaged.

Secondly, it seems reasonable to suppose that the concept of *da she* which has been suggested here as the major determinant of Sichuan's 'backwardness' in co-operativization, although to some extent an alternative Sichuanese form of APC, was in fact developed from a misunderstanding of Mao's intentions. Although the *da she* in Sichuan were clearly very different (both in scale and organization) to those envisaged by Mao, he did encourage the creation of 'large co-operatives' on at least two separate occasions. One of the articles selected for inclusion in the collection *Socialist Upsurge in China's Countryside* dealt with the 'Advance' APC of Chaoyang *xiang* in Jiangsu (with 578 peasant households) and was entitled 'The Superiority of Large Co-ops'. In his preface to the article, written in September 1955, Mao wrote,

This is a very well-written article, well worth reading.

Most of our present semi-socialist co-ops have only 20 or 30 families in them, because co-operatives of that size are easy to run and they give the administrative staff and the members an opportunity to gain experience quickly. But small co-ops have fewer members, less land and not much money. They cannot operate on a large scale or use machinery. The development of their forces of production is still hampered. They should not stay in this position too long, but should go on to combine with other co-operatives.

Some places can have one co-op for every township. In a few places, one co-op can embrace several townships. In many places, of course, one township will contain several co-ops.

Not only the plains sections can form big co-operatives, the hilly regions can form them too. The township of Anhwei province where the Futseling Reservoir is located is all hills. Yet a big farming, forestry and animal husbandry co-op has ben established there that stretches dozens of miles in each direction.[74]

The second occasion on which large co-operatives were encouraged was in the Twelve Year Plan. Article 2 stipulates that areas which were not 'advanced' in co-operativization (at the turn of 1955–6) should established experimental higher stage large co-operatives in 1956, with upwards of a hundred peasant households.[75]

It is thus suggested that although Mao may not have approved of (or even intended) the kind of *da she* created in Sichuan, Sichuan's leaders did in fact believe they were acting in the spirit of Mao's policy if not exactly implementing that policy itself, and that Mao to some extent appreciated their intentions. Certainly, later events would appear to support such an hypothesis. Far from being disciplined for the course of co-operativization. Sichuan's leaders were actually praised by Mao. In his second speech at the Chengdu Conference in March 1958, Mao criticized Zhou Xiaozhou, party first secretary of Hunan, for his opposition to agricultural co-operativization. In contrast he held up and praised 'X X X of Sichuan' (presumably Li Jingquan) who had persevered with higher stage collectivization despite many difficulties.[76]

That this indeed is a likely interpretation of co-operativization in Sichuan seems reinforced by adjacent chapters. The previous chapter has suggested that Sichuan's leaders came to support Mao's position in national politics increasingly after 1955. The following chapter extends the argument to cover the wider contemporary debate about China's future strategy for development. Remarkably, though it appears that Sichuan did not share Mao's views on decentralization, they none the less supported him strongly in that debate. As here, it thus seems likely that any attempt to use the process of policy formulation and implementation in order to influence the direction of policy was not so much a function of provincial conditions, but of the relationship between specific leaders at the centre and in the provinces.

4

DECENTRALIZATION AND NATIONAL POLITICS

Provincial leaders are often credited with having campaigned for decentralization before its implementation in 1957–8. It has been suggested that in the national debates on China's future that occurred during 1955–57, an alliance developed between Mao and provincial leaders.[1] According to that scenario, Mao enlisted the support of provincial party first secretaries for his plan for economic development, in which the '1956–1967 Outline for National Agricultural Development' (the Twelve Year Plan) played a major role, and that in return he supported their requests for a 'decentralization of power to provincial authorities'.[2]

The simplicity of that argument is compelling. Provincial leaders had after all forced the pace of agricultural cooperation during the 'High Tide' in line with Mao's policy preferences. The Twelve Year Plan had originated from meetings between Mao and provincial leaders in November 1955 and January 1956.[3] At the 8th Party Congress in September 1956, when the Second Five Year Plan was being drafted, provincial leaders were encouraged to articulate their specific problems and desires in the context of the future plan, and to a large extent they complied.[4] Moreover, between the end of 1955 and the 3rd plenum of the 8th Central Committee, when Mao's development ideas were adopted, there was a series of meetings between Mao and provincial leaders, where the shape and form of development after 1957 were discussed.[5]

Were that argument sustainable it might prove one possible explanation for the emerging relationship betwen Mao and Sichuan's leaders. However, this chapter suggests there is little evidence of a generalized provincial demand for decentralization, let alone that mutual support for decentralization and the Twelve Year Plan provided a basis for agreement between Mao and provincial leaders as a whole. Nor for that matter does the description of such an agreement apply to the relationship between Mao and the leaders of either Guizhou or Sichuan. Neither campaigned in favour of provincial-level decentralization. On the other hand, Sichuan's leaders clearly were more in favour of Mao's position in national politics at this time than most. For example, they supported the much-vaunted Twelve Year Plan at a time when to do so was not the national norm. In contrast, Guizhou's leaders (as always) not only had a lower profile in national politics, but appear to have taken a more conservative stance.

<h2 style="text-align:center">THE TWELVE YEAR PLAN</h2>

During 1955–7 there were in fact four versions of the Twelve Year Plan. The first contained 11 articles, had been drafted by Mao in Hangzhou presumably during the autumn of 1955, and was presented by him to a meeting of the party first secretaries of 15 provinces at Tianjin in November 1955.[6] That meeting produced a new draft containing 17 articles. The third, drafted by the same participants in January 1956 contained 40 articles – it was in fact later referred to as the '40 Articles' as well as the Twelve Year Plan – was presented to the Politburo on 23 January, and to a Supreme State Conference on 25 January, having been discussed by a Central Committee conference of intellectuals and scientific workers during 14–20 January 1956.[7] It was that version which was prominent during Mao's attempt to accelerate development during the first half of 1956. The fourth 'revised' version appeared in October 1957 with the return to Mao's line but did not differ substantially from the earlier version.[8] It was a 'revised' version because several items which had been particularly derided by Deng Zihui in his June review of agricultural co-operativization, such as the much promoted double-bladed double-wheeled plough, had been deleted.[9]

Although primarily concerned with agriculture, the Twelve Year Plan also contained recommendations for China's development in a wider social context. In particular it emphasized both the need for rapid agricultural development and social mobilization: two of Mao's major points at the time. The Twelve Year Plan together with 'On the ten major relationships' of April 1956 can be regarded as indicating Mao's position before the Great Leap Forward.

Here it is the political symbolism of the Twelve Year Plan between April 1956 and October 1957 which is of particular importance. Before April, the Twelve Year Plan had been publicized and discussed nationally as part of the 'First Leap Forward',[10] which also included the attempt to accelerate implementation of the first five year plan and rapid agricultural co-operativization. However, in the spring the brakes were applied on the drive for rapid development,[11] and the Twelve Year Plan was dropped nationally until its readoption at the 3rd plenum. According to Schurmann: 'On October 27, 1957 the *Jenmin jihpao* published an editorial on the revised program for the development of agriculture in 1956–1967 – the first public reference to it since its disappearance from view in the spring of 1956.'[12] Although correct in substance, Schurmann's statement is in slight error in that the Twelve Year Plan was mentioned publicly during this period. For example, at the 8th Party Congress in September 1956 several leaders referred to the plan by name and their speeches were published. However, with few exceptions, their references were either downright critical or neutral, referring to the Twelve Year Plan in the context of agricultural development. Thus of the central leadership, Zhou Enlai was disparaging about the plan,[13] whereas Liu Shaoqi by comparison was more positive.[14] Eight provincial leaders (from six provinces) also mentioned the Twelve Year Plan.[15] Most references were neutral, but one, by Ye Fei, the first secretary of Fujian was extremely critical, blaming the unrealistic over-enthusiasm engendered by the Twelve Year Plan for most of his province's economic problems during 1956.[16]

Given the overwhelmingly predominant negative attitude to the Twelve Year Plan during this period it is more than somewhat remarkable not only that Guizhou and Sichuan should have had contrasting attitudes but that they differed to the extent they did. As far as can be ascertained, Guizhou followed the national norm during April 1956–October 1957, yet Sichuan quite spectacularly did not. Sources on Guizhou are not rich for this period. None the less, it only proved possible to find two Guizhou-related references to the Twelve Year Plan. Both were neutral references, referring to the Twelve Year Plan in the context of agricultural development. In February 1957, it was reported that thirteen *xian* had reached the 1967 norm for grain output per *mou*, without any further comment on the Twelve Year Plan.[17] Whilst in his speech to the 8th Party Congress, Zhou Lin noted that despite improvement in grain production during the previous years, '. . . this is still far from the grain yield provided for in the Draft Outline on National Agricultural Development of 800 *jin*, and we need to unceasingly strive for more'.[18] No further elaboration on the importance of the Twelve Year Plan was forthcoming, despite the fact that the measures Zhou had described as having led to the initial improvement – the development of small-scale irrigation works and the extension of the irrigated area, the improvement of agricultural techniques such as new tools and the use of fertilizers, and the extension of the arable land by reclamation – were precisely those stipulated in the Twelve Year Plan.

Sichuan, on the other hand, had a positive attitude, which moreover was clearly articulated, towards the Twelve Year Plan throughout April 1956–October 1957. Unlike Guizhou, and presumably most other provincial leaderships, Sichuan's leadership saw the Twelve Year Plan as a guiding principle. There was hardly a major statement by a provincial leader (whether at national level or within the province) that was not extremely positive about it, and the provincial media in general continued to extol the Twelve Year Plan's virtues. For example, in October 1956 it was reported that as a result of implementing the Twelve Year Plan, Hongguang APC had already reached the future plan target of 800 *jin* of grain per *mou*.[19] Perhaps significantly, Hongguang was one of the places visited by Mao when he was in Sichuan during February and March 1958.[20] More spectacularly, in December, an article on Jiaotong APC not only revealed that there was a provincial twelve year plan in operation but that it had resulted in the APC harvesting 1,000 *jin* of grain per *mou*, and 1,000 *jin* of sugar cane per *mou*.[21] When higher stage collectivization was achieved in Sichuan, this too was greeted as a victory for the Twelve Year Plan, and it was pointed out that collectivization had been completed a year ahead of the plan's target date.[22] In his speech to the NPC in June 1956, Li Dazhang said,

It can be seen from the conditions of production, that within 7 years grain output per *mou* can reach 800 *jin*, and more than 900 *jin* within twelve years, so that the plan can be completed. Because of high production in all areas, for example, there are twelve APCs in Chengdu Special District where average yields per *mou* have reached more than 1,100 *jin*, we believe we can meet the requirements of the Outline on National Agricultural Development on the increased production of grain.[23]

Whilst later in his 1956 provincial government work report, Li Dazhang stressed the importance of the Twelve Year Plan to the successful implementation of co-operativization in Sichuan.[24] However, the Twelve Year Plan was not just seen as being significant for agricultural development, but also of importance and applicable to politics in general. For example, Li Jingquan, in his speech to the 8th Party Congress, described the Twelve Year Plan *inter alia* in glowing terms:

The shining light of the party centre's general line for the transitional period, in particular last autumn's report by Chairman Mao 'On the question of Agricultural Co-operation', and the important documents published by the party centre, 'Decision concerning problems of transforming capitalist industry and commerce', 'Directive concerning problems of intellectuals', and 'The Draft Outline on National Agricultural Development', has victoriously led us to welcome the high tide of socialist transformation.[25]

Moreover, he was the only one among 34 provincial leaders who spoke at the congress to open his remarks with a reference to the Twelve Year Plan.[26] In the political section of his 1956 government work report, Li Dazhang also stressed the importance of implementing articles 4 and 5 of the Twelve Year Plan, which were those dealing with policies towards 'landlords, rich peasants and remnant counter-revolutionaries'.[27] Finally, in January 1957, in a speech to a provincial conference of 'progressive workers', Li Jingquan extolled the virtues of the Twelve Year Plan, not only with respect to agriculture, but also with reference to the importance of the 'mass line'.[28]

The extent to which Sichuan and Guizhou had differed in their attitudes towards the Twelve Year Plan before October 1957 clearly emerges in their different responses after its national re-adoption at the 3rd plenum. In Guizhou, the change in line necessitated a 2nd session of the party congress, which 'warmly welcomed' the Twelve Year Plan – a phrase more normally appropriate in the publication of new policy documents – as the prelude to a 'New High Tide' in industrial and agricultural production.[29] The 36th plenum of the Guizhou CCP committee drew up a provincial twelve year plan for agricultural development on 14 December and this was published later in the month.[30] In Sichuan, on the other hand, there was no extraordinary party congress. Instead the national resurrection of the Twelve Year Plan on 25 October was greeted immediately and enthusiastically in the *Sichuan Daily* on 26 October. The 28th meeting of the Provincial People's Council in mid-November considered a report on the successful execution of the provincial twelve year plan during the previous two years and approved its revised draft.[31] The revised and updated provincial twelve year plan was adopted and published by the provincial party committee in early December.[32]

PROVINCIAL DEMANDS

Provincial aspirations for the second Five Year Plan were voiced at the 8th National Party Congress in September 1956. Decentralization had been one of Mao's major proposals in his 'On the ten major relationships' of April 1956,[33] in order to encourage local initiative. Despite the setbacks generally to Mao's policies after the spring of 1956, decentralization was not abandoned. Thus, in his concluding speech to the 3rd NPC in June, Zhou Enlai had made it quite clear that the leadership was still committed to some form of decentralization.[34] However, the major question was as to what form of decentralization should be implemented. Schurmann has suggested that in the national debate two forms of decentralization were advocated: to enterprise level and to the provincial authorities.[35] However, this distinction is only really useful when considering generally the debate amongst the national leadership and blurs to a certain extent the demands made by provincial leaders. Basically there were three attitudes prevalent among provincial leaders at the 8th party congress. Some, such as Tao Zhu (Guangdong)[36] did ask for more provincial control of provincial resources. However, many more, such as Tan Qilong (Shandong),[37] Lin Tie (Hebei),[38] and Yang Shangkui (Jiangxi),[39] requested greater central aid, in particular for the construction of water conservancy projects. Finally, there were those, such as Ye Fei (Fujian)[40] and again Yang Shangkui, who were concerned with the need for greater local flexibility at the lowest levels of the political and administrative hierarchy, particularly with respect to planning and pricing policy. Quite clearly these demands do not fit neatly into Schurmann's typology, nor are they mutually exclusive.

In their speeches to the congress neither Zhou Lin nor Li Jingquan mentioned, let alone requested, decentralization to provincial level. Unsurprisingly, given their common preoccupations with remoteness, transport problems, and under-developed industrial sectors, their demands were similar although of different intensity. Zhou Lin's major request was for greater central investment in the province, particularly for large-scale flood control and water conservancy construction in the mountains.[41] Li Jingquan's speech had two major demands. The first was for increased central aid and investment in the province, particularly in order to develop the province's industrial base, its internal transport system, and communications with the rest of China. Li justified his request not just by reference to the provincial supply crisis, but also by emphasizing the importance of Sichuan's agricultural production to the rest of the country. The experience of the provincial supply crisis was also used by Li as evidence to support his second, more general demand. Like Ye Fei and Yang Shanggui, Li advocated more flexible planning and pricing policies. As a result of pricing policy, Li was concerned that the urban areas had become over-advantaged at the expense of the peasantry, and that agricultural production might consequently fall. With respect to planning, he argued that enterprises should have greater control of their own resources, particularly profits. Li advocated enterprise control over a portion of their profits in order to allow for more flexible systems of re-investment and workers' bonuses according to the nature of each enterprise. In that way he envisaged that the levels of both individual income and total production could be raised.[42]

Guizhou and Sichuan clearly then did not have an agreement with Mao about mutual support for the Twelve Year Plan and decentralization. Although Sichuan would appear to have supported the Twelve Year Plan, its leaders showed no sign, either at the 8th party congress or otherwise, of being in favour of a 'decentralization of power to provincial authorities'; whilst Guizhou favoured neither. Nor does there appear to have been mutual support more generally. At most only 15 provincial leaders participated in the formulation of the Twelve Year Plan. With few exceptions it is not known who they were, nor what was their attitude to decentralization.[43] In any case, it is clear that few provincial leaders supported provincial-level decentralization at the 8th party congress.

GUIZHOU AND SICHUAN IN THE NATIONAL DEBATE, 1955–7

In the light of the Cultural Revolution it is easy to view the 1955–7 policy debates as being between those who were either for or against Mao's policies. Although this is an oversimplification (not least because individuals' attitudes could and did change during the period, and, apart from Mao, policy preferences are rarely visible as programmatic)[44] such a distinction can none the less provide a useful guide. Mao did make most of the running during 1955–7; and debate did tend to polarize between (in each other's words) the 'snail pacers'[45] and the 'rash advancers',[46] defined by reference to the speed of development.

As early as 1958 MacFarquhar pointed to the importance of the Twelve Year Plan as a touchstone of the political debates during 1955–7.[47] Certainly, in a source which became available during the Cultural Revolution, Mao acknowledged his personal investment in the Twelve Year Plan. Speaking in Chengdu in March 1958, he criticized the setback to his programme for economic development during the previous two years, when he said: 'In 1956, three things were blown away – the slogan of "More, Faster, Better, and More Economical", the progressive faction, and the 40 Articles.'[48] As became apparent with the publication of Volume 5 of the *Selected Works of Mao Tsetung* in 1977, Mao's speech at Chengdu had echoed and paraphrased his speech at the 3rd plenum of the 8th Central Committee on 9 October 1957.[49] In the earlier speech he had mentioned 'committees for promoting progress' rather than 'the progressive faction', but the meaning was essentially the same. Narrowly defined, Mao was presumably referring to those like himself who had been attempting to accelerate the implementation of the first five year plan. In a wider context, he was criticizing the more conservative attitude to development and equating it with 'retrogression' and in his view the reactionary nature of the Nationalist Party. The slogan of 'More, Faster, Better, and More Economical' was coined by Mao at the 6th plenum of the 7th Central Committee in the autumn of 1955 as the industrial counterpart of rapid agricultural co-operativization in order to increase production.[50] Attitudes to these three aspects of Mao's programme, together with those towards agricultural co-operativization and rectification, may be considered as indicators of the differences between Mao's supporters and antagonists, or rather the poles of 'adventurism' and 'conservatism'.

Largely because of the magnitude of internal problems, the responses of Guizhou's leaders to the national debate were extremely muted, particularly by comparison with Sichuan's. Indeed, as previously indicated, the drive for integration at provincial level – occasioned by central demands on provincial leaders, rather than from below – resulted in provincial introspection, and there is more than a suggestion that during this period national-level politics passed Guizhou by. With the exception of Zhou Lin's interview in the national press on rectification during May 1957, Guizhou's leaders were not in the mainstream of national politics, nor were developments in the province in the forefront of national political developments. On the contrary, it would seem that possibly agricultural co-operativization and most certainly rectification occurred slower and later in Guizhou than elsewhere.

None the less it would appear that on balance Guizhou tended towards the more conservative position in national politics in so far as the attitudes of its leaders are observable. At the very least it can be argued that Guizhou's leaders did not adopt a pro-Mao stance when a choice was relatively freely available. Thus, it has not proved possible to find one reference to the slogan of 'More, Faster, Better, and More Economical' before October 1957; Guizhou did not attempt to forward the implementation of the first five year plan during the first half of 1956; it did not champion the Twelve Year Plan before October 1957; and the province's rectification campaign, when it eventually started, was more concerned with criticizing the minority nationalities and other 'rightists', rather than with problems of cadres' work-style. On the other hand, neither Guizhou's leaders nor the provincial media uttered warnings about 'rash advances' or 'adventurism'. Moreover, the province's preoccupation with extremely high rates of increased grain production could be considered as 'adventurist', since its forecasts for 1956 and 1957 were an attempt to duplicate the impressive rates of growth achieved during 1949–54, when the initial base line had been extremely low and good weather prevailed. However, there is no evidence that such 'adventurism' was an attempt to speed development as a response to Mao. On the contrary, given the province's obvious lack of response to Mao's initiatives in general, such a drive (however unrealistic) would seem more explicable as a response to the centre's general demand to 'Do the best according to local conditions.'

In complete contrast, the attitudes of Sichuan's leaders were clearly articulated. Moreover, it would seem that Sichuan's leadership not only favoured Mao's position in national politics during this period, but most likely were in active alliance with him. As has been indicated, Sichuan promoted the Twelve Year Plan, against the national trend, during April 1956–October 1957. Moreover, the slogan of 'More, Faster, Better, and More Economical', also 'blown away' nationally during the same period was, like the Twelve Year Plan, in constant use in Sichuan. For example, in his 1956 provincial government work report, delivered in November, Li Dazhang said in relation to economic construction that the province '... had acted in accordance with the Party Centre and State Council's directive to make socialist construction "More, Faster, Better, and More Economical", in order to bring forward and complete the First Five Year Plan'.[51] Again, in December 1956, Chongqing's industrial successes during the previous nine months were attributed to having followed the general line of 'More, Faster, Better, and More Economical'.[52]

Similarly, Sichuan was one of the first provinces to attempt to accelerate the implementation of the first five year plan in November 1955, and clearly seemed reluctant to abandon that attempt after April 1956.[53] Furthermore, rectification in Sichuan would also seem to have supported Mao's position, not only in 1957, but also during the previous year. This emerges particularly from a comparison with Guizhou. In Sichuan, rectification had been discussed throughout 1956, and was in large part said to be occasioned, by defects in cadres' work style during co-operativization. Despite a lack of national agreement on the form of rectification, a campaign was underway in Sichuan immediately after the November PPC.[54] Moreover, in the spring of 1957, Sichuan actively supported Mao's rectification directive. In Guizhou, on the other hand, the province's problems during 1956, particularly with the economy and the national minorities, were not blamed on the party's cadres, although there was perhaps more cause. The provincial rectification campaign did not really start until August 1957, when it took the form of an 'Anti-Rightist' movement, mainly directed at the minority nationalities during 1957.

Of necessity, much of the evidence presented here as an argument that Sichuan's leadership adopted Mao's position during this period must be circumstantial and inferential. However, when taken together with similar evidence of some kind of symbiotic relationship between Mao and Li Jingquan, it would all seem to add up to too much to be mere coincidence. As mentioned in the previous chapter, Mao praised Li for his implementation of agricultural co-operativization in Sichuan. Even more remarkable is Mao's Chengdu speech of 22 March 1958. Then, in speaking about provincial politics, and the role of the provinces on the national stage, Mao said: 'Comrades working in local areas will eventually come to the centre. Those working in the centre will eventually die or be overthrown, Khrushchev came from a local area.'[55] It is reasonable to assume that since Mao was speaking in Sichuan, he can hardly have been unaware that a direct parallel could be drawn between Li Jingquan and Khrushchev. The latter came from the Ukraine, which is the Soviet Union's most important region for grain production, to become a Politburo member. Only two months after Mao's speech (in May) Li Jingquan also became a member of the Politburo,[56] and, as was frequently stressed during this period by its leaders,[57] Sichuan certainly is China's 'rice-bowl' – *tianfu zhiguo*, the 'Storehouse of Heaven'.

PART II

AFTER DECENTRALIZATION

5

1958–60:

THE GREAT LEAP FORWARD

In some ways, and particularly from the perspective of elite-level politics, the period from the 3rd plenum of the 8th Central Committee in October 1957 to the Enlarged Politburo Meeting of May 1966 (when the Great Proletarian Cultural Revolution (GPCR) was launched onto the wider stage) parallels developments during 1955–7, although much extended over time.[1] After the 3rd plenum an attempt was made to force the pace of development mainly through social mobilization, notably by Mao and his supporters. As in the 'High Tide' of agricultural co-operativization, an increasingly fast pace was set by the provinces who repeatedly raised their targets for production. However, as in the late spring of 1956, doubts about the wisdom and efficacy of the strategy set in during the first half of 1959. These culminated at the Lushan Plenum of August 1959, and thereafter until the 9th plenum in January 1961 the Great Leap Forward (GLF) was advocated somewhat more cautiously. At the 9th plenum the GLF strategy was shelved, as had been the attempt to advance the First Five Year Plan in the summer of 1956. Debate on China's future strategy was the focus of the central committee's 10th plenum in September 1962, and like the 8th Party Congress of September 1956 in the context of the 1955–6 debate on development, resulted in a setback for Mao's 1958 ideas on development. However, as in the earlier period, Mao retaliated, refused to accept the failure of the GLF strategy and stressed rectification of cadres. As divisions within the leadership deepened, particularly over the Socialist Education Movement, Mao was once again able to force his ideas onto the CCP despite considerable opposition.

On the other hand, the two periods are not identical. There was no equivalent of the 'Hundred Flowers' of May 1957 in the later period. Nor was there an equivalent of the 'Three Bitter Years' in the earlier period. The debate which developed during 1961–5 about China's future centred to a large extent on differing interpretations of the lessons to be learnt from the GLF. Moreover, the readoption of Mao's line in and after 1965 was not a result of economic priorities, nor was it adopted by a united party.

Against the background of national politics, this and the following two chapters outline the major concerns of the leaders of Sichuan and Guizhou during this period. The first two of these chapters outline the preoccupations of the two provinces' leaders, and their reaction to national politics from the 3rd plenum until the end of 1965.[2] The divide between these two chapters is the 9th plenum of the 8th central committee which saw as decisive a change in the party's line as that which launched the GLF. Chapter 7 examines the evolution of rural people's communes during this period in Sichuan and Guizhou.

As will be seen in the next chapter, the 9th plenum also marks a definite sea-change for the participation of the provincial leaders of Sichuan and Guizhou in national politics. In particular, it seems likely that politics (and certainly Southwestern politics) became regionalized to a considerable extent after 1961. Though little is known about the six large party regions – nominally regional bureaux of the CCP's central committee, but located in the regions rather than Beijing – which existed during the early 1960s, the evidence presented in Chapter 8 is that they played an important role in the relations between centre and province. In this specific case, the Southwest regional bureau was very much an institution dominated by Sichuan's provincial leadership, and Guizhou was at least partially subordinated to its control.

Sichuan's role in the southwest region was, of course, nothing new.[3] It had, for example, been growing in regional influence even before 1958. However, with the onset of the GLF it was purposively assigned the leading economic role in the region. That influence spilled over onto other areas of activity during the GLF, and became institutionalized thereafter.

The major theme which emerged in Part I was the contrast between Sichuan and Guizhou in terms of their involvement in national politics. That contrast entails the developing relationship (possibly firm enough to be identified as an alliance) between Mao Zedong and the provincial leaders of Sichuan, in particular its party first secretary, Li Jingquan. Once again that theme continues in Part II, covering the period from 1957 to the eve of the GPCR. However, here an important complementary theme is the regionalization of politics.

More immediately, the period of the GLF was one in which provincial autonomy was feted. However, this chapter (and indeed Chapter 7, on rural people's communes) does not demonstrate provincial-level resistance to the centre. On the contrary the exercise of provincial autonomy – specifically, variations in the policy process – are perhaps better viewed as a function of integration (or at least the desire for integration) in the political system. During the GLF, both Sichuan and Guizhou were repeatedly, in effect, carried away on a tide of political optimism and encouraged to experiment. Though both provinces participated enthusiastically, particularly before August 1959, the result often created new restraints on provincial leaders. In particular, Sichuan and Guizhou became more dependent economically on the centre. Moreover, though there may have been little provincial-level resistance to the centre, the GLF certainly saw resistance within the wider populations of both provinces. To some extent that too limited the possibilities for provincial politicians. However, it is noticeable that Guizhou's leaders drew back from the strategy of the GLF markedly sooner than their counterparts in Sichuan.

THE GREAT LEAP FORWARD

Although the Great Leap Forward in Industry and Agriculture was officially endorsed at the 2nd session of the 8th Party Congress in May 1958,[4] the movement had been underway and the phrase in common use, first at provincial and later at national level, since the 3rd plenum of September–October 1957. Once again, as in 1955–6, there would appear to be some evidence of collusion between Mao and provincial leaders. Provincial responses to the re-adoption of Mao's Twelve Year Plan would seem to have been enthusiastic. Provincial twelve year plans were published and high targets set. Within a couple of months, the targets for agricultural development had been revised upwards and the GLF extended to industrial production. From a provincial perspective, the enthusiasm generated and the constant upward revision of targets that started in the winter of 1957–8 characterized the period of the GLF, despite the setbacks (and reality) which became increasingly apparent towards and after the end of 1958.[5] Moreover, as before, there were a series of meetings between Mao and several of the provincial leaders that pre-empted the formal decision-making process. The most important of these were the Hangzhou and Nanning Conferences in January 1958 where the 'Sixty Work Articles' (in effect the blueprint for the GLF) were drafted and the 'General Line for Socialist Construction' (also later adopted in May) discussed.[6] It was at this time that the key slogans of the Great Leap Forward were spelled out. Mao spoke not only of 'catching up with Britain within 15 years' but also of completing the Twelve Year Plan ahead of schedule, both of which were emphasized in his speech to the Supreme State Conference at the end of the month, when he outlined the strategy of the GLF.[7] It also seems likely that it was at the Hangzhou and Nanning Conferences that the slogan of 'walking on two legs'[8] was first applied to economic development – implying in that context the simultaneous and rapid development of industry and agriculture, heavy and light industry (with priority to the former), national and local industry, and the use of both modern and traditional methods of production; and the slogan of 'Basically transform the rural areas after three years of struggle' was coined. Indeed the genesis of that last slogan provides further evidence suggestive of collusion between Mao and provincial leaders, or at least one in particular. Acording to Mao (speaking at the 6th Plenum of the 8th Central Committee in December 1958) it had been first proposed by 'a comrade from Henan' (presumably Wu Zhipu, its party first secretary) at the Nanning Conference.[9] Mao may certainly have pressed his ideas on provincial leaders during the winter of 1957–8, however it also seems likely that those provincial leaders who attended the various meetings at that time (unfortunately, there is no detailed record of which provincial leaders were involved) made their views known to Mao.

1958 clearly marked the high tide of Mao's policies before the GPCR. The Great Leap Forward had started in the winter of 1957–8. In May, at the 2nd session of the 8th National Party Congress, the General Line for socialist construction – 'to build socialism by exerting our utmost efforts and pressing ahead consistently to achieve greater, faster, better and more economical results' – was proposed by Liu Shaoqi in his political report and adopted.[10] Finally, in late August the People's Commune movement, which had been rapidly gaining momentum during the summer,[11] was sanctioned. The Socialist education movement became a 'Communist education movement' as China seemed poised in its self-perception to enter a new stage of development.

However, it became clear towards the end of 1958 and in the first half of 1959 that all was not as officially described or desired. In his speech to the Supreme State Conference on 5 September 1958, Mao had claimed the 'basic realization' of the Twelve Year Plan, and on the basis of that year's increased grain output predicted that it would be possible to double grain production yet again during 1959 over 1958. Moreover, he looked forward to 'surpassing Britain in all but shipbuilding, cars, and electric power within two years',[12] instead of the originally prescribed fifteen years. By the 6th plenum of the 8th Central Committee which met in December, and following nation-wide 'visitations' by national leaders, optimism was being tempered by caution, and Mao himself was no exception.[13] Commune reorganization was discussed and production targets for 1959 lowered.[14] Although the national leadership was still outwardly united, as in 1956, there were those who advocated 'less haste, more speed'. A compromise was maintained at the 7th plenum in April 1959, however, opposition to the Great Leap Forward became open at the Lushan Conference from June to August.[15] Largely because that opposition was personalized against him, Mao was able to salvage the strategy of the GLF. Indeed, although the 8th plenum (which followed the Lushan Conference) admitted that there had been mistakes, revised the 1958 production figures and economic plans for 1959, and decided on commune reorganization, it still called for a further GLF in the face of 'rightist opportunism'.[16]

However, in retrospect the 8th plenum marked the start of the formal retreat from the strategy of the GLF. Where each province had previously been urged to become 'self-reliant', now emphasis was placed on the slogan of 'The whole country is a single chess-board', stressing interdependence and proportionate and planned development.[17] Instead of 'catching up Britain within 15 years', stress was laid on completing the Second Five Year Plan two years ahead of time – despite the fact that it hardly had been mentioned since 1957.[18] Opposition to the strategy grew not only within the party's national leadership, but also from below as bad weather, unrealistic production targets, and the results of 1958's over-enthusiasm combined to take their toll. The latter were particularly significant for their impact on the food supply. During 1958 the peasantry had been assured that there had been a bumper harvest, and so had tended (albeit unwittingly) to consume a significantly higher proportion of the actual production than in previous years. Agricultural and industrial production did not 'leap forward' in 1959–60 and by the summer of 1960 it became clear to the national leadership that a change in line was necessary. At a party meeting in Beidaihe, which included provincial leaders, it would appear that the decision was taken to abandon the GLF along the lines later adopted by the 9th plenum.[19] Most importantly, instead of 'walking on two legs', the strict order of economic priorities was to be agriculture, light industry, and heavy industry;[20] and there was to be a campaign against the 'leftist excesses' of 'communism, commandism, privilege, blind direction, and exaggeration'.

SICHUAN

In his speech to the 8th plenum of the 8th central committee in August 1959, Mao Zedong stated that three provinces, of which one was Sichuan, were 'Leftists'.[21] His speech was to a large extent one of self-defence against the criticisms of Peng Dehuai relating to the GLF and it seems reasonable to argue that his comment that others were the 'Leftists' was made in order to support his assertion that he was 'a middle-of-the-roader'.[22] Moreover, Mao described the three provinces as 'Leftist' specifically with reference to the management of communes. None the less, in so far as the terms 'left' and 'right' are applicable, Mao's judgement of Sichuan as 'Leftist' would seem to be justified, not just with reference to people's communes (as will be suggested in Ch. 7 it is hard to argue otherwise) but generally throughout the period of the GLF. Before Lushan Sichuan was in the forefront of national political developments associated with the GLF, invariably promoting slogans and policies before their national adoption. After Lushan, Sichuan did more than retain a formal pro-GLF stance, as did some other provinces,[23] Guizhou included. On the contrary, although it reduced its economic expectations and reorganized communes, Sichuan's politics to the end of 1960 differed little from the period before Lushan.

The major preoccupations of Sichuan's leaders during this period were with the creation of a GLF in Sichuan in order to build not only a more self-reliant province, but also a regional industrial centre for the Southwest; communization and the development of people's communes; and with the political counterpart of the GLF, rectification and political education. Developments in Sichuan during the GLF paralleled 1955–7 to a remarkable extent, including a supply crisis in 1959–60. However, presumably because of its adherence to the strategy of the GLF, Sichuan's leadership made light of this second supply crisis.

It was not used, as had earlier been the case, as an argument for a change in line, nor was it as widely publicized through the provincial media. On the contrary, its existence was attributed to cadres' defective work style and mentioned only in the context of the need for an even 'Greater Leap Forward'.[24]

Winter 1957–8

As throughout China, the events of the winter 1957–8 formed the foundation on which the GLF in Sichuan was based. However, even so (and particularly by comparison with Guizhou) the pace at which development was forced in the province was quite remarkable. Statistics emanating from the period of the GLF are far from reliable, none the less they do provide a guide to aspirations. Tables 7 and 8 provide data on targets and (contemporarily reported) output for selected items in Sichuan and Guizhou respectively. As Table 7 indicates, it seems likely that Sichuan's plan for 1958 was revised at least twice between the 28th meeting of the provincial people's council in November 1957, and the adoption of the 'General Line' in the province at the 2nd session of the 1st provincial party congress during April 1958.[25] By comparison, Guizhou's plan for 1958, set at the end of 1957, was mainly agrarian and not revised. Although Guizhou also set targets for the twelve year plan at the same time and Sichuan did not, that did not signify reluctance on the latter's part. In November 1957, Sichuan claimed to have 'basically realized' its original twelve year plan,[26] and by early 1958 announced the possibility that the revised plan could be completed within the year.[27]

Regardless of the global figures, it is quite clear that vast quantities of economic and political resources were invested in the GLF between November 1957 and April 1958. Even before the 28th meeting of the provincial people's council, it had been decided to

Table 7 *Targets and contemporarily recorded output of selected items in Sichuan during the Great Leap Forward*

	Steel (tons)	Coal (million tons)	Grain (million *jin*)	Cotton (million *dan*)
1957 output	355,600[1]	7.73[1]	46,000[1]	1.35[3]
1958 target (November 1957)			50,000[4]	1.45[4]
1958 target (January 1958)		8.3[5]		
1958 target (Summer 1958)	1,400,000[6]		69,000[7]	
1958 output – first reported figures	702,900	20.0	90,000	2.5
1959 target[8]	1.07 mn	35.0	126,000	3.3
1958 output – revized figures	370,471[9]	13.6[0]	64,600[10]	2.2[10]
1959 output[11]	1.01 mn	31.97	70,000	2.3
1960 target[11]	1.25 mn	43.3	77,000	3.5

Notes:
[1]. SCRB 25 June 1959, p. 1
[2]. SCRB 1 January 1958, p. 1
[3]. SCRB 27 November 1957, p. 1
[4]. SCRB 16 November 1957, p. 1
[5]. SCRB 22 January 1958, p. 2
[6]. SCRB 3 July 1958, p. 1
[7]. SCRB 5 May 1958, p. 1
[8]. SCRB 24 June 1959, p. 2
[9]. SCRB 27 May 1960, p. 2
[10]. SCRB 6 September 1959, p. 1
[11]. SCRB 26 May 1960, p. 2

launch a 'High Tide' of winter water conservation[28] and a provincial conference on water conservation and agricultural work held in early November in preparation.[29] At its 28th meeting, the provincial people's council not only adopted a provincial economic plan for 1958, but enlarged on the coming winter's agricultural work.[30] It emphasized that the early realization of the twelve year plan was dependent on a five point plan of action. Water conservation work, as elsewhere, was the top priority. There was to be a general mobilization to repair all small-scale water conservation projects and an effort made to increase the irrigated area, in order to increase both the cultivated area and yields. Increased fertilizer production was stressed, particularly through pig-breeding. Cultivation was to be

Table 8 *Targets and contemporarily recorded output of selected items in Guizhou during the Great Leap Forward*

	Grain (*Yijin*)	Steel (produced by modern methods – tons)	Pig iron (tons)	Coal (million tons)
1957 output	106[1]			
1958 target	117[2]			
1958 output – first reported figures	210[3]	20,000[4]	550,000[4]	6.5[5]
1959 target[5]	340	200,000		9.0
1958 output – revized figures[6]	150	10,000	600,000	6.5
1959 output	103[7]	40,000		
1960 target	119[8]			
1962 target (set January 1957)[9]	115			
1967 target (set January 1957)[9]	240			

Notes:
[1]. GZRB 4 January 1958, p. 1
[2]. GZRB 4 December 1957, p. 1
[3]. GZRB 28 October 1958, p. 1
[4]. GZRB 23 November 1958, p. 1
[5]. GZRB 9 January 1959, p. 1
[6]. GZRB 30 September 1959, p. 1
[7]. GZRB 8 April 1960, p. 2
[8]. GZRB 10 December 1960, p. 2
[9]. GZRB 4 January 1958, p. 2

improved by both an expansion in the area of reclaimed land and a higher rate of land utilization. It was claimed that on the basis of experience gained in 1957, the Multiple Cropping Index could be raised from 169.66 to 176.4 in 1958. Finally, the application of improved techniques, such as tools and seeds, and of 'good management' were emphasized. In the light of the experiences of the previous two years (especially with respect to collectivization) it is interesting to note that cadres were warned that 'This time (they should) pay attention to local conditions', particularly in the mountain areas.

Each area was encouraged to carry out its own small scale water conservation construction projects, and Nanchong, as so often, was held up as the model for emulation.[31] There was indeed a general mobilization, not only for water conservation, but also in the campaigns for fertilizer accumulation, against the 'four pests', and later in the spring farming. In December, 13 million were said to be involved in the agricultural 'Great Leap Forward';[32] in early January, 18 million;[33] and by late January, 20.5 million.[34] In addition to small scale construction projects, larger projects were undertaken such as the construction of a 60 km canal at Jiajiang, and a reservoir at Mingshan.[35] Agricultural techniques were also improved. For example, the provincial agricultural department encouraged the increased cultivation of 'two quarters' rice', and double-cropping was extended to 147 of Sichuan's 194 *xian*, whose output (it was claimed) had consequently increased.[36] Eventually, it was claimed that the agricultural 'High Tide' had become a 'great Leap Forward' and was even more successful than had been originally intended. Thus, for example, in July Li Dazhang reported that during the winter, the irrigated acreage had been expanded by more than 11.27 million *mou* (the original target set in November had been 7.6 million *mou*), whilst water and soil conservation had been generally executed over 22.88 million *mou*.[37]

In industry, a similar GLF was planned and would appear to have been implemented. At first the expansion of local industry was emphasized in order to support agriculture, as in the provincial industry department's directives issued at the end of November.[38] Rural electrification was an important item on the agenda. 600[39] and later 1,000 small scale hydro-electric stations were planned for Sichuan's rural areas in 1958.[40] This represented one-third of the total to be built in the whole country and compared to the 76 erected in the first nine months of 1957.[41] The increased production of agricultural tools was also a major concern, with the provincial handicraft industry department preparing the production of 33.6 million small agricultural implements.[42] Later, as the Great Leap Forward widened with the desire 'to catch up and pass Britain within 15 years' (popularized in the province after early December)[43] heavy industry was emphasized. Iron, steel[44] and coal[45] were designated as growth points, with greater efforts to be made to utilize Sichuan's mineral resources.[46] For the first time, technical instruments (at the Chengdu Measuring Instruments and Precision Tools Plant visited by Mao when it opened in March)[47] and motor vehicles[48] started to be manufactured in the province. If anything, the amount of enthusiasm generated and the extent of target raising were even greater with respect to industry than to agriculture. Thus, for example, at the end of January it was decided to increase the value of industrial production in Chongqing by 50% during 1958 over 1957.[49] However, by the end of February this target had been raised to 70%, as a result (so it was claimed) of a more than 30% overfulfilment of the February plan.[50] In the event, it was claimed that throughout the province during the period from January to May, the gross value of industrial production had risen 26.5%, pig iron output had risen 37.06%, coal production 39.4% and electricity 21.5%, all when compared to the same period in 1957.[51]

Political investment – enthusiasm, participation and rectification – was integral to the winter's GLF. Mass enthusiasm and spontaneity were seen as being essential to the continuing development of the great leap. As early as the end of October Li Jingquan stressed the importance of activism and enthusiasm to increasing agricultural production in a rousing speech to a meeting of 'cadres from three levels' in Fouling,[52] while Liao Zhigao (another provincial secretary) was engaged in similar activity in Neijiang.[53] Rectification and the *xiafang* movement entered a new phase and became more intense. As the 29th meeting of the provincial people's council in December recognized both were desirable ends in themselves in order to combat 'bureaucratism'. However, the GLF also required a high level of ideological consciousness and the downward transfer of cadres to strengthen basic-level production units.[54] Local party committees held rectification meetings, such as that organized in Chongqing from 8–30 November, that criticized the 'mistaken revisionism and departmentalism of certain leadership cadres'.[55] Although no provincial leaders were removed from office or expelled from the party, several cadres from the procuratorate and the cultural and educational systems were.[56] Throughout the winter, basic-level rectification continued apace, covering the whole of the province by the Spring Festival,[57] and increased production was firmly linked to the level of political education. Thus, for example, in February it was claimed that as a result of rectification, production had increased and made it more possible to advance the realization of the twelve year plan.[58] Similarly, although 80,000 cadres had been transferred down to the 'front line of production' by the end of August,[59] the December meeting of the provincial people's council decided to increase the number of transferred cadres to 250,000 during the winter.[60] Over the following months the movement gathered momentum. By February it was being claimed that provincial 'specialist organs' (with no further identification) were being sent down to lower levels as complete units.[61]

Once again, as in the years immediately beforehand, during November 1957–May 1958 Sichuan was not only in the forefront of national political developments, but would also appear to have promoted policies that reflected Mao's preferences. Although not necessarily alone in its advocacy of the GLF, and the slogan 'to catch up and surpass Britain within 15 years' before their national adoption, both were common themes before January 1958. Moreover, although not formally announced until after Liu Shaoqi's report to the 2nd session of the 8th National Party Congress on 5 May, it would appear that the Sichuan party committee had adopted the 'General Line for Socialist Construction' in mid-April[62] as a result of discussions at a provincial conference of cadres from four levels originally held from 21 January to 13 February.[63] Finally, it is interesting to note that during the winter of 1957–8 the double-wheeled double-bladed plough was publicized and praised in Sichuan as a technical improvement in agriculture. Thus, for example, Shangliu *xian* claimed to have increased production by 10% and saved half as much manpower as an ordinary plough in the winter great leap through use of the double-wheeled double-bladed plough.[64] The double-wheeled double-bladed plough had been associated with Mao ever since its promotion in the 1956 version of the Twelve Year Plan. Although it had been omitted from the October 1957 revised version of that plan, it re-appeared in the 'Sixty Work Articles'.[65] The latter, as already noted, had emerged from discussions between Mao and provincial leaders at the Hangzhou and Nanning Conferences during January 1958. Presumably other provinces also publicized the double-wheeled double-bladed plough at this time, though which are unknown, and it would seem that Guizhou in contrast did not.

Sichuan as a regional economic base

The impact of the GLF on Sichuan's economic performance was, of course, nothing like as optimistic as even the most charitable interpretation of Table 7 might suggest. On the other hand, the aims and aspirations of Sichuan's leaders at the time were relatively clear.

Under the first five year plan, the main emphasis in Sichuan's economic development had been on agricultural growth rather than the much-needed industrial construction: the province's agricultural production grew twice as fast as that of China as a whole.[66] Industrial development had been a minor consideration, and heavy industry relatively neglected '... because during the period of the first five year plan Sichuan province was still not a key-point construction area'.[67] By the end of 1957, heavy industry only accounted for 15.2% of the total value of production in the province, compared to 27.4% in China as a whole.[68] As the crisis of 1956–7 indicates the province was almost totally dependent on imports of equipment and machinery to meet its industrial requirements, as well as of raw materials both for industrial purposes and the manufacture of consumer goods.[69] Such industrial development as did take place was almost solely agriculture based or supporting, and food processing was the province's largest industrial activity by 1957.[70]

Under the second five year plan this strategy was to be radically altered. Chongqing, Chengdu and Xichang were to be developed as industrial centres, not only for Sichuan, but also, as the authors of the *Economic Geography of Southwest China* written in 1959 to that specific end, pointed out for the whole of the Southwest region.[71] The development of both heavy and extraction industries were the new priorities, so that the province would not only become self sufficient in catering for its own equipment needs, but also '... develop an industrial base for the industrialization of all Southwest China ... [with the] emphasis on ferrous metallurgy, machine building, the petroleum and chemical industries, and the building of hydro-electric power stations'.[72] Although small-scale industrial activity was far from being ignored in Sichuan during the GLF – for example, Nanchong special district became a national model for its creation of 43,000 rural-based 'factories' within two months during 1958[73] – such development required considerable capital investment. This need was reflected in the proportion of budgetary expenditure earmarked for capital construction which rose from 24.2% during 1952–7 to 62.8% in 1958 and 73.2% in 1959.[74] Furthermore, the number of above-norm projects (i.e. those costing over 10 million *yuan*)[75] under construction increased dramatically. 63 such key construction projects were started in 1958,[76] 36 in 1959,[77] and 76 planned for 1960.[78] Apart from the nationally acclaimed development of Chongqing as the 'industrial metropolis of the southwest',[79] the most widely publicized of these projects were the Chongqing Iron and Steel Works and the Yangtze River Bridge. It was claimed that the Iron and Steel Works had been successfully developed (including the construction of its steel furnaces within forty days) without state investment, the intensive use of machinery or the support of technical personnel from higher levels.[80] The construction of a second bridge over the Yangtze at Chongqing was celebrated for its completion in November 1959, ten months ahead of schedule, having only been started in September 1958.[81]

The adoption of the General Line in Sichuan at the April 1958 session of the provincial party congress outlined the priorities in support of that programme for development. Agricultural production was to be increased in order to finance industrial expansion, and the Twelve Year Plan was to be completed within three years 'or even earlier'. In industry, there was to be a GLF such that within five years, the value of industrial production should exceed that of agriculture in the province.[82] In the event it is clear that as throughout China there were problems in creating a GLF. Although it was claimed at the time that the Twelve Year Plan had been 'basically realized' in 1958,[83] as late as 1973 Sichuan still claimed to be one of the provinces 'that had not reached the targets of the Twelve Year Plan'.[84] Even in the fastest year of economic advance – which however one interprets the statistics in Table 7 would appear to be 1958 – the value of industrial production actually increased at a slower rate than that of agricultural output, 55.7% over 1957 as opposed to 69.9%.[85] The general problems which became manifest at Lushan and were reflected in Sichuan by revised figures for output in 1958,[86] revealed an even more serious problem. Whereas, in the summer of 1959 Sichuan's industrial development was seen as being generated from within the province,[87] after September 1959 it was recognized that expansion would be largely financed from the centre. In both 1959 and 1960 approximately half Sichuan's income came from central funds.[88] Thus, for example, in 1959, locally derived income amounted to 56.6 thousand million *yuan*, and central support to 53.9 thousand million *yuan* in the provincial budget.[89]

Politics in command

Apart from communization and subsequent concerns, Sichuan's leaders, as at the start of the GLF, continued to stress the importance of political education and enthusiasm throughout this period. In September 1958, the Socialist Education Movement which had contributed to the initial GLF became a Communist Education Movement[90] – an example of the 'Communist Wind' later criticized by Mao and others when caution started to set in.[91]

If anything, the importance of placing 'politics in command' was stressed to a greater extent after the Lushan plenum than before. Liao Zhigao in his report to the 3rd session of the 1st provincial party congress in February 1960 emphasized that in order to achieve a continued GLF:

... cadres in posts of leadership at all levels must seriously study Mao Zedong's works, improve their method of leadership, and raise their ideological level. They should master Mao Zedong Thought, and sum up and solve the theoretical problems found in the course of socialist construction in order to execute the party's general line correctly. Party organs at all levels should detail theoretical personnel to create the necessary conditions for the elevation of the ideological and theoretical level of all party members.[92]

Similarly, Li Dazhang in his 1960 provincial government work report, whilst admitting that there had been problems attributed these to the bad weather conditions of 1959 and cadres' defective work style. Above all he stressed the importance of enthusiasm for the GLF rather than pessimism in the fourth section of his report. As in 1956–7, Li blamed basic-level cadres for the problems arising from food supply shortages, over-emphasis on grain production, lack of freight movement, and advocated further rectification as the solution.[93]

Moreover, after Lushan the movement to study the Thought of Mao Zedong was expanded, having originally started in 1958.[94] In that, Sichuan was not unusual. However, its development in the province did have one peculiar characteristic, not known to have existed in other provinces – a proto-'Little Red Book'. At first in Sichuan, the movement to study Mao Zedong's works appears to have developed from the attempts by the Chongqing YCL to raise the political consciousness of young people and children, and to instill in them the revolutionary values of hard work and struggle. Stress was laid on 'becoming Chairman Mao's good children and following the CCP' and 'understanding why the past must not be forgotten and the future not be left out'. The campaign was built around a selection of quotations from Mao's writings.[95] Later, in

February 1960, the movement was broadened into a province-wide campaign for the study of Mao Thought. Mao's ideas were acclaimed as having brought about a victory in the GLF, and in particular for 'having attained the principal targets set in the second five year plan ahead of schedule'.[96] As the passage previously quoted from Liao Zhigao's speech indicates, the campaign was a major item of discussion at the 3rd session of the 1st provincial party congress.

As elsewhere, the placing of 'politics in command' resulted in continued rectification and the downward transfer of cadres; and mass mobilization, not only for agricultural and industrial production, but also in the newly-expanded militia. Thus, for example, in January 1960 it was stated that

The basic purpose of sending cadres down to the lower levels to take part in labour is to reform our ranks of cadres and to establish an army of cadres who are both red and expert ... [it] is especially important for cadres of non-proletarian origins, who despite long participation in political and theoretical study, particularly during the 1957 rectification campaign, still have not solved the problem of their stand and world-outlook.[97]

The downward transfer of cadres reached its height towards the end of 1960, when a further 37,000-plus provincial level cadres, including '1,200 hardcore leadership cadres' went down to the front line of production.[98] Again, the people's militia expanded in the 'Everyone a soldier' movement, with the 1st Sichuan Militia Representative Conference being held in January 1960. The militia's purpose, it was stated, was not just one of defence but also, like the PLA 'to take part in production, in the promotion of productivity and in the maintenance of public security'.[99] Presumably as a result of the emphasis on 'placing politics in command', party recruitment was increased in Sichuan during the GLF. 150,000 new party members were recruited between June 1958 and July 1959,[100] and 110,000 in the first five months of 1960.[101] On a conservative estimate, the total provincial membership of the CCP would appear to have grown to 1.25 million during 1960, approximately 1.8% of the population.[102]

Sichuan's stress on placing 'politics in command' continued even after the summer of 1960, when it would appear that the decision had been taken nationally to backtrack on the GLF. In an emergency telephone conference held in September, Li Jingquan and Li Dazhang both emphasized the continued energetic promotion of a GLF in industry and agriculture. In order to ensure an 'all-round victory' they proposed a five-point plan which included 'Whipping up work enthusiasm'; 'Commending the advanced and criticizing the backward'; and strengthening leadership and supervision by carrying out an ordinary inspection each day, and a major inspection every five days.[103]

GUIZHOU

For Guizhou's leaders the period of the GLF provided a political turning point. Although, as the data in Table 8 indicate, there were clearly limits to economic growth, the national-level change in line enabled, or forced, Guizhou's leadership to adopt different perspectives. Rectification, the campaigns against 'local nationalism', mass mobilization campaigns, and the emphasis on political education were important techniques in the integration of the province. The development of a provincial industry, however small and inefficient, not only contributed to provincial-level integration, but through the improvement of transport and communications with neighbouring provinces also aided the province's integration into China as a whole. As a result, Guizhou attempted to shed its quasi-colonial status during this period, and certainly was much more in the mainstream of national political developments than previously. Although by no means as radical in its responses to national politics as Sichuan, and distinctly more conservative after Lushan, Guizhou's leadership reacted immediately and enthusiastically to the GLF after the Nanning Conference of January 1958. Moreover, throughout the period its reactions to national political developments were more conformist than beforehand. There clearly was an attempt on the provincial leadership's part to respond positively to central directives, even when, as with communization (to be discussed in Chapter 7), implementing such policies as the centre desired was impossible.

The GLF of spring 1958

As previously indicated, Guizhou's response to the national re-adoption of the Twelve Year Plan was slower and less enthusiastic than that of Sichuan. The change in line was presumably adopted at the 1st session of the 2nd provincial party congress in December.[104] Certainly, thereafter enthusiasm for the twelve year plan, increased agricultural production and a new 'high tide', were reflected in the provincial media.[105] A provincial local industry conference was even convened, in order to encourage the development of light industry to support the proposed 'high tide' in agricultural production.[106]

However, in January 1958 Guizhou started to take the GLF to heart. A winter water conservation work campaign was started which was almost immediately said to be near completion, thus necessitating the raising of targets and an extension of the campaign.[107] Preparation for a 'high tide' in industrial as well as agricultural production was announced,[108] and it was claimed that an 'ideological leap forward' leads to a 'construction leap forward'.[109] The importance of rectification and the downward transfer of cadres were stressed, and in a speech to a meeting for cadres about to *xiafang*, Zhou Lin pointed out that without these '. . . socialism could not be built, Britain could not be caught up with in 15 years, or the 40 articles realized'.[110] In the downward transfer of cadres, particular stress was laid on the problems of mountain areas, and they were the first recipients of cadres and technicians.[111]

Although targets had already been raised in water conservation work, the decisive turning point in Guizhou's GLF came with the 5th plenum of the provincial party committee in February. Thereafter, as in Sichuan, production and target-setting seemed to develop a life of their own, rising at an increasingly fast rate until, in Guizhou's case, the spring of 1959. The 5th plenum laid plans to 'Basically change the appearance of Guizhou's economy in three years of bitter struggle and struggle upstream to realize the agricultural development outline in five years'. Within three years the GLF in Guizhou was to result in a doubling of the amount of irrigated land; the removal of the 'four pests' and malaria; increased fertilizer accumulation; a surplus of agricultural production in each *xiang*; a seven-fold increase in industrial production; and Guizhou was to become the 'Shanxi of the south' in coal production.[112] In addition, grain targets for the fulfilment of the twelve year plan in 1962 and 1967 were adopted.[113]

As in Sichuan, considerable political and economic resources were invested in launching the GLF. The first stage was a campaign to 'expand the socialist activism of masses and cadres'. All were criticized for only wanting to be average rather than achieving the best possible results. Cadres, in particular, were criticized for fearing mass mobilization, and not being prepared to trust the masses. Such attitudes were attacked as 'rightist errors' and 'conservatism' that had to be exterminated.[114] The aim of such rectification and attempt at enthusiasm was to encourage mass mobilization. In that it seems to have succeeded. By May, 600,000 had been mobilized in 'inspection groups' to travel throughout the province to both propagandize 'the general line' and 'the mass line' and to 'participate in work and ensure that the correct policies are implemented'.[115] In the water conservancy campaign, it was claimed that over one million small pools, canals and reservoirs had been built irrigating (according to one source) 9 million *mou*[116] of land, or (according to another source) 15 million *mou*.[117] (Although as a comparison between tables 7 and 8 suggests, Guizhou's reporting was more cautious and conservative than Sichuan's, it was clearly no more reliable.) Manure collection was said to have amounted to 49,000 *jin* per *mou* during the first half of the year, as opposed to the 10,000 originally planned by the 5th plenum.[118] Similarly, 110,000 small-scale rural-based industrial enterprises were started; the 'four pests' were said to have been completely exterminated and malaria 'basically eliminated'.[119] In Guiyang alone it was claimed that through 'the efforts of tens of thousands', 1.2 million rats, more than a million grain-eating sparrows, 200 tons of fly larvae, and 250,000 metres of mosquito-breeding ditches had been destroyed in the three spring months.[120]

Rectification and political education

Rectification and political education were major concerns of Guizhou's leadership, not just at the start of the GLF but right through to 1961. However, rectification and associated campaigns served a dual purpose in Guizhou. As eleswhere, the GLF would have been very different without the emphasis on political consciousness. In addition, in Guizhou these campaigns were crucial in the attempt to combat 'local nationalism'. This dual role of rectification was clearly spelt out by Zhou Lin in his report to the 1st session of the 2nd PPC in September 1958.

The rectification campaign is essential to all activities. It is a power house for all action. In fact enthusiasm for the 'high tide' of production came about as a result of the anti-rightist campaign ... It served to educate the masses so that they understand the merits of socialism ... and a more positive attitude to socialism has resulted. They have given up their entrenched attitudes resulting from their place of residence and their occupations ... The new type of personality has become the major power source in industrial expansion. The rectification campaign also strengthened party leadership in government organs and enterprises. The policy of 'Better troops and simpler administration' was implemented.[121]

Although Zhou, in his report suggested that the anti-rightist campaign that had started in August of 1957 was now completed, that did not mean that the campaign against 'local nationalism' was over, any more than it signalled the end of rectification. As Ye Kulin, president of Guizhou highest people's court made clear in his 1959 work report, 'local nationalism' was a 'counter revolutionary activity' and treated as such.[122] 'Local nationalists' in other words have moved from being designated as 'rightists' to clear 'enemies of the people'.

As in Sichuan, and elsewhere, the emphasis on 'politics in command', resulted not only in continued rectification campaigns and the downward transfer of cadres, but increased recruitment into the CCP, the expansion of the people's militia, and labour participation schemes for cadres. For example, although the socialist education movement does not seem to have become, as in Sichuan, a 'communist education movement' in late 1958, basic-level rectification continued apace, and in early 1960 a campaign started for the study and propagation of Mao Zedong Thought amongst the peasantry.[123] Between January and May 1960, 21,000 new members were recruited into the CCP in Guizhou, and a further 80,000 were awaiting entrance as candidate members.[124] In February 1960, the 'Everyone a soldier' movement led to the convention of Guizhou's 1st Militia Work Conference. As elsewhere, it was not just the security role of the militia that was seen as important, but its role as an 'efficient force on the socialist construction front' as part of 'Chairman Mao's theory of the people's revolutionary war'.[125] Finally, Guizhou not only transferred cadres 'down to the front line of production' – 75,000 from the provincial-level in 1959 alone[126] – but at the 2nd session of the 2nd provincial party congress in April 1960 popularized the '2–5 working style' for cadres. Cadres were to spend two days each week in political study and administration and five days in active production.[127]

A further aspect of putting 'politics in command' which was of particular importance to Guizhou was the emphasis on education and literacy. Although that emphasis was generally part of the GLF, its impact was greater in Guizhou than elsewhere. Before 1958 only 4% of the provincial population could read and write;[128] there were only 792[129] primary and middle schools; only 3.83% of the population (that is the total as opposed to simply the school-age population) attended primary schools (as opposed to a national average of 10.3%), and only 0.09% attended middle schools (compared to 0.63% nationally).[130] During 1958, the provincial education department set to the task of improving educational facilities with a will. According to Tian Junliang, the director of the provincial education department, in a speech to the NPC, 60% of school age children had been enrolled in primary schools.[131] By September, Zhou Lin claimed that 11,000 primary schools and 2,600 secondary schools had been established during the year.[132] By 1959, the province had 21,000 primary schools, with 15% of the provincial population enrolled, and 1.3% in secondary schools at the year end.[133] Even more remarkable, by September 1958 it was claimed that illiteracy had been 'basically eliminated' amongst the young and middle-aged.[134]

'Our method is simple: start from nothing and work hard!'

Throughout the GLF the economic development of Guizhou was promoted as a model of the virtues of having been 'poor and blank'. Thus, the quotation in the title of this section is from a commune cadre in Guizhou's mountain areas who was interviewed about the 'revolutionary spirit needed to build socialism'.[135] Nor was Guizhou a model for agriculture alone. Writing in *People's Daily* in 1958, the director of the provincial propaganda department, Wang Xiaochuan, emphasized the advantages of having been 'poor and blank' for industrial development. In particular he stressed the power of mass mobilization.

The peasants were busy day and night over iron and steel production. Even children aged 8 or 9 were happy to stay by the blast furnaces and help with the supply of coal and iron-ore. They said proudly 'I have had a hand in the victory on the iron and steel battle front.' In those days of continuous rainfall, when the roads were muddy, a great transport army of men and women, young and old, marched day and night. As a result of Guizhou people's heaven-rending strength, a great victory has been achieved on all production fronts.[136]

Similarly, when Zhou Enlai visited the province in May 1960, he was quoted as having said that 'Guizhou has a good climate [sic!], rich resources and diligent people', and that provided the various nationalities in the province united behind the CCP and worked hard, the province 'would catch up with other provinces in the pace of socialist construction'.[137]

Although mass mobilization was certainly an important element of the GLF in Guizhou, it seems relatively clear that after 1957 the development of an industrial base in the province was never intended to be self-generated. Any product of the localized and small-scale rural-based industries was a bonus, however dubious that might have been. Right from the start of 1958, and in contrast to Sichuan, Guizhou's industrial development was dependent on central aid and investment, of both capital and technical resources. Although the provincial financial and planning systems virtually ceased to produce even unreliable statistics after the Lushan plenum, in 1958 alone, 63% of provincial income came from central funds.[138] Without exception every major industrial project started in the province during the GLF was said to have been 'undertaken by the central government', and most publicized the involvement of technicians from outside the province. Thus, for example, the large-scale development of the Anshun coal mine received not only central funding but technical assistance from Shanxi.[139] Similarly, the construction of railways connecting Guizhou with Sichuan, Yunnan, and Guangxi;[140] the Guiyang Iron and Steel Plant;[141] the Guiyang Chemical Fertilizer Plant;[142] and various other large-scale above-norm projects were centrally funded.[143] Technical specialists and workers were brought into the province, not only from Sichuan, whose considerable assistance was acknowledged,[144] but from Shanghai, Jilin, and Shandong.[145]

On the other hand, there can be little doubt that Guizhou's leaders were caught up in the atmosphere of enthusiasm generated by the GLF. Whereas in February 1958, the plan had been to increase industrial production by 700% within three years, by May this target had risen to 800%.[146] Similarly, in agriculture, whereas the provincial party's 5th plenum had set a target of 210 million *jin* of grain for 1967,[147] by the end of the year, it was being claimed that production had already reached that level, and Wang Xiaochuan was even talking of producing 500 million *jin* of grain in 1959,[148] though this target was never adopted by the provincial party. It was even claimed that the province had produced 20,000 tons of steel in 1958,[149] even though the province's first steel plant was only opened in 1960.[150] The 8th plenum of Guizhou's party committee in January

1959 represented the 'High Tide' of the province's enthusiasm in the GLF. At that time the steel target was set at 200,000 tons (still without the appropriate equipment) and the target for grain at 340 million *jin*, in order to achieve 'an even greater, even better, more all-round leap forward than in 1958'.[151]

In the event, developments in national-level politics and particularly the poor harvest of 1959 in the province, rapidly deflated the enthusiasm of the GLF. In the two months following the Lushan plenum, there was a series of emergency telephone conferences (approximately one a week reported in the press during September and October) between provincial and *xian* level cadres concerned in agricultural production. One reason was presumably in order to urge caution. Another was presumably because once again, as in the three years before 1958, the weather had proved that there were severe limitations to agricultural growth in Guizhou. Indeed, it would appear that 1959's grain production had not only been over two-thirds down on the target set in January, but had also fallen below the 1957 level of output.[152] Despite Zhou Lin's claim in the national media that Guizhou had exported grain ever since 1953,[153] Vice Governor Dai Xiaodong, in delivering the provincial government work report for 1959 pointed out that: 'During the past years the state has not received any grain from Guizhou province. Instead it has suffered deficits . . . [Moreover] the loss of food grains this year will be even greater than in previous years.'[154]

As a result the 2nd session of the 2nd PPC acknowledged that there were problems in agricultural production, and adopted a series of emergency measures such as Sichuan had done in 1956. Thus state procurement prices for rice, millet, beans and other foodstuffs were raised by approximately 5–6%. Similarly, the province's commercial department launched a mass transportation movement using horse and ox-drawn carts, as well as people.[155] Unfortunately for Guizhou, the problems that had caused agricultural failure in 1959 were not capable of both easy solution and rapid advance. As outlined by Dai Xiaodong in a speech to a provincial conference of Representatives of Advanced Units in Socialist Agricultural Construction held in January 1960, these included not only problems with prices and the market, but also severe labour shortages in agricultural work, and a rash of diseases affecting crops. Prevention of the latter – which included rice dwarf-disease virus, maize streak virus, olethpic Steinhaus, and flea-beetle – was presumably hampered by labour shortages in agriculture. Although Dai called for a further agricultural leap forward under the party's 'General Line' and leadership for 1960,[156] the weather once again intervened – a drought unusually covering the whole province throughout the whole summer.[157]

Sichuan, Guizhou and the results of the GLF

There can be little doubt that, particularly before August 1957, the leaders of both Sichuan and Guizhou enthusiastically promoted the GLF. That really is not surprising. The change in line adopted at the 3rd plenum and the Second Five Year Plan promised to bring not only much of what they had previously requested, but also more general solutions to the various problems they faced. However, there can also be little doubt that the early enthusiasm for the GLF was not matched by its results. Indeed as the next chapter indicates the impact of the GLF was such that it created severe problems for provincial leaders in both Sichuan and Guizhou and led to the reorganization of the leadership in Guizhou.

Two problems in particular were common to both Sichuan and Guizhou during the GLF. In the first place, there was the effectiveness of capital investment, largely provided from central funds. Although considerable capital was invested in both Sichuan and Guizhou in order to develop industry, capital was wasted in large amounts as planners were overtaken by the general enthusiasm of the GLF. In addition, the provinces were consequently that much less independent economically than they might otherwise have been. Capital investment and central aid were not always utilized to the best effect.

Perhaps the best example of inefficient investment and 'industrial enthusiasm' in either province was the development of the Central Sichuan Oilfield at Nanchong during the middle of 1958. Explorations for oil had been carried out in Sichuan since September 1957. On 10 March 1958 an exploratory hole turned into a gusher.[158] Almost as if on cue, two further major fields were claimed within the next six days.[159] The new oil-field was hailed as a great victory in the GLF, and the three oil structures were estimated to cover 2,200 sq. kms. A spokesman for the Ministry of Petroleum was quoted as saying: 'Central Sichuan is our country's new oil field. The scale of the prospecting wells' producing oil is unprecedented in history.'[160] By the end of March, 120 wells had been sunk, work had started on constructing roads to connect with both the river and rail networks, three refineries were under construction, and the oil field was expected to yield 10,000 tons of oil in 1958.[161] Aid and investment were poured into the project. For example, 3,400 specialists were sent from Yumen, including 40 drilling teams, an oil-testing team, a complete motor convoy, and personnel for a machine repair workshop.[162] By April, the expected long-term annual capacity of the field had risen to 300,000 tons, and a much larger oil refinery planned for construction in Nanchong.[163] By June, two refineries were already said to be in production.[164] The growing number of gushers and rising expectations of the field's capacity continued throughout the early summer. As a result, work started on extending the transport network around the field (for example, a short distance air service was opened on 2 July between Chengdu and Nanchong); more storage tanks were built; and it was planned to develop Nanchong into a city of over 200,000 in three to five years.[165] However, the vast effort put into developing the oil field appears to have come to nought for after July 1958 it was never again mentioned in the media at either provincial or national level. It seems reasonable to assume that, as is quite common in oil exploration, the oil existed only in isolated pockets sufficient for several gushers but no more. A story of similar waste applied to the development of the Maotiaohe hydro-electric station – a large scale project – in Guizhou. Started in 1959 it was abandoned after 1960.[166]

A second problem common to both provinces was that of popular resistance. Although Sichuan and Guizhou's leaders may have favoured the GLF, it is relatively clear that substantial sections of the populations did not share their views. In Guizhou, every party and people's congress during 1959 and 1960 devoted considerable time and space to 'refuting erroneous views' articulated within the province about the GLF and people's communes. Thus, for example, in his 1959 government work report, Dai Xiaodong criticized the views that 'The building of people's communes transcends reality ... they result from a gust of wind ... they result from the orders of cadres they have no advantages.'[167] Again, in his report to the April 1960 session of the provincial party congress, Zhou Lin pointed out that ' ... many bad elements ... still resist reforms. They grab every chance to destroy socialist construction. Some are still in the party, and even after education by the party, continue to resist reforms.'[168] Zhou Lin even wrote an article in the *People's Daily* which, in the course of criticizing resistance to the GLF, *inter alia* detailed the differences of opinion and opposition that had emerged in one rural people's commune.[169] In Sichuan, provincial leaders and the provincial media were similarly concerned to rebuff resistance within the province to both the GLF and people's communes.[170]

Despite any similarities between Sichuan and Guizhou during the GLF, the contrast between their two roles in national politics persisted. Although the leaders of both Sichuan and Guizhou supported the GLF through to the 9th plenum, after the Lushan plenum subtle but significant differences appeared in their attitudes. Where Sichuan continued to emphasize the politics of the GLF much as it had before August 1959, Guizhou's attitude became more cautious and conservative. The difference appears relatively clearly in the contrasting slogans referred to in each province's provincial government work report during 1960. In Guizhou, Chen Puru stressed the importance of taking 'the whole country as a chessboard' and 'agriculture at the base'; and even resorted to stressing the importance of 'doing the best according to local conditions', presumably in order to attempt to justify the province's economic performance during the previous year.[171] None of these slogans were mentioned in Li Dazhang's provincial government work report in Sichuan.[172] Instead he stressed the continued importance of 'walking on two legs' and 'taking steel as the key link': slogans which did not reflect the change in political rhetoric nationally that followed the Lushan plenum of August 1959. Moreover, as will become clear in Chapter 7, Sichuan and Guizhou's policies on the rural people's commune similarly diverged. These political differences may well have become even more significant after 1961. Then as Guizhou's internal problems increased so too did the influence of Sichuan's leadership in Guizhou. It is far from impossible that more partisan considerations informed the reorganization of Guizhou's leadership by the southwest regional bureau in 1965.

6

1961–5: THE PRELUDE TO
THE CULTURAL REVOLUTION

For provincial leaders the period from the 9th plenum of the 8th central committee in January 1961 to the outbreak of the GPCR must have been extremely difficult. Atrocious weather, poor harvests, and the strains imposed by the GLF caused economic problems and dislocations of such a magnitude that it was only toward the end of 1964 that Zhou Enlai could imply an economic recovery to pre-GLF levels.[1] Indeed, throughout this period provincial leaders in Sichuan and Guizhou (as well as more generally) when they stressed economic advance tended to do so with respect to 1949 as the base, rather than as during the GLF with respect to the period of the First Five Year Plan.[2]

Moreover, the strains and tensions which developed within the leadership and eventually resulted in the GPCR, also led to a bewildering series of often conflicting central directives, as for example in the evolution of the Socialist Education Movement.[3] It is clear that provincial leaders were vulnerable in the context of national politics. The wonder, to some extent, is not that most were removed during the GPCR, but that more, such as soon will become apparent, Guizhou's leadership, did not succumb sooner. Certainly, Mao's suggestion in 1964 that several provinces were 'rotten' was intended to lead to the reorganization of their leaderships.[4]

Once again, as throughout the period after 1954 there is a marked contrast between the leaders of Sichuan and Guizhou with respect to their preoccupations and reactions to national politics. However, under the crisis conditions that often pertained during the early 1960s that contrast became even sharper. Indeed, as has already been suggested, the contrast between Sichuan and Guizhou may well have become a source of tension within the Southwest. Sichuan's leaders continued to argue a radical stance in national politics, not only within Sichuan, but also through their domination of the Southwest regional bureau and in Guizhou. That province's leadership adopted a more conservative position. Moreover, it also appears to have increasingly run into problems of internal political control, to the extent that it was either unwilling or unable to satisfy either central directives or the regional bureau. The crisis came to a head in February 1965 when the regional bureau stepped in to reorganize Guizhou's leadership.

As previously indicated the 9th plenum marked a change in line, probably previously agreed at the Beidaihe Conference of the Central Committee in the summer of 1960.[5] The plenum adopted the policies of 'readjustment, consolidation, filling out and raising standards' and of 'taking agriculture as the base, industry as the leading factor' with respect to economic development. Investment in capital construction was to be reduced, particularly for the development of heavy industry, and emphasis was placed on increased agricultural production and its associated light industry. In addition, the plenum decided to establish six regional party bureaux, and to implement a nation-wide rectification (that had already started in some areas) against the excesses that had become apparent in the preceding years. However, there was as yet no official political retreat. Despite acknowledging that there had been problems in 1959 and 1960, the communiqué of the 9th plenum still paid obeisance to the 'Three Red Banners of the party's general line, the GLF and the people's communes'.[6]

However, by the June Central Work Conference it would seem that a debate had started within the national leadership about the lessons to be learnt from the GLF.[7] Certainly it was well under way by the time of the central committee's enlarged work conference of 7,000 cadres in early 1962, when Mao and others gave speeches clearly designed to unite the party.[8] In very general terms, that debate concerned whether the GLF had 'failed' for human or natural reasons, and whether or not the strategy could or should be readopted in a modified format.

The 10th plenum of September 1962 represented both the nadir of the 'Three Red Banners' reputation in the period before the GPCR, and the start of Mao's emphasis on rectification and 'class struggle'. Unlike the communiqué of the 9th plenum that of the 10th did not mention the 'Three Red Banners'.[9] The plenum stressed agricultural production, adopted new draft regulations for rural people's communes (the stages in the reorganization of rural people's communes will be considered in Ch. 7), and rectification. As Baum points out, regardless of debates within the leadership, the evidence presented to the 10th plenum was sufficient to convince all of the need for rural rectification.[10] Mao, in particular, spoke at the plenum about the need to heighten ideological vigilance because of the possibility of a restoration of the reactionary classes, summed up in his call, 'Never forget class struggle'.[11]

The concern with rural rectification led to what later became the Socialist Education Movement. From the autumn of 1962 through to the winter of 1964 this movement, originally aimed at the corrupt practices and administrative inefficiencies of basic-level rural cadres, passed through several different stages, at each of which greater stress was placed on ideological education. Moreover, as the movement developed greater emphasis was placed on the role not only of the peasantry, who were to aid cadres' rectification, but also of higher-level cadres. Eventually by the winter of 1964 Mao's concern with rectification had moved to provincial-level cadres and above – 'Those in authority taking the capitalist road'.[12]

The emphasis on rural rectification was thus one factor which led to the development of the GPCR. However, at the same time as emphasizing the importance of 'class struggle' in the countryside, Mao was also concerned with rectification in cultural activities, in particular with respect to education; and literature, art and drama.[13] Thus, for example, after 1963 various campaigns were launched to 'revolutionize' Chinese art forms, notably under the leadership of Jiang Qing. In late 1963 she had organized the East China Drama Festival 'to encourage the creation of a new revolutionary theatre', and in the summer of 1964 the Festival of Beijing Opera on Contemporary Themes, which had given birth to the modern revolutionary Beijing opera.[14] Similarly in education after 1963, greater emphasis was placed on training 'revolutionary successors' and creating students who were both politically conscious and technically competent, both 'Red and Expert'.

In retrospect it is hard to view the events from 1963–6 in any other way than as the prelude to the Cultural Revolution. Largely this is because knowledge of that period depends to a large extent on sources emanating from the GPCR.[15] Thus, what becomes emphasized is Mao's relationship with Jiang Qing and the PLA, the apparent deepening divisions within the leadership, the start of the

Cultural Revolution (that is the Socialist Education Movement in this context) at Beijing University in 1965,[16] and the debate over 'Hai Rui's dismissal from office'.[17]

SICHUAN

Although the 9th plenum signalled the end of the GLF nationally, this was not immediately apparent in Sichuan. Until the end of July 1961, Sichuan's leaders continued to call for a GLF in industry and agriculture. Thus despite the cutback on capital construction in industry nationally, Sichuan's coal industry department was praised for advancing its capital construction plan by the end of June.[18] However, at the end of July the provincial party committee recognized the severity of the agricultural situation and its economic perspectives changed drastically. After an emergency telephone conference on 22 July between the provincial leadership and cadres from the special districts and *xian*, the provincial party committee met on 29 and 30 July and issued a 'Directive on production self-help and beating natural disasters'. Li Dazhang's speech to the party committee explaining the change in economic priorities – 'taking agriculture as the base' – was printed in full in the provincial paper. The severity of the crisis was underlined by the fact that in the headline he was referred to as 'Comrade Dazhang' – an unprecedented occurrence in Sichuan.[19] Since Li Dazhang, the provincial governor and a provincial party secretary, was the highest ranking local cadre who was also a native of Sichuan (unlike Li Jingquan, the first party secretary) the intention was presumably to provide a symbol of unity between the province's leadership and its population in a period of crisis. In general, the use of an individual's personal name in this manner was in itself rather unusual at that time. The three leading national figures, Mao Zedong, Zhou Enlai, and Liu Shaoqi, were known familiarly as Chairman Mao, Premier Zhou, and only the last as Comrade Shaoqi. Li's emphasis was followed in a similar speech by Huang Xinting, the commander of the military region.[20]

Thereafter, the priority in industrial production was to support agriculture. The provincial industry department made this quite clear five days after the party committee's directive was published.[21] Almost the whole of the provincial press in the following few months was given over to raising agricultural production, overcoming natural disasters, maintaining procurement and supporting agriculture;[22] and all units, whether commune-based or not, and including both local PLA units[23] and the provincial public security department,[24] were involved. Even so, the provincial leadership seems somewhat reluctant to abandon its commitment to the GLF and the 'General Line', particularly by comparison with Guizhou, which had virtually done so ever since late 1959. Thus in mid-October, Li Dazhang sounded no retreat in his speech to the provincial people's consultative conference, 'China has trod a new path since 1958'.[25] Again, in advocating increased agricultural production and procurement in September 1961, the call was for 'More, faster, better and more economical'.[26] A slogan which was still in use provincially as late as August 1962.[27]

Throughout 1961–5 in fact, and despite definite changes in economic perspectives, Sichuan showed some reluctance to abandon the rhetoric of the GLF. Moreover, although there was more emphasis on 'proportionate and planned' economic development, not all the mass line techniques of the GLF were completely abandoned. The development of commune management apart, the major concerns of Sichuan's leaders during this period were with agriculture production, the Socialist Education Movement, and political consciousness in general. In a real sense those three concerns are inherently connected. The agricultural crisis of 1961–3 led to the concern with rural rectification, which then in turn became seen in the wider context of raising ideological consciousness and political education more generally.

Agriculture

Although heavy industrial production and development was by no means ignored to the same extent during this period as it had been before 1958, Sichuan's main economic priority was with agriculture. Moreover, as before and after 1958 (although not during 1958 itself) increased agricultural production was emphasized not only for provincial consumption, but also in order that its surpluses could be exported to meet other provinces' demands. Thus towards the end of the GLF it was reported that 'Sichuan has mobilized a "grain army" of 500,000 to ship grain to meet the needs of Beijing, Shanghai and Tianjin and state key-point construction areas.'[28] Similarly, even during 1961 and 1962 when agricultural production in Sichuan was admitted to be well below normal,[29] an integral part of the 'patriotic grain procurement campaigns', was the emphasis on the importance of grain exports.[30]

Nationally, Zhou Enlai later described 1959–61 as the years of bad weather, natural disasters and poor harvests.[31] Although Sichuan's leaders had admitted to difficulties arising from natural disasters during 1959 and 1960,[32] it was the period from mid 1961 to mid 1963 which was explicitly regarded as one of crisis. The siege mentality which set in with the late July 1961 party committee plenum lasted until the summer of 1963. By September, Li Dazhang was able to report to the 1st session of the 3rd PPC that the improvement in the market situation had been 'remarkable' with the development of both industry and agriculture exceeding not only the preceding year's production but also the estimates made at the beginning of the year.[33]

It is hard to assess the extent of agricultural problems, for although it is clear that production was hit by an eight-month drought during 1961,[34] agricultural production suffered not only from 'natural disasters', but also from a certain amount of peasant resistance. Drought in 1961 was followed by a much shorter (two month) drought in the spring of 1962,[35] but that was hardly sufficient to explain the apparent slump in production. Although in 1963 it was claimed that the 1962 grain procurement target had been achieved,[36] no details were published in either 1961 or 1962, and only one area (Wanxian) was publicized for having reached its grain output and procurement targets.[37] Moreover, data on agricultural production after 1963 would seem to indicate both that growth was very slow and had sunk to low levels in the early 1960s. For example, the area of land planted with sugar cane in 1964 although 51% up on 1963, was still only 385,000 *mou*[38] compared to 510,000 *mou* in 1952 and 620,000 *mou* in 1957.[39] Even Sichuan's rice production (in the 1950s normally 60% of all food grains) had only just risen above the 1957 level by 1965, at approximately 30,550 million *jin*.[40]

Throughout the crisis of mid-1961 to mid-1963 various measures were taken to aid both production and procurement. As elsewhere, it was stressed to the peasants that production, procurement and distribution would be handled according to the principles of 'three guarantees and one reward' and of the 'Three fixed'. From its side, the provincial leadership encouraged schools, factories and other urban enterprises to 'link-up' with 'backward' production units.[41] As in the supply crisis of 1956–7 local industrial departments convened material Resources Regulation and Exchange conferences in order to facilitate the two way flow of goods between urban and rural areas;[42] and local 'integrated transport networks' – the 'living evidence of the vitality of the policy of "walking on two legs"' – were once again promoted. As a cadre from Jiangbei *xian* (which was promoted as a national model for its promotion of traditional, low cost means of transport) is reported to have said: 'The long-term aim is naturally to create a far-flung national transport network using the most modern means of transport. Meanwhile, to get the job done 'anything that goes, goes', as some local transport enthusiasts put it.'[43] Moreover, in general lower transport costs were fixed for agricultural goods.[44] Similarly, as part of the policy of 'industry and commerce serving agriculture' the provincial chemical industry's fertilizers and phosphates were supplied to the rural areas at reduced prices.[45]

Although there is no evidence that Sichuan's leaders advocated production quotas be set for individual households, during this period, as there is for Guizhou and as was claimed during the GPCR,[46] it is not impossible that this may have occurred in some areas. However, one new departure in production policy was the selection of priority areas for resource allocation in 1963. 65 *xian* were selected as 'key-point cotton and grain *xian*' receiving top priority in the distribution of state support to agriculture – that is tools, fertilizers, pesticides, draught animals, ploughs, machinery and other agricultural implements – and over half the available provincial total. Increased agricultural production over the province as a whole was the stated aim of this policy for it was pointed out that these *xian* (concentrated in the Chengdu basin) had '... historically supplied the state with grain etc., and have been the most important production areas, providing 48% plus of all the province's agricultural output'.[47]

By November 1963, the agricultural situation had improved to the extent that the provincial grain department could announce the fulfilment of the grain procurement plan ahead of schedule.[48] Thereafter, the province's emphasis on agricultural production continued, but in a much less frenzied and urgent manner. Greater emphasis than previously was placed on diversification of cultivation. Raw cotton cultivation, as before, remained a priority along with grain, however now other products, such as oil-bearing crops, sugar cane, and sideline production were also promoted.1[49] One can only assume that the provincial leadership was once again attempting to drive home the lessons learnt from over-concentration on grain and cotton during co-operativization and communization.

Moreover, during 1963–5 much greater emphasis was placed on technical inputs into agriculture. A determined attempt was made at the electrification and mechanization of the rural areas;[50] and technical experimental units were established throughout the province in order to both provide technical assistance to communes and to train agriculturally competent new basic-level cadres.[51] Interestingly, although the most famous of these, at Huohua commune in Nanchong (which became a national model in 1964) was criticized during the GPCR for 'putting production before politics' and ignoring Mao Zedong Thought,[52] at the time it was publicized for precisely the opposite qualities.[53]

None the less, there was still (unsurprisingly) room for mass mobilization techniques of development. Thus, for example, the Luosi hydro-electric station was a medium-scale rural construction project based on mass mobilization and minimal capital investment. Although it does not seem to have acquired the national coverage of many of Sichuan's other projects, it was certainly promoted in the province as a model for emulation.[54] Nor were national models of that kind, such as Dazhai, ignored in Sichuan as was later claimed in the GPCR.[55] In 1964, a peasant representative was sent to Dazhai on a visit. On his return he reported its achievements, experiences and the lessons to be learnt to a mass meeting of 'no less than 100,000 people'.[56] Moreover, the province adopted its own Dazhai-type models in the campaign to 'Learn from Yanlong to catch up with Sima'. These communes had been chosen for emulation provincially because of their original backward condition which had been transformed by 'putting politics in command'.[57]

The Socialist Education Movement

As during the GLF, the concern with agriculture and increased production was not seen by Sichuan's leaders in the isolation of its economic context but was integrally associated with the Socialist Education Movement. In general it would appear that the Socialist Education Movement of 1957–9 was gradually de-escalated thereafter and had disappeared altogether as a rural campaign by 1960–1. However, in Sichuan that was clearly not the case. The Socialist Education Movement of the GLF continued as an important rural campaign right through until 1962–3 when it became merged with the second and better known Socialist Education Movement that in some respects led directly to the Great Proletarian Cultural Revolution. As during the GLF, the Socialist Education Movement in Sichuan during the 1960s, particularly before the 10th plenum was directed at increasing cadres' and peasants' political consciousness in order to increase production.[58] However, in the period from early 1961 to early 1963, when Mao's 'First Ten Points' were developed,[59] it was also directed at combating the excesses and defects in cadres' work-style which had become apparent during the GLF, such as commandism.[60]

Presumably as elsewhere, it was in general a rectification of rural cadres such as had been implemented regularly in the previous decade. On the other hand unlike elsewhere (as far as can be ascertained) even before the 10th plenum the movement in Sichuan had started to develop the specific characteristics associated with later stages of the national movement. Indeed, although sources of information on the implementation of the Socialist Education Movement in Sichuan from 1962 on are resticted, it would none the less appear to be the case that its development differed significantly from the pattern of central dictates outlined by Baum.[61] In the first place there is nothing to suggest that either Liu Shaoqi's 'Revised Second 10 Points' – the 'Big Four Clean Ups' – or Mao's final 'Twenty Three Points', were implemented in Sichuan. Certainly, there was no major reorganization of the provincial party leadership (the major point of Mao's 'Twenty-Three Points') in Sichuan during 1965, as there was in Guizhou. On the other hand, Mao had not mentioned Sichuan as either a 'rotten' or a 'leftist' province in his speech of late 1964, and there is no reason to suppose that he regarded all provincial leaders in that light. Moreover, despite the accusation made during the GPCR that there had been a 'Big Four Clean-Ups' in Sichuan, the evidence for that assertion is dubious at best. Only one case was ever cited as proof of a 'Big Four Clean-Ups' in Sichuan, and that was the reorganization of the Yibin party committee in 1962,[62] which predated the 'revised Second 10 Points' by two years. Whilst secondly, although both the 'First' and 'Second Ten Points' (of May 1963 and September 1963 respectively) do seem to have been largely implemented in Sichuan, in both cases it would appear that local experimentation preceded national adoption. If this were so it would not be too surprising since the period from the

10th plenum to May 1963, and indeed the development of the Socialist Education Movement until late 1964 was largely one of experimentation.[63]

It would appear that the 'First Ten Points' were adopted nationally at a central work conference in May 1963. This was the stage in the development of the movement that the 'Four Clean-Ups' (*si qing*) were first introduced to purify rural cadres. According to Baum, the most important aspects of the 'First Ten Points' were that there was to be mass participation in the rectification of cadres, and that cadres should spend a significant portion of their work-time down 'at the front line of production'. In order to facilitate mass participation in rectification, the poor and lower-middle peasant organizations were to be revived, who were themselves to become involved in self-rectification at the same time through the study of past histories. Such studies were designed to bring home to the peasantry how they (or their forebears) had suffered under previous regimes and the advantages that had been gained from collectivization and communization.[64]

As far as can be ascertained most of those practices were already being propagandized in Sichuan before May 1963. As early as May 1962, peasants were being exhorted to aid production team cadres to raise their political and ideological levels.[65] In March 1963, Hongguang Commune (so often a provincial model of rural social development since the early 1950s) was publicized as a model of the masses' supervision of cadres' work;[66] and the slogan of 'Depend on the poor and lower-middle peasants' raised in the 'First Ten Points' had been promoted provincially.[67] By the beginning of April 1963 Poor and Lower-Middle Peasant Conferences to organize more permanent associations, had been held throughout the province,[68] and cadres were urged to 'Fully rely on the poor and lower-middle peasants to strengthen production team management'.[69] For their part cadres were urged to participate in physical labour under the slogan 'When cadres maintain participation in labour, ideology doesn't get rusty and work gets better'.[70] As elsewhere and elsewhen (for example in Guizhou during the later stages of the GLF) a '2–5 system' of work was promoted for cadres, whereby they spent 2 days of each week in administrative duties and 5 in production.[71] Finally, although history had been used generally as an educative device even before May,[72] thereafter it was specifically applied to the Socialist Education Movement. Peasants were encouraged to write or relate their family's histories to highlight the transformation of the rural areas and warn about the dangers of 'feudal and capitalist restoration'.[73]

The 'Second Ten Points' of the Socialist Education Movement were adopted in a central directive of September 1963.[74] According to Baum's interpretation, although the effect of the 'Second Ten Points' may have been to by pass certain of Mao's aims this was not their intention. On the contrary, he argues that Phen Zhen and Deng Xiaoping, who were largely responsible for drafting the central directive, were trying to formalize the processes of experimentation and rectification within the Socialist Education Movement. The important developments outlined within the 'Second Ten Points' were the creation of work teams to carry out the *si qing*, and new emphases on the 'struggle between the two lines in the countryside' and party reform. Cadres were to engage in political study first, then move to on-the-spot experimentation, and finally from work teams to go down to basic levels to widen rectification,[75] i.e. the small 'Four Clean-Ups'. In any case, the 'Second Ten Points' were presented as complementary to the 'First Ten Points' and not the antithesis.

Interestingly, during the GPCR, it was claimed that in June 1963 the Southwest Bureau had met and circulated a directive on arrangements for a rural 'Four Clean-Ups', which was later 'copied almost verbatim' in the 'Second Ten Points'.[76] Although it has not been possible to find any record that Peng Zhen and Deng Xiaoping visited the Southwest between May and September 1963 (as was alleged during the GPCR), it is not impossible that there was a certain amount of collusion between them and Southwestern leaders. Certainly, some aspects of the 'Second Ten Points' and the small *si qing* were being promoted in Sichuan before September 1963. On the other hand, it cannot be claimed that all were. For example, there is no evidence of either a '5-Anti Campaign' amongst cadres or of '3-level cadre meetings'[77] being held either before or after September 1963. Those aspects of the 'Second Ten Points' and the small 'Four Clean-Ups' which were implemented in Sichuan were the campaign to promote '5-good' commune members; the emphasis on the 'struggle between the two roads'; and the organization of work teams to manage the *si qing*. Although Baum suggests that '. . . a mass propaganda campaign designed to promote the selection and public recognition of 'five good' commune members and cadres at the basic levels' was initiated in the spring of 1964 as part of the small *si qing*,[78] such a campaign had been under way in Sichuan since the beginning of 1963.[79] Similarly, the importance of supporting the proletarian revolutionary line as opposed to 'capitalist revisionism' in the Socialist Education Movement had been emphasized since June 1963.[80] Finally, it would seem that work teams had been organized to carry out rural rectification by July 1963.[81]

During 1964 and 1965 the Socialist Education Movement in the rural areas proceeded along similar lines to its development during 1963, though perhaps in a more intense fashion. Thus for example, the family histories of selected poor and lower-middle peasants became reference materials via the *Sichuan Daily*,[82] and the class struggle between the 'two lines' became an increasingly important emphasis of the Socialist Education Movement.[83] The '2–5 system' of work for cadres was enlarged to include cadres above the basic level,[84] and provincial leaders went out of their way to emphasize the importance of participation in labour. Li Dazhang, for example, was quoted as having said: 'Only by persisting in collective productive labour can cadres carry the socialist revolution on all fronts to the end and fundamentally prevent the 'peaceful evolution' of socialist society into capitalist society and nip revisionism in the bud.'[85] However, by mid-1964, the rural Socialist Education Movement had become less distinguishable from the general concern with political education and the desire to 'Use class and class struggle to educate as a principle – implement the class line everywhere.'

Political consciousness

Presumably as elsewhere,[86] during 1963–5 there was an increasing concern in Sichuan with political consciousness and education, the importance of 'class struggle' and the slogan of 'let politics take command' once again, not just with respect to the rural areas but throughout the province's activities. Thus, for example, political departments were established in the province's industrial, commercial and communications departments and enterprises in 1964;[87] and 'educated youth' continued to be sent 'Down to the countryside and up to the mountains'.[88] As in agriculture, so too in industry, were cadres directed to participate in production. The '3 fixed and one replacement' labour system for cadres was popularized and became a national model for emulation. Such a system

... calls for fixing the time, work posts, and duties of cadres participating in labour and employing them in place of regular members of production shifts

... [in order that] every revolutionary cadre heighten his ideological consciousness ... and strive to make himself ... a new-style economic worker of the proletariat who is capable of doing manual labour and mental work and is both red and vocationally proficient.[89]

Two particular and interesting, given national political developments, aspects of the general concern with raising political consciousness in Sichuan during this period were the movement to 'revolutionize' art and literature, and the renewed emphasis on Mao Zedong Thought. The movement to modernize and revolutionize art and literature in Sichuan started in 1962 with the celebration of the anniversary of Mao's 'Talks at the Yanan Forum',[90] and largely paralleled Jiang Qing's efforts thereafter. At first the movement focussed on modernizing traditional Sichuan Opera, and various experiments were tried at representing the 'contemporary themes' of 'workers, soldiers and peasants' on stage.[91] At the time of the East China Drama Festival, the Sichuan literary and arts magazine publicized the concept of 'modernized theatre';[92] and after the summer of 1964 and the Festival of Beijing Opera on Contemporary Themes, the creation of Modern Revolutionary Sichuan Opera was advocated along similar lines and for similar reasons.[93] Though drama continued to be of importance in this context right up to the GPCR, a similar direction was given to art and literature in general. For example, in November 1965, a commune in Pi *xian* produced an exhibition of 100 human-size sculptures of a landlord and peasants before Liberation in order to portray class struggle in action.[94] This was the famous 'Rent collection courtyard', much publicized during the Cultural Revolution, and put on permanent exhibition in the local Exhibition Hall for Class Education.

Finally, after a break for part of 1963 there was renewed emphasis on the study and content of Mao Zedong Thought. In his speech to the 1st session of the 3rd provincial committee of the Chinese People's Political Consultative Conference, Li Dazhang once again emphasized the 'brilliant leadership' of Mao Zedong Thought.[95] By the 2nd session of the 3rd PPC in October 1964, when the province was called upon to 'hold still higher the red banner of the Thought of Mao Zedong'[96] it was as if the study movement had never been shelved. Later in 1965, the campaign reached new heights as Mao Zedong Thought was once again credited with new victories. For example, the official report of the 3rd session of the 3rd PPC stated, in language reminiscent of the GLF that

While carrying out the three major revolutionary movements of class struggle, production struggle and scientific experiments, the people have scored one victory after another... Since last October, all nationalities in the province have raised still higher the radiant banner of Mao Zedong Thought and have followed the general line for socialist construction on an over-all basis by stepping up their enthusiasm for work, aiming high, and striving for more, faster, better and more economical results.[97]

The importance of studying Mao Zedong Thought was not only emphasized at this session, particularly amongst the young in order 'to train successors to the cause of revolution',[98] but also elsewhere, as for example at the Chengdu Military Region Work Conference in September 1965.[99] In general, the province was exhorted, in Guo Linxiang's words, to 'Raise further the level of studying Chairman Mao's works'.[100]

At the end of 1965 there was thus little in the behaviour of Sichuan's leaders to suggest that the overwhelming majority would be branded as 'Anti-Maoists' in the near future. On the contrary, Sichuan's reluctance to abandon Mao's ideas of 1958, its implementation of the Socialist Education Movement throughout the 1960s, and generally its expressed attitudes to policy initiatives associated with Mao suggest support for Mao rather than opposition throughout this period.

GUIZHOU

At the start of the Cultural Revolution all provincial leaders were said to have been opposed to Mao because of the policies of retrenchment implemented during 1961–3: a somewhat biased perspective given that it is reasonable to assume that there was a consensus, which included Mao, for those measures at the earlier time. Given that the national-level debate during 1961–5 centred on the interpretations and relevance of the GLF then it seems more reasonable to take provincial leaders' post-GLF attitudes to the GLF and its policies as a guide to their position in national politics. By this measure, Sichuan would appear to have been on the radical wing of the party. Although there were clearly changes in Sichuan's economic perspectives after 1960, the political rhetoric of its leaders hardly changed. There was only a short period during 1963 when the 'Three Red Banners' and associated slogans were not aired by Sichuan's leaders, and positive emphasis on the GLF, Mao's leadership and Mao Zedong Thought increased after September 1963. In contrast, Guizhou's leadership appeared very cool towards the GLF, at least until Zhou Lin was replaced as first secretary, temporarily by Li Dazhang, and then permanently by Jia Qiyun, in 1965. For example, Chen Puru in his report to the 2nd session of the 3rd PPC in October 1964 stressed the policy of 'readjustment, consolidation, filling out and raising standards'[101] rather than the importance of the 'Three Red Banners' as had Li Dazhang at the Sichuan PPC in the same month.

If the suggestion that Guizhou's leadership was cool towards the ideas of the GLF before February 1965 is correct, then that would at least partially explain both Mao's condemnation of the provincial leadership as 'rotten' in December 1964,[102] and its reorganization in February 1965. At that time, Zhou Lin was removed as both Governor and party first secretary and nine new leaders (one of whom was only temporary, Li Dazhang – the Governor of Sichuan) appointed. However, it is not a total explanation since other provinces similarly labelled managed to avoid provincial leadership changes.[103] None the less in piecing together what is known about Guizhou during this period, and in particularly concentrating on Zhou Lin's replacement, it would appear that provincial leaders were faced by serious economic and political problems which they were unwilling or unable to handle. Guizhou's concerns with agricultural production and political integration in the first half of the 1960s were almost identical to those during 1955–7. However, now agricultural conditions were so severe that they adversely affected not only production but also, as a result of the measures taken to alleviate the situation, the provincial leadership's political control. Moreover, central demands on Guizhou were now much stronger than before the GLF. Whereas before 1958 rectification could be and was delayed in order to 'do the best according to local conditions', in this period the non-implementation of the Socialist Education Movement proved Zhou Lin's stumbling block

Problems and solutions

There can be little doubt that Guizhou's agricultural production suffered a severe depression after 1959, from which it had not really recovered by the start of the GPCR. Conditions in 1959 and 1960 have already been mentioned. In 1963, it was claimed that during the previous three years Guizhou had suffered from serious droughts.[104] Given the province's climate and normal precipitation (together with Yunnan and Guangdong it has the highest average annual rainfall in China)[105] this is not impossible, just unlikely. What is more possible is that there was not enough rainfall to support all the extra paddy fields developed in the 1950s, and that in this sense the province suffered from drought. Even in 1965 when the total water-cultivation acreage had been reduced, over half Guizhou's paddy fields were dependent on rainfall rather than irrigation, and their unit yield was admitted to be low.[106] Certainly the few available figures on agricultural production suggest a reverse on the claimed advances of even the pre-GLF period. In 1963 it was acknowledged that both the cultivated area and output of grain crops had fallen.[107] In mid-September 1964, it was said that 6.8 mn *mou* had been sown with grain during the year,[108] and even though not a year-end figure that still does not compare well with the 24.6 mn *mou* of grain crops cultivated in 1957.[109] Finally, in late 1965 there were said to be 12 mn *mou* of paddy fields in Guizhou,[110] compared to the 20 mn claimed for 1957.[111]

Various measures were taken to meet the economic crisis of the early 1960s. Those publicized included the importation of essential supplies from Sichuan along the Wu River,[112] and the mobilization of workers from the towns to help in agricultural production. It seems likely that for many of those sent from the towns to the countryside the move was permanent, as, for example, the 250,000 sent out from Zunyi as 'emergency shock troops' to aid agriculture during 1961.[113]

It also seems likely that less well publicized policies were implemented to meet the crisis, including a much more liberal attitude not only towards the peasantry in general, but also towards the province's minority nationalities in a complete reversal of the policies of the GLF. It was repeatedly claimed during the GPCR, and to a much larger extent than in Sichuan, that Guizhou's leadership had enlarged private plots, and organized production quotas for individual households rather than production teams or brigades.[114] Given the severity and duration of the crisis, particularly in comparison with Sichuan, this does not seem too unlikely. Moreover, Guizhou's leadership had advocated (and presumably implemented) the setting of household quotas for sideline production – described as 'production marketing contracts' – already in the later stages of the GLF.[115] Certainly, the more tolerant attitude of the early 1950s was readopted towards the minority nationalities in order to elicit their compliance. To this end an additional 20,000 cadres were recruited from among the minority nationalities in the province to work at the basic-level.[116]

Leadership changes

However, it would seem, if the late 1965 self-descriptions of the changed Guizhou (that is after Zhou Lin's dismissal) are anything to go by, that all previous attempts to raise either production or enthusiasm through a policy of *laissez-faire* were not successful, and that the situation in fact worsened. Thus, for example, in announcing a 'good harvest' (without further details) for 1965, this was contrasted with the 'apathy and lethargy among cadres' in previous years which had produced poor results.[117] In discussing the impact of the *si qing* on Guizhou, great emphasis was placed on eradicating the 'recently prevalent pessimistic attitudes' that had pertained in the province, and the notion that 'people are lazy'.[118] Finally, the tolerant policy towards the national minorities also seem to have been counter-productive, for once again they appear to have risen in revolt. Several of Zhou Lin's critics during the GPCR attacked him for being too lenient towards minority nationalities. In the course of their accusations they referred to such armed resistance. One was Wang Dezhou, a militia company commander, who speaking at a Mao-study Activists Congress in December 1967 said

.... class enemies, in order to oppose the people's communes .... organized a counter-revolutionary armed revolt .... Zhou Lin, however, claimed 'this incident is a dispute between nationalities, not a class struggle. You may not open fire on them.' .... I and many other militiamen could not understand this. The enemies had taken up arms and were killing people. Some PLA soldiers had been sacrificed .... I then led the militia to work with the PLA in the battle to suppress the revolt.[119]

One solution to Guizhou's problems, which it would seem to a large extent resulted from poor basic-level leadership in the aftermath of the GLF, might well have been the Socialist Education Movement. However, it would seem to be a measure of the seriousness of the province's problems that it was unwilling or unable to implement any part of the Socialist Education Movement before February 1965. When the Socialist Education Movement was launched in Guizhou it was with the help and assistance of cadres from outside the province and under the direction of the southwest Bureau, and moreover, started with Zhou Lin's dismissal. According to Li Dazhang he had headed a work team of the Southwest Bureau to visit Guizhou in October 1964 and recommended Zhou Lin's replacement, for his failure to implement the Socialist Education Movement.[120] Certainly it was only after February 1965 that contemporary sources started to mention the campaign in Guizhou, and this is confirmed by sources from the GPCR. In most of the GPCR accounts February is mentioned as the starting date for the implementation of the 'Twenty-Three Points',[121] and July 1965, when Jia Qiyun replaced Li Dazhang as first secretary, as the beginning of the rural 'Four Clean-Ups'.[122] The late implementation of the Socialist Education Movement in Guizhou is, however, perhaps best indicated by the fact that it was not until the beginning of September 1967 that a poor and lower-middle peasant association was established in Dongren.[123]

In February 1965 then, although no one else was removed from the leadership, new provincial leaders were appointed from outside the province. In addition to Li Dazhang and Jia Qiyun (from Sichuan), these included Li Li (who replaced Zhou Lin as Governor) from the organizational department of the Central-South Bureau; and Cheng Hongyi, previously Vice-Mayor of Beijing. Moreover, according to reports of the 27 July 1965 provincial work conference that detailed the implementation of the Socialist Education Movement in Guizhou, it would appear that basic-level cadres from other provinces in the Southwest were brought into the province in order to provide the work teams for the *si qing*. Unsurprisingly, GPCR sources seem to indicate that this was a cause of considerable tension at the basic-level within the provinces.[124]

Li Dazhang's appointment was, however, only temporary and presumably a function of his position on the Southwest Bureau's secretariat. In July he was succeeded by Jia Qiyan. Thereafter, even in the few months to the end of 1965, provincial pronouncements adopted a new air of optimism, based once again as in the GLF on the virtues of having been a 'backward area'. Thus, for example, in the campaign to 'Learn from Dazhai' it was reported that

Su Shicheng from Weining Hui and Miao Autonomous county, Guizhou's highest, coldest, and poorest place, went to Dazhai. On his return he said, 'Our conditions are better than theirs so what we lack is the new Dazhai spirit of Chen Yonggui and the Dazhai party branch.' Guizhou can not only learn from and surpass Dazhai, but learn from and surpass the West Sichuan plain, the richest, most fertile place in that province.[125]

However, the new provincial leaders' optimism could be but short-lived for within the year they had come under attack in the GPCR. Thus, for example, Jia Qiyun was *inter alia* criticized for '.... having publicly resisted Chairman Mao's instruction that political work is the lifeline of all economic work ....'[126] A particularly strange accusation to level at the man, who when he became director of the State Statistical Bureau in 1959, said in his first public speech to the staff of the bureau: 'Statistical Work is a weapon of class struggle and of political struggle. Our statistical reports must reflect the great victory of the party's general line and the progress of everything led by the party. They definitely should not be a mere display of objective facts.'[127]

7

RURAL PEOPLE'S COMMUNES

The evolution of policy on the rural people's communes (PC) in and after 1958 is an excellent example not only of provincial participation in the national policy process, but also of the specific roles played by Sichuan and Guizhou in that process. The contrast in attitudes and policies between the leaderships of the two provinces is similar to that which has already emerged in other contexts. However, it is not identical. Before late 1958, and the retreat from the earlier ideal of the commune, Sichuan's leadership ran ahead of national politics and was more radical. Guizhou's was more cautious and conservative. After late 1958 it was Sichuan which dragged its heels in adapting to changes in commune policy, and Guizhou which ran ahead of national developments. On the other hand, that difference is only to be expected in the circumstances. It resulted from Sichuan's more radical perspective on national politics, as compared to Guizhou's conservatism.

In the 'High Tide' of 1955–6 provincial leaders had clearly influenced national policy through their implementation of first co-operativization and later collectivization. But whereas at that time provincial leaders had shaped policy largely through their control of the pace of development, the entire history of the commune movement between 1958 and 1963 is a monument to provincial leaders' involvement in national policy-making.[1] In the first place, as Schurmann and Walker amongst others have long since suggested[2] and Xue Muqiao more recently (1979) confirmed,[3] the very notion of a rural people's commune emerged during 1958 as a result of experiments carried out in some provinces, apparently with Mao's support, and presented to the Politburo very much as a *fait accompli*. Whilst secondly, the structure and function of the PC and its constituent parts was very much a subject of debate and discussion within the CCP after their establishment had been approved by the Beidaihe resolution of August 1958.[4] As a result national policy on the PCs was in an almost constant state of flux between the 6th plenum of December 1958 and the 10th plenum of September 1962. Provincial leaders played an important role in that process not only through their participation in the discussions that led to formal decisions, but also through their experiments and attempts to implement previous policy that preceded those discussions. At almost every stage in the commune's evolution, a formal national decision was followed by provincial attempts at implementation that led to further national discussion, provincial adaptation, and eventually a new decision on PCs.[5]

Before outlining that process from a national perspective it is perhaps useful to indicate that there is, and was at the time, considerable confusion about the nomenclature, size and functions of the commune's sub-divisions. To simplify, in 1958 the commune was conceived as, and has remained, generally a three-tiered organization. Each commune is sub-divided into production brigades, which in turn are sub-divided into production teams. On balance it would appear that in August 1958 Mao had intended that the existing higher stage collectives would become the PC's production teams and basic accounting units; whilst production brigades would be formed by the amalgamation of production teams into administrative areas at an intermediate level between the commune and the production team.[6]

Confusion exists for several reasons. In the first place, as Hsia indicates in some detail there was considerable terminological confusion before 1963 as between the production brigade and the production team.[7] Of greatest significance, the former was sometimes referred to as *shengchan dadui* (literally, 'large production group'); the latter sometimes as *shengchan xiaodui* (literally, 'small production group'); but both were also sometimes referred to, even simultaneously, as *shengchan dui* (literally, just 'production group'). Apart from creating problems for the western observer, it seems likely that cadres themselves may have been confused, particularly during the winter of 1958–9 by the use of the term *shengchan dui* to refer to both the production brigade and production team.

The second reason for confusion is that when communes were first established, whereas some provinces did follow Mao's intentions and turn their former higher stage collectives into the PC's new production teams, others did not. For example, in some cases the former higher stage collectives were divided to create the PC's new production teams, and in others the higher stage collective became the new production brigade: thus in general creating smaller communes. Moreover, some provinces did take the production team as the commune's basic accounting unit (as Mao had intended) but others preferred the production brigade. (To some extent it is possible that those differences resulted from the terminological confusion just described.) Unfortunately, as far as clarity is concerned, it would appear that there was no correlation between a province's preference for either the production brigade or the production team as the basic accounting unit within the commune on the one hand, and its decision on how to create production brigades and production teams from the existing higher stage collectives on the other. The result was a bewildering variety of production brigades and production teams in terms of size and function.

As if these problems did not make analysis of the communes between 1958 and 1963 difficult enough, there is a third reason for confusion (that is in many ways the more generalized case of the second). As had already been indicated and will become clearer later, the evolution of the commune nationally was very much a process of trial, experiment and discussion in which provincial leaders played a substantial role. The result was a wide variety of size and functions not only when communes were first established, but also over time as national policy on the commune developed. Thus, to take one example, official emphasis on ownership within the commune changed from the commune level in August 1958; to all three levels of ownership at commune, production brigade and production team in August 1959; to the production brigade alone in December 1960; and to the production team in September 1962.

By 1963, variations in terminology had disappeared, those in function had been considerably reduced, but those in size remained (if somewhat reduced) and that situation has remained relatively stable since. However, to avoid further confusion (that may result from equating the PC after 1962 with its predecessor) it should be pointed out that in general the post-1963 production brigades and production teams are roughly equivalent to the pre-GLF higher stage collectives and lower stage co-operatives respectively. In this chapter, production brigades and production teams will be defined by their status in the hierarchy of the PC – the latter being the smallest unit of management, and the former the intermediate level within the commune – rather than in terms of their functions or absolute size. The latter clearly changed several times after 1958. Moreover, it is the provincial leadership's political attitude to the commune and its constituent parts that is of prime interest rather than the commune's economic functions or performance.

COMMUNIZATION

The 'Decision of the party centre on the question of establishing rural people's communes' was adopted by the Politburo at an enlarged meeting (that included all provincial first secretaries) in Beidaihe on 29 August and published in *People's Daily* on 10 September 1958. However, it would seem clear that the movement to establish larger and more collective (not just for agricultural production but for almost all economic, political, and social activities) rural units had been growing since the early spring. At the Nanning Conference, Mao had called for the amalgamation of APCs into larger units, and during the spring and summer had visited various provincial experiments. The most famous of these was the *Weixing* (Sputnik) commune in Henan, whose draft regulations became those for the model commune publicized in early September, and which was promoted even before the announcement of the Beidaihe resolution.[8] Indeed Mao's reported statement of 9 August 1958, usually translated as 'People's Communes are good' but perhaps (as Schram indicates) better rendered as 'People's Communes are better', arose from one such visit to Shandong where he recommended that 'people's communes' be established rather than 'large co-operatives'.[9]

The essential genesis of the PC in the enthusiasm of the GLF was not just the economies of scale to be gained from larger agricultural units, but also the creation of the basic units for the transition to communism. The major difference between APCs and people's communes was that the latter were not just to be large units of agricultural production, but also units for the 'organization of collective life'[10] in the rural areas, hence the descriptive phrase *yi da, er gong* – 'large and communal'.[11] According to the Beidaihe resolution there was to be no private property; and an article in *Red Flag* on the *Weixing* commune even indicated the free supply of food.[12] Moreover, the Beidaihe resolution also optimistically looked forward to the commune's future in '... the transition from collective ownership to ownership by the whole people ... the completion of which may take less time – three or four years – in some places, and longer –

five, six years or even more – in others'. However, the resolution did warn that: 'Even with the completion of the transition to people's communes, these (like state-owned industry) are still socialist in nature – the principle of 'from each according to his ability and to each according to his work' still is in operation.'[13]

Well before the end of 1958 communization had been completed throughout China with some 26,000 PCs established. However, there had clearly been problems involved in that process. For a start, the average size of PC envisaged by the Beidaihe resolution had been 2,000 peasant households; but already by the end of September the average size had risen to almost 5,000 peasant households.[14] Nation-wide inspection tours by national leaders led to doubts about the speed and efficiency of communization. In early November, those doubts were first voiced at a meeting in Zhengzhou. As a result Mao (though probably hedging his bet) urged the need for caution, the continued importance of remuneration for work, and that the transition to communism could not come about overnight – all of which indicated that the provinces, or at least some provinces, had become 'adventurist'.[15]

Similar doubts about the success of the PCs, particularly focussing on problems of management and distribution within the commune, were discussed at Wuchang at the end of November and beginning of December when the 6th enlarged plenum of the central committee was held with the provincial first secretaries in attendance. At the plenum, Mao called for the consolidation of the communes in general and the need to avoid exaggeration.[16] The plenum's resolution called for a consolidation of the PCs over the coming five months; pointed out that the production brigade was a 'business accounting unit' within the commune; and stressed the concept of 'management at different levels' (as opposed to just the commune level as previously) with the production brigade responsible for certain commune indus-try and the team for labour organization. Although the Wuhan resolution was much less optimistic about the transtion to commu-nism, stressing that 'socialist ownership by the whole people ... will now take fifteen, twenty or more years to complete, as from the present', ownership within the PC still resided at commune level.[17]

It would appear from a letter written by Mao to provincial first secretaries in March 1959 that not only had there been considerable confusion (and possibly misunderstanding) about how the com-munes should be consolidated, but also a debate had developed amongst provincial leaders. Some provinces advocated taking the production brigade as the basic accounting unit of the commune, others the production team as Mao had earlier advocated.[18] In the event, the 7th plenum, meeting in April, which the provincial first secretaries once again attended, decided that the production brigade should be the basic accounting unit.[19] The result was that there was a reduction in the number of PCs to about 24,000, with each having on average 21 production brigades and 100 production teams.[20] However, far from signalling an end to the process of consolidation as had been intended at the 6th plenum, the 7th plenum's communiqué indicated that consolidation would continue.[21]

DE-COMMUNALIZATION

By the Lushan (8th) plenum of the central committee in August 1959, there was considerably less emphasis on the 'communal' aspects of the PCs. In many places, the communal mess-halls (where they had been established) had been abandoned and strict limits were being set on the ratio of food supply to wages in remuneration for commune members. However, it is clear that different practices applied in various provinces, and even possibly within provinces. Moreover, for the first time national policy emphasized that there were not only three levels of management within the same commune, but also three levels of ownership.[22] On the other hand, as Hsia indicates, the 8th plenum confirmed the production brigade as the most important management level within the commune.[23]

The bad harvests of 1959 and 1960 necessitated the re-establishment of communal mess-halls after the early autumn of 1959. However, in every other way the period after the Lushan plenum saw a decrease in both the 'large and communal' nature of the commune. Moreover, any emphasis on the notion of the commune as the basic unit for the transition to communism disappeared. By December 1960, the production brigade rather than the commune had become the major level of ownership within the commune,[24] and the 9th plenum of the central committee in January 1961 initiated discussion on new draft regulations for the PCs.[25] Following a Central Work Conference in Canton during March 1961, central leaders visited the provinces, consulted with local leaders,[26] and drew up the first draft of these regulations on 12 May 1961.[27] This draft presumably advocated that the production team become the basic level of management within the commune, for after April 1961 that was the emphasis reflected in the national media.[28] Thus, for example, a *People's Daily* editorial in March 1961, not only indicated the importance of the policy of 'three guarantees and one reward' towards the peasantry, of private plots for peasants, and a system of work-points for the calculation of remuneration, all to be organized by the production team, but also emphasized its share of ownership in the commune.[29] Moreover, by August, the production brigade was being described as a 'management unit for federated economic organizations', whereas the production team was said to 'directly organize production'.[30]

Discussion, investigation and debate continued through 1961 and 1962 until the adoption of the new 'Regulations on the work of the rural people's communes' at the 10th plenum of the Central Committee in September 1962. In sum the new regulations left the commune almost solely as a politico-administrative unit, the production team as the principal level for the management of production (and of ownership), and the brigade as a co-ordinating level for teams within the commune. On the other hand, the 1962 regulations did allow a considerable amount of leeway to the provinces in their implementation. Thus, for example, depending on local conditions there could be one or two levels beneath the commune, and various functions could be exercised by either the production brigades or production teams.[31] However, even before the 10th plenum, it had become clear in January 1962 that the production team was already the basic accounting unit.[32] As a result of these changes by the end of 1962 the communes had diminished in size and subsequently grown in numbers. There were now 74,000 PCs with on average 10 production brigades and 95 production teams each.[33]

During 1963–5 there would appear to have been few changes in national policy towards the structure and function of either the commune, production brigade and production team.[34] Moreover, although early 1960s innovations, such as the system of work points, were generally implemented, communes clearly differed greatly in their size and organization.[35] Although at some stage before 1971 the number of communes was decreased once again (to around 51,000) it is not clear when precisely this occurred, and it seems unlikely to have been before 1966.[36]

SICHUAN AND GUIZHOU

Although it is possible to outline the development of policy towards the rural people's communes from a national perspective, it is clear that there were considerable variations at each stage in their development. The establishment of communes and the process of their consolidation, that eventually resulted in a retreat from some of the original precepts of the concept, did not occur uniformly in each province in clearly definable stages. As a result, from a national perspective there appears to have been considerable confusion and less tight central direction of the commune's development than even during the 'High Tide' of 1955–6. Indeed that aspect in the development of commune policy is apparent right from the start of communization, for many provinces explicitly reacted to the slogan accredited to Mao – 'People's Communes are better' – rather than to the Beidaihe resolution. Thus, for example, the Hebei party's 'Directive on the building of people's communes' stated that: 'Particularly after Chairman Mao issued his important directive on rural people's communes, their development has become all the more rapid.'[37] Consequently commune policy in Sichuan and Guizhou will be considered thematically rather than chronologically, concentrating on the establishment of PCs; provincial attitudes to the function of communes; and the development of policy on management and ownership within the commune. By no means intended as a comprehensive survey of commune policy in the two provinces, these aspects have been selected because they indicate variations both between Sichuan and Guizhou, and from the national norms. Given what has already been suggested about the general perspectives of their leaders, it is no surprise to find that there is a considerable contrast between the two provinces. On the one hand, Sichuan appears to have been part of the 'Maoist conspiracy' that promoted the formation of PCs before September 1958, and thereafter to have adopted a more radical stance towards the communes than most, being reluctant to 'de-communalize' at each stage of that process. Guizhou, on the other, appears constantly more cautious and conservative. It was slow to establish PCs, and had already started to 'de-communalize' by the time communization was complete.

The establishment of Rural People's Communes

The contrast between Sichuan and Guizhou is particularly apparent with respect to their establishment of communes. Whereas Guizhou initially claimed to have completed rural communization by the end of September 1958,[38] it seems likely that this process did not in fact end until February 1959. In Sichuan, not only was communization completed by the end of September 1958,[39] but it would appear that the process had started well beforehand, on a trial basis in March, and provincially after July.

The emergence of the PC in Sichuan was a process which not only started early in 1958 but also provides further evidence suggestive of a political alliance between Mao and the province's leadership. In the spring of 1958 and following both the Nanning and Chengdu conferences, Sichuan like several other provinces[40] had started to amalgamate APCs into larger administrative units – 'federated cooperatives' (*lian she*) – so that resources of labour and capital could be pooled to mutual benefit; and to abolish private property, such as pigs, that now became collectively owned.[41] In addition, 'large collectives' (*da she*) were created that were not just administrative federations of existing APCs, nor *da she* such as those that had existed in the province during 1955–6,[42] but new units in their own right, involving complete economic, administrative and social reorganization.[43] By the beginning of July, Li Jingquan later estimated, that about a third of the province's rural population had joined such units, most of which were at *xiang* level, but some at *xian* level. Private plots and pigs had gone into collective ownership; communal dining-rooms and nurseries had been established; and small-scale rural industries started by these new *da she*.[44] As elsewhere in China at that time, it seems likely that many of Sichuan's *da she*, particularly the larger ones, were in fact People's Communes by another name.[45] However, unsurprisingly (given that such organizations were not yet official national policy) contemporary evidence to support that hypothesis is limited, for their activities were not greatly publicized at the time but only after August 1958 when many communes were eager to describe an early genesis. Certainly the speed with which communization in Sichuan, once officially started, was completed would seem to suggest that the ground for the creation of People's Communes had been well (and long, in relative terms) prepared.

The most famous of Sichuan's new *da she* was at Hongguang in

Pixian. Formally established during April 1958, through the amalgamation of three federated cooperatives,[46] it was visited by Mao either shortly before, during, or soon after its creation.[47] It seems reasonable to assume that Mao either approved of its existence or encouraged its development in the direction it took. It would obviously be useful to know whether the development of the Hongguang *da she* resulted directly from Mao's visit or from an earlier local initiative. Unfortunately, it is not possible to date either Mao's visit or the emergence of the *da she* precisely enough to come to a firm conclusion. The contemporary evidence (from early April) is limited to newspaper reports that Mao had visited Hongguang, but no date is given. However, on balance it seems likely that Mao visited Hongguang during mid-March 1958[48] at the time of the Chengdu conference, and hence that the *da she* developed after his visit.

By the end of July, each *xiang* in the province had a *da she* and the process then started to turn them into PCs. This was revealed in the provincial party's committee's regulation for the establishment of PCs, decided on 11 September 1958. These provided for the completion of communization by 1 October; experiments with *xian*-level communes and federations of communes within each *xian*, although the PC was initially regarded as replacing the *xian*; but (unlike Guizhou) exempted the minority nationality areas from immediate communization.[49] Unsurprisingly, in the event the task of turning *da she* into PCs was not arduous and was completed well before the end of September. Both the early start and the early transformation would seem to be confirmed in Li Dazhang's 1959 provincial government work report, where he claimed that communization had been completed: 'By the end of September after only something over forty days' work ...'[50]

The name 'people's commune' was first mentioned (without further comment) in the provincial newspaper on 15 August,[51] and popularized on 19 August 1958.[52] However, it was not adopted provincially until after the Beidaihe resolution and the publication of the provincial regulations on 13 September. Thereafter, the provincial party committee published various reference materials to aid and educate local cadres in the establishment of PCs, such as the provincial propaganda department's 'Outline for propagandizing the establishment of people's communes'.[53] By the end of September 4,038 PCs had been established with an average of approximately 3,000 peasant households each.[54]

All this would appear to be in complete contrast to what occurred in Guizhou. As far as can be ascertained there was no attempt at amalgamating APCs before late August 1958 – at least there is no official record of such activity. Moreover, before 24 August (that is during the Beidaihe meeting of the Politburo which took the decision to establish PCs) Guizhou seems to have an attitude towards communes (or their like) that was either cool or bemused. The first mention of 'people's commune' occurred in the provincial paper on 19 August. Interestingly, although the article was based on the identical NCNA report as that which appeared on the same day in the *Sichuan Daily* (date-lined Zhengzhou, 18 August) it was differently presented. Whereas Sichuan's article had appeared right across the top of the first page and was headlined 'Run People's Communes Well', the story in the *Guizhou Daily* appeared under the more more cautious headline of 'Xinyang special district starts a movement to establish people's communes', and in the bottom left-hand corner. Moreover, the Guizhou version of the NCNA report did not contain all that appeared in the *Sichuan Daily*. In particular, it omitted the passages referring to the amalgamation of APCs earlier in 1958 that had led to the creation of the PC, and those which concerned the advantages of the PC's communal activities, such as mess-halls and kindergartens.

Sometime shortly thereafter, Zhou Lin, who was presumably at Beidaihe with the other provincial first secretaries, must have realized that official backing was going to be given to the people's commune, for on 24 August it was announced that Guizhou had established its first PC.[55] It was claimed that local cadres had started discussing the pooling of resources on either 17 (according to one article)[56] or 18 August (according to another article in the same paper)[57] and that: 'After hearing that Chairman Mao had said that running people's communes was a good idea, the masses thought that if Chairman Mao says it's a good thing to run people's communes, why shouldn't we have a people's commune?'[58]

By early September, and still before the publication of the Beidaihe resolution, it was announced that all Guiyang's suburbs had established PCs.[59] Moreover, together with the publication of the Beidaihe resolution, it was announced that 'there were many counties where communization will be completed within the next few days'.[60] However, unlike in Sichuan, no provincial regulations on communization or reference materials were published in the provincial press.

Although it was announced that communization had been completed by the end of September, and that 2,389 PCs had been established by 10 October 1958,[61] in retrospect this seems to have been little more than an administrative fiction. The reasons for suggesting this, quite apart from the lack of any detailed media coverage of communization at the time, rest with later statements by provincial leaders. In his 1959 provincial government work report, Dai Xiaodong, in reviewing communization said: 'Within two months 20,000 APCs were organized into 534 rural people's communes.'[62] Again in his 1960 report to the provincial party congress, Zhou Lin stated: 'Rural people's communes in our province developed very rapidly following the [Beidaihe] resolution, communization of the rural areas was accomplished in a short period of less than two months. The 24,112 APCs in our province were organized into 537 people's communes.'[63] There may be numerical differences between these two retrospective accounts, but they are not as great as that between the contemporary sources and these later speeches.

It seems reasonable to suggest that what actually happened in September 1958 was that the existing APCs were simply federated into organizations (not unlike the *lian she* that had been established in Sichuan and elsewhere earlier in the year) which for political convenience were called people's communes, and that between October 1958 and February 1959, communes were themselves created from those organizations. There is additional evidence to support this hypothesis, although of course nothing could be, or was, published contemporaneously in the provincial press. In the first place, Guizhou's 'original' PC had been said to have emerged from the amalgamation of five higher stage collectives.[64] However, according to a later statement in Guizhou's communization the higher stage collectives became the commune's production team, and on average each PC (of 537) had 186 production teams.[65] Secondly, in his 1958 provincial government work report, delivered in late September 1958, Zhou Lin had not foreseen the immediate completion of communization. On the contrary he had said: 'The development of people's communes had become a trend. Within one or two months, we are going to establish people's communes throughout the rural areas of the province.'[66]

Thirdly, a conference called by the provincial party's rural work department in October 1958 to discuss the consolidation of the PCs by spring 1959 decided that the commune's production brigades and teams (which did not yet exist) should have approximately 500 and 100 peasant households each.[67] Yet when it was claimed that the PCs had been consolidated, by February 1959, on average each production brigade actually had 172 peasant households and each production team 38.[68] Finally, in his 1960 report to the provincial party congress, Zhou Lin had said '... communization in the province was achieved in a very short time. The province experienced various handicaps at the beginning of the commune movement: these were corrected by February 1959.'[69]

Admittedly, all this evidence is somewhat circumstantial and inferential. However, there is little else to explain the apparent disparate reports of communization in Guizhou during August 1958 to February 1959. Moreover, if it is true, as suggested, that communization in September 1958 was in effect an administrative fiction, then it also follows that the consequent consolidation of the PCs did not result in the kind of administrative and social re-organization that had occurred earlier in Sichuan. By February 1959 when PCs were finally consolidated (that is in reality, established) in Guizhou, it was not commune-level activities that were emphasized in the province but those organized by production brigades. Yet from the available evidence it would appear that the commune's new production brigades were by and large the former higher stage collectives.[70] When the later statement (of 1960) referred to in the previous paragraph claimed that higher stage collectives became the commune's production teams, what that really meant was that the former higher stage collectives had been subdivided to create the commune's new production teams. In the light of this evidence, and what follows, it seems likely that commune administration and the re-organizsation of peasant life in Guizhou were never quite on the same scale as in Sichuan.

The commune as a social unit

As previously indicated, an important aspect of the PCs envisaged in the Beidaihe resolution was that it should serve as the basic unit for the transition to communism. Hence the emphasis on its 'large and communal' nature. Such aspirations had clearly begun to recede even by the time of the 6th plenum at Wuhan in December 1958, and were de-emphasized totally after August 1959, although for economic reasons certain communal characteristics (e.g. mess-halls) were either maintained or revived. Here too, there would appear to be a contrast in the attitudes of Sichuan's and Guizhou's leaders towards the potential of the people's commune.

In the first place, when communes were first established in the two provinces there was a distinct difference in the emphasis placed on their function(s). In Guizhou, presumably because the commune movement had to a large extent taken the provincial leadership by surprise, almost nothing was said about the communal or political nature of the PC. The very first PC established in Guizhou was praised because, in the words of its party secretary: 'all the production tasks we have to do are better done by and in larger units', and its main reasons for existence seemed to be the avoidance of labour shortages which had become apparent in the winter of 1957–8 and the desire for higher yields.[71] In October, when the provincial party rural work department organized its conference on the consolidation of PCs, nothing at all was said about their communal nature, and its conclusion was that 'consolidation can lead to a production "high tide"'.[72] Indeed it would appear that it was only when Deng Xiaoping visited the province in early November and suggested the establishment of communal mess-halls that the idea was taken seriously.[73] Even so, during the winter of 1958–9, the only area that was publicized for its adoption of the free supply system was the one he had visited (Zunyi),[74] and it does not seem to have been adopted provincially until later in 1959. In complete contrast, Sichuan had right from the start stressed the political and communal nature of the PCs. As the provincial regulations for establishing PCs made explicit, the PC was to replace the *xiang* and not only take over the existing communal activities (such as mess-halls and nurseries) but also '... combine the rural market's industry, handicraft industry and commerce; services, schools, clinics etc'.[75]

Secondly, the two provinces differed in their attitudes to the commune as the 'bud of communism'.[76] In general Guizhou followed the national trends. Thus in his September 1958 provincial government work report, Zhou Lin referred to the people's commune as '... the best form of organization in the present stage of socialist construction. It will also be a basic unit of the future communist society.'[77] By the 1959 PPC, the 'future communist society' was no longer mentioned. Instead it was emphasized that: 'Although ownership at commune level contains some elements of all-people's ownership, the people's commune are still a collective form of ownership.'[78]

Finally, by Spring 1960, in his report to the provincial party congress Zhou Lin was emphasizing the length of the process whereby the ownership level within the commune would rise so that 'eventually collective ownership could become people's ownership'.[79]

Although in and after 1960 Sichuan moderated its attitude in line with national policy, during 1958–9 the emphasis was that the establishment of communes indicated that communism was much closer at hand. In Sichuan, the PC was not seen as just the building block for the future communist society, but, in Li Jingquan's words, 'the early shoots of communism itself'.[80] Thus, for example, in October 1958, an article in the provincial party's theoretical journal emphasized that it the management of people's communes was '... handled correctly, we can soon bring about the highest ideal – a communist society!'[81] Again, the provincial party's 'Directive on collective life, welfare and rest periods for rural people's communes' of December 1958 was issued explicitly on the grounds that 'the better the people's living conditions, the more enthusiastic and energetic they will be in building communism.'[82] Moreover, this emphasis persisted even after the Lushan plenum.[83] In an article clearly designed to counter Peng Dehuai's criticisms, Li Jingquan not only defended the view of the commune as 'the early shoots of communism', but emphasized that the PC had brought political, as well as economic advance:

The movement to set up people's communes brought about important changes in the relations of production and in the superstructure. That is to say, existing collective ownership was expanded and raised to a higher stage, and some elements of ownership by the whole people began to appear. Thus what was originally an organization of agricultural production alone turned into the basic unit of China's social structure ...[84]

However, it should perhaps be emphasized that by 1960 both Sichuan and Guizhou had fallen into line in terms of their attitude to PCs as a social unit. No longer were they seen explicitly as the shape of the future society, even in Sichuan. Although in his 1960 provincial work report, Li Dazhang (unlike Chen Puru in his to the Guizhou PPC)[85] still described the PCs as 'large and communal', his emphasis was on the different levels of ownership within the commune, rather than on all-people's ownership, which was not mentioned.[86] On the other hand, Sichuan had maintained and Guizhou started communal mess-halls. In March 1960 it was reported that 98% of Sichuan's rural population ate in 440,000 communal mess-halls;[87] whereas between April and December 1960 the number of communal mess-halls in Guizhou rose from 11,000[88] to 106,000[89]. In both cases, moreover, a strict limit was set on the proportion of the 'free' food supply so that it should account for no more than 30% of a single peasant's remuneration.[90]

Management and ownership

Given the difficulty of unscrambling commune policy on a national level, it might be thought that its development were more clearly visible from the provincial perspective. However, the profusion of terms which is apparent nationally[91] also occurred within both Sichuan and Guizhou. Thus for example quite apart from the confusion between *shengchan dui, shengchan dadui,* and *shengchan xiaodui,* which was a general phenomenon, one finds in Guizhou and Sichuan that both production brigades and production teams were referred to as *shengchan dui,* area teams (*qudui*), 'commune-parts' (*fenshe*), divisions (*fenying*), and construction departments (*shetuanbu*), more often than not simultaneously. As previously indicated here the lowest level of the commune will be referred to as the production team and the intermediate level as the production brigade regardless of the term formally applied. Although at one stage Guizhou's party committee rural work department suggested that the commune might have three[92] (rather than the more general two) sub-divisions, there is no evidence that this was ever implemented. Certainly in Sichuan provincial regulations only provided for three levels in the commune's administration.[93]

Moreover, the confusion as to the precise functions of each level of the commune, which characterized commune policy nationally between the 6th and 8th plenums of the central committee, was also apparent within both Sichuan and Guizhou. Although the Wuhan resolution of December 1958 signalled the start of the retreat from the 'High Tide' of the commune movement, with its call to 'consolidate' (or perhaps more accurately 'check out') the PCs and an emphasis on their three levels of organization, it provided no clear guidelines on how this should be implemented. This lack of specific direction was repeated at provincial level in Sichuan and Guizhou. Thus Guizhou's provincial party committee at its 8th plenum in early January 1959 called for the consolidation of the communes in line with the resolution of the 6th (national) plenum, but provided no specific guide to action, and indeed encouraged experimentation.[94] It was not until after the summer of 1959 that Sichuan and Guizhou appeared to clarify provincial policy on PCs. Thereafter the development of commune policy signified an eventual retreat from the original notion of the PC in three important respects. In rank order of closeness to the concept of the commune as expressed in August 1958 these were the decentralization of management functions and the organization of production; the decentralization of the level of ownership within the commune; and the re-emergence of private property, private plots and household production in general. In all three cases it would appear that Guizhou ran ahead of national trends whereas Sichuan lagged behind.

Before considering each of these three developments, it is interesting to note how Sichuan and Guizhou reported their reactions to the 6th plenum's resolution on consolidating the PCs. A comparison between the relevant sections in their respective provincial government work reports for 1959 reveals Sichuan's continued preference (though suitably amended) for the commune and Guizhou's less enthusiastic attitude. In Sichuan, Li Dazhang reported that after the 6th plenum

... work was carried out throughout the province to overhaul the rural people's communes systematically in all respects. After more than half a year's exertion, a marked success was achieved in the overhaul of the communes. Throughout the province, in the course of overhauling the communes, wide and deep publicity was given to the essence of the party centre's resolution. Through the solution of all kinds of concrete problems, cadres as a whole together with the masses have come to understand that at the present stage people's communes still have to practise the socialist system of collective ownership. They have thus achieved uniformity in ideological understanding. In accordance with the principle of 'unified leadership, different levels of administration, and different levels of accounting', all kinds of business management systems have been preliminary inaugurated and perfected; the areas of authority of commune, production brigade, and production team have been defined. As a result the division of labour among the different organizational levels of the commune is rational, and the division of responsibility clarified. In accordance with the principle of distribution according to labour and exchange at parity, the distribution system has been preliminarily inaugurated and perfected in people's communes.[95]

Where Li Dazhang had stressed three levels of management and made light of distribution problems, Dai Xiaodong was much harder on the PCs' initial problems and indicated that Guizhou had retreated much further than Sichuan, emphasizing the decentralization of ownership within the commune. Dai reported that after the 6th plenum.

... the overhaul of people's communes started throughout the province last winter. The principles of different levels of administration, of different levels of accounting, of distribution according to labour, of greater reward for harder labour were implemented. The system of ownership of the means of production in people's communes at three levels – ownership at the level of production brigade being the fundamental one, ownership at commune level being less extensive, and ownership at the level of production team being the least important – was implemented. In this way, the excessive centralization of administrative authority and mistakes in the system of distribution, which were shortcomings that became apparent just after people's communes were built and resulted from the lack of experience of cadres and masses, were thoroughly overcome. As a result people's communes were soon on their way to perfection and consolidation. They showed more clearly their immense superiority for the organization of production and construction, the advance of economic and cultural development in the villages, and the improvement of peasants' standard of living.[96]

As has already been suggested it seems dubious at best that the commune level was ever a major level of management in Guizhou. Clearly it would appear, according to a later source, that even commune-run industry had been decentralized to production brigade management by early 1959.[97] Throughout 1959 and early 1960 the production brigade would appear to have been the most important management level within the commune – that is the level at which production was organized – in Guizhou,[98] as indeed it was in Sichuan. However, Guizhou decentralized the organization of production to the level of the production team during the summer of 1960, much earlier than appears to have been the case either in Sichuan or nationally. By September 1960, Guizhou's production brigades were left mainly responsible for small-scale industry, the organization of construction work, and the co-ordination of production team's activities, whilst production became the team's responsibility.[99] Production contracts and guarantees were fixed between brigade and team, and it was the production team which drafted plans and arranged their execution. The reason given for this change was that it was only at front line of production that bureaucracy was minimized and 'on-the-spot management' could take place, the masses be fully involved, and 'basic-level initiative be given full play'.[100] To quote an editorial from the *Guizhou Daily*: 'The production teams are the combat units at the most basic level of agricultural production.'[101]

In complete contrast, it would seem that the production brigade remained the major level of management within Sichuan's communes until the end of 1961. Thus, it was made explicit in September 1961, as the annual procurement gathered momentum, that production contracts and guarantees were between communes and production brigade, and that the brigade was 'the pivot of the system for the organization of production'.[102] However, it is apparent that by early November 1961 the emphasis had shifted to the production team as the major unit for the organization of production.[103] The main production contract was now between brigade and team,[104] and although at first the brigade was also contracted to the commune,[105] its function rapidly developed into one of co-ordination among teams particularly with respect to construction.[106]

A similar contrast between Sichuan and Guizhou is apparent with respect to the decentralization of the level of ownership within the commune. As had already been noted, Guizhou had stressed the ownership function of the production brigade in early 1959. It seems reasonable to assume that the production brigade became the major level of ownership within the commune in Sichuan as well sometime in 1959, although it has not proved possible to find an explicit reference to this effect before March 1960.[107] However, after 1959, Guizhou decentralized the level of ownership to the production team well before Sichuan. For most of 1960, the production brigade remained the basic accounting unit,[108] however in December 1960, it was announced that the production team was to be the 'fundamental level of ownership within the commune'. In an article in the provincial party's theoretical journal ostensibly stressing the importance of the three level ownership system within the commune, the change was justified by reference to the principle of 'Do the best according to local conditions': 'We may find an expression of this in the old proverb which says; "A man should do his best and the land should be fully utilized."' It was pointed out to cadres that they should understand that peasants had a long experience of agricultural cultivation; and it was emphasized that: 'It must not be assumed that bigger is better.'[109] At the same time, while stressing that 'People's Communes have shown their superiority', the director of the provincial rural work department pointed out that there could be no hurried transformation from collective to all people's ownership:

... Mao Zedong has strongly emphasized that there must be a period of transition before a people's commune can change its three-level ownership system based on the production team into an ownership system based on the commune.[110]

Interestingly, at the same time that Guizhou was decentralizing the level of ownership to the production team ahead of the national trend, by reference to the commune's 'Three-level ownership system', one of Sichuan's communes was being popularized as a national model in the same context. In that case, however, the Sichuanese commune was singled out for its implementation of the 'three-level ownership system' because it had the production brigade as the basic level of ownership within the commune.[111] Indeed, Sichuan appears to have promoted the production brigade as the basic level of ownership within the commune right up to the summer of 1962, long after other provinces had decentralized ownership to the production team. Although it is not possible to determine exactly when the change occurred in Sichuan during 1962, at the beginning of July the provincial press certainly propagandized the production team as the commune's basic accounting unit.[112]

Finally, there is the question of the restoration of private property, private plots and household production. Unsurprisingly, there is little detailed information available, particularly with respect to private property. However, from the information that can be gleaned it would seem that once again Guizhou was quicker off the mark than Sichuan. As reported in Chapter 6, it seems likely that household sideline production had restarted by the summer of 1959. At least by that stage individual households were being encouraged to make contracts with local commercial departments for the supply of products from sideline industry.[113] Certainly in October 1959, Zhou Lin was recommending that individual peasants be given their own small plots of land for cultivation, when he went on an inspection tour of Jinsha *xian*.[114] Sichuan, on the other hand, which had socialized sideline production well before August 1958, appears to have been slow to return any livestock or land to private ownership. However, pigs were back under household management by September 1961.[115] On the other hand, sideline industry in general appears to have remained under collective management, at least by the production team, well into 1963[116] if not later. The only references to private sideline production during 1963–5 were to the raising of pigs and no other activities were mentioned in that context.[117]

Variations in commune policy

There were then considerable variations from the national norms in commune policy in both Sichuan and Guizhou. However, it would be misleading to view those variations as provincial-level resistance to central policies. In the first place, they were variations from national norms not from central directives. Until September 1962, national policy was not clearly defined and was definitely a matter for debate and discussion. Central directives specifically encouraged local variations by positively demanding experimentation so that further discussion could take place. Indeed one could argue that to a certain extent provincial variations in the implementation of commune policy reflected compliance with central demands rather than resistance. Moreover, both before and after the 10th plenum of the central committee, national policy on PCs recognized that it would be too difficult, if not impossible, to impose uniformity throughout the country. Hence the wide variety of communes reported by visitors during 1963–5.[118] Secondly, just as central directives to provinces encouraged experimentation and variations, so too did provincial instructions to their subordinate units.

None the less, it is possible to view these variations as evidence of provincial leaders' attempts to influence national policy. Indeed, once again, one could argue that to a certain extent this was required of them by the 'centre' (in so far as this is a meaningful concept at such a time of heated discussion) in the formulation of national policy on the PCs. The variations from the national norms in the implementation of commune policy in Sichuan and Guizhou are thus clear examples of their 'relative autonomy'. Whereas the attitudes of Guizhou's leadership were predominantly shaped by conditions in that province, Sichuan's 'relative autonomy' appears to have been exercised with more regard to the continuing national debate.

In Guizhou, the leadership had been caught slightly off guard by the launch of the commune movement. They responded by basing PCs on the already existing APCs, thus ensuring minimal re-organization and dislocation. Moreover, their rapid retreat from the original principles of the commune may well have been a positive response to peasant resistance under the strains imposed by the GLF. Examples of peasant resistance were frequently cited by provincial leaders during 1959–60, though it should be added in order to criticize them. One such, cited by Zhou Lin in late 1950, was a proposal submitted by a peasant to the provincial party committee who advocated the establishment of a free market in the countryside, and the establishment of production contracts between the commune and what were described as 'production households'.[119] Although this proposal was said to amount to the sin of 'de-collectivization' it was not so far from the solution to Guizhou's rural problems that was eventually adopted. It is not known whether total de-collectivization was ever advocated by Guizhou's leaders, but already by the end of 1960 it was reported that the average production team had only 30 peasant households, and the smallest 10–20.[120] This was a considerable retreat not only from the 'high tide' of the commune, but also from the APCs as they had existed in Guizhou before August 1958,[121] given that by this time the production teams were already the basic ownership units.

On the other hand it cannot be argued that everything advocated by Guizhou's leaders arose from, or was even compatible with, provincial conditions. The classic example of this was the promotion of deep ploughing, advocated nationally during the GLF.[122] In Guizhou as was repeatedly emphasized, a major reason for communization was in order to mobilize peasants to extend the area of 'deep ploughing', and this included the mountain areas.[123] It is hardly surprising that one of the most cited peasant criticisms was of opposition to this policy.[124]

It has already been suggested that a major determinant of Sichuan's enthusiasm for the commune movement during 1958 was the relationship that is presumed to have existed between Mao and the provincial leadership. Indeed the existence of that relationship would seem to be confirmed by Li Jingquan's defence of the commune after the Lushan plenum of August 1959. Here Li not only stressed the success of communization, but the importance of Mao's role in that victory.:

Comrade Mao Tse-tung has developed the Marxist theories of uninterrupted revolution and the development of revolution by stages. It is precisely under the guidance of the Thought of Comrade Mao Tse-tung which integrates the theory of the development of the revolution by stages and the theory of uninterrupted revolution that we are leading the revolution from victory to victory. The people's communes are a great, remarkable victory, a proof that this integration by Comrade Mao Tse-tung will always led to success.[125]

However, Sichuan's attitude and politics towards the PCs are not totally or readily understandable in the light of that suggested relationship. In the first place, Sichuan was relatively slow to adopt the name 'people's commune', waiting until after the Beidaihe resolution (unlike even Guizhou). On the other hand, this delay may only signify the cautious actions of a Politburo aspirant, for Sichuan had fulfilled Mao's task in deed if not in name. Secondly, the more enigmatic is Sichuan's attitude after 1958. Early in 1959, Mao had advocated the production team as the base in the consolidation of the communes, yet Sichuan had opted for the production brigade. Later on, Mao had advocated greater caution, yet Sichuan showed itself reluctant to retreat from the initial principles of the commune. The advocacy of the production brigade may well have resulted from the general confusion of terms; and it could be argued that Sichuan's post 1958 radicalism on the commune was an attempt to support Mao's real (as opposed to his stated) position.

Although such arguments are not palpably false they do seem to add up to a case of special pleading. Rather, Sichuan seems to have adopted a line which whilst it certainly did not oppose Mao's intentions was more radical. In any case, it seems hard to justify that line by reference to provincial conditions as opposed to national politics. Even given the wealth of Sichuan's production, and assuming that its economic crisis during 1959–1961 was less than that which occurred generally, it still seems a remarkable feat of organization and will that in 1962 the province's production brigades (which to at least the end of 1961 remained the commune's basic ownership unit) were on average almost four times as large as the higher stage collectives of early 1958. Although in 1963, Sichuan's communes, production brigades, and production teams were considerably reduced in size, that was in line with national policy as directed after the 10th plenum.[126] The post-1963 changes in Sichuan's commune policy may well have partially met peasant demands. However, it can hardly be argued that those demands influenced Sichuan's leaders to implement policies at variance with those adopted nationally.

8

THE SOUTH-WEST REGION
AND THE
SOUTHWEST REGIONAL BUREAU

Two themes have informed the account presented in the preceding
three chapters of Sichuan and Guizhou after the start of the GLF.
One is the seemingly perennial contrast between their roles in
national politics. Sichuan was in the forefront of debate and development, Guizhou usually (if less so during the early GLF) more
cautious. Whereas Sichuan favoured radical policy preferences,
Guizhou supported the more conservative (if sometimes only by
default). To some extent their particular outlooks have been attributed to, on the one hand, the 'special relationship' between
Sichuan's leaders and Mao Zedong, and on the other, the internal
problems faced by Guizhou's leadership. The second and complementary theme is the growing influence of Sichuan and its
leadership in the southwest region. As in national politics, that
influence was exercised on behalf of radical causes and Mao Zedong
within the southwest region, particularly after 1961 through
Sichuan's leadership's manipulation of the southwest regional
bureau.

This chapter aims to justify that second theme in greater detail. It
is a possibly rash argument to pursue, not least since very little is
known about the regional bureaux of the early 1960s. Before the
GPCR very little was said even officially about the structure and
function of the regional bureaux, other than that they existed. It was
only during the GPCR, in the attacks that were made on provincial
and regional leaders, that further information came to light as to the
activities of the regional bureaux. As a result, almost all the evidence
on the structure and functions of the southwest bureau has been
drawn from sources emanating during the GPCR.[1]

The 9th plenum of the 8th Central Committee in January 1961
decided *inter alia* to establish six regional bureaux of the central
committee.[2] One of these six was for the southwestern provinces of
Sichuan, Guizhou, Yunnan and Tibet. There is some evidence that

this was only the formal announcement of a decision taken earlier (in 1960), and that in fact the regional bureaux had already been in operation for some time.[3] Certainly, although little is known about their functions, there were Economic Co-ordinative Regions – one of which was for the southwest as later conceived – established during the GLF. Thus the *Economic Geography of the Southwest Region* and six similar volumes had been written and published between 1957 and 1960 explicitly because Economic Co-ordinative Regions had been established.[4] Mao spoke twice to meetings of the leaders of the (Economic) Co-ordinative Regions in late 1958;[5] and made reference *en passant* to their activities elsewhere during the GLF.[6] However, the precise relationship between the Economic Co-ordinative Regions and the GLF and the Central Committee's Regional Bureaux of the 1960s is unclear. Little is known about the latter, and even less about the former (other than that they existed). There may have been some continuity between the two organizations. On the other hand, there were more Economic Co-ordinative Regions than Regional Bureaux, though most (as in the case of the southwest) covered the same territory, at least in theory.

The establishment of these regional bureaux did not necessarily signify the return to regional, as opposed to provincial, rule at the immediate sub-central level. They were nominally organs of the central committee (although physically located in the regions) and not formally regional party committees as had existed during 1949–54. There was no attempt to re-establish the regional pattern of administration that had existed before 1955: the organization of the state and military *apparats* at local levels remained as it had since 1954. None the less, the evidence presented here suggests that, at least in the Southwest, politics was regionalized and the bureau came to act as a regional party committee to some extent. Necessarily, because of Sichuan's predominance in the region, that perspective implies different consequences for the provinces within the Southwest.

THE SOUTHWEST AS A REGION

The idea that the four provinces of Sichuan, Guizhou, Yunnan and Tibet formed a Southwest Region was relatively new. During the period of regional administration between 1949 and 1954, Tibet was not included as part of the Southwest. Although the *Economic*

Geography of the Southwest Region stated that one intention in creating the Southwest Economic Co-ordinative Region was in order to aid both Tibet's development and its integration regionally and nationally,[7] it is interesting to note that it did not provide detailed analysis of Tibet as it did for the other southwestern provinces. Moreover, although the concept of the Southwest Region had existed before 1949, more often than not this had referred to Yunnan, Guizhou and Guangxi, rather than to the provinces it later comprised.[8]

Before 1949 Sichuan, Guizhou, Yunnan and Tibet were a formal rather than a functional region.[9] They had common experiences as border, colonial zones. They were areas of immigration for the ordinary Chinese, and of exile for recalcitrant officials. Apart from Sichuan in general (although it is also true for parts of what later became incorporated in that province) the area had never been fully integrated into the Chinese tradition. All had considerable non-Han populations, and as frontier areas experienced non-Han resistance and rebellion. However, in so far as there were regional ties these were similar memories of separate events rather than shared memories of common experiences. Before 1949 therefore the southwest as later conceived can hardly be considered a region. Historically its main characteristic was extreme localization rather than integration. Its major economic centre was undoubtedly the Chengdu Basin, but communications within the region (as well as with the rest of China) were hardly existent. As a result, as Skinner indicates, in so far as the southwest can be conceptualized in terms of 'regions', there were two rather than one economic regions: the one based on the Chengdu Basin, and the other on the Yunnan–Guizhou plateau, the latter being much less integrated than the former.[10]

However, after 1949 a determined effort was made by the CCP to create a functional region of the southwest. Right from the start it was intended that the region should be centred on Sichuan. Indeed this was a major point in the CCP's strategy for the region's integration.[11] Thus, for example, the province was developed in the early 1950s as the centre for regional trade meetings which served both political and economic ends;[12] and the development of railways and communications in general was centred on the Chengdu–Chongqing railway axis.[13] Although in a different political context, Sichuan was fulfilling one of its traditional roles as the base for the integration of the southwestern provinces. Under the first five year plan, when the region was not a 'key-point' construction area, the few 'above-norm' projects in the Southwest were designed to improve communications between Sichuan and the provinces within the region, as well as between Sichuan and the rest of the country.[14] Even before that, the conquest of Tibet had been organized initially from Chengdu. Moreover, as has already been noted with respect to Guizhou, Sichuan's economic wealth was of importance to the extremely undeveloped economies of the southwest provinces, which it supplied with 'cotton, salt and other daily necessities'.[15]

Sichuan's role as the region's economic centre was further enhanced after 1957.[16] The large-scale development of heavy as well as light industry in Sichuan was intended to create an economic base for the region, centred in particular on Chongqing. Thus, for example, the Chongqing Iron and Steel Works was greatly expanded, not only to meet provincial requirements but as a manufacturer for the whole region.[17] Moreover, Chongqing was developed as the regional economic centre precisely and explicitly because it straddles the major lines of communication within the region: east–west along the Yangtze, and north–south along the new railway system.[18]

Regardless of the impact of the GLF on economic production, the strategy of developing Sichuan as the region's economic base did reinforce the pattern of economic dependence within the region. Yunnan and Guizhou supplied raw materials for Sichuan industry. Thus, for example, the development of the Chongqing Iron and Steel Works depended in part on the supply of iron ore and coal from north Guizhou.[19] However, that was of secondary importance compared to Sichuan's supplies of manufactures, salt and agricultural products to the other provinces. Moreover, as has already been noted with respect to Guizhou, the development of the other provinces' local industry relied heavily on aid and assistance from Sichuan. It seems reasonable to assume that this pattern of economic dependence became particularly important during 1959–61 when Guizhou, and presumably Yunnan, both of whose agricultural let alone industrial production had never been strong, relied to a large extent on Sichuan's supplies.

SICHUAN'S POLITICAL LEADERSHIP OF THE SOUTHWEST

Sichuan's economic domination of the Southwest is hardly surprising. Apart from anything else it is the only province with a high and stable agricultural output, and a long commercial history. Moreover, it does in any case contain two-thirds of the region's total population.[20] Politically too, Sichuan's predominance characterized the Southwest as it emerged during the 1950s. In the first place, it is observable that Sichuan acted as a feeder province for the appointment of leading cadres to the other southwest provinces after 1950. For example, Xie Fuzhi moved from East Sichuan to Yunnan where he became first secretary in 1955. He was succeeded in 1959 by Yan Hongyan, previously a secretary and vice governor in Sichuan. Nor is that pattern confined to the appointment of provincial party first secretaries. Thus, in 1952 Qin Jiwei moved from South Sichuan to become a commander of the Kunming Military Region; and Lu Ruilin, who had been a vice chairman of the Xikang people's government became a commander of the Yunnan Military District in 1955.

Secondly, there is some evidence, although by no means conclusive, that Sichuan's leaders had influenced or attempted to influence those of other provinces in the southwest. For example, during the commune movement the first major references to the term 'people's commune', and the phrase 'People's Communes are better' that appeared in the Southwest's provincial party papers all occurred on the same day and used the same NCNA report.[21] This in itself does not indicate Sichuan's influence over Yunnan and Guizhou. However, the Sichuan paper had previously mentioned, though without further comment, that Mao had visited a people's commune, whereas the press in Guizhou and Yunnan had not.[22] Moreover, the NCNA report carried by all three provincial papers specifically cited the *People's Daily* as its source on the development of the commune movement, but was datelined 'Zhengzhou, 18 August'. This is unusual because the first report of Mao's approval for the people's commune appeared in the *People's Daily* on 13 August 1958.[23] At the very least such simultaneous action but delayed reaction suggests the possibility of collusion. Given that (as outlined in Chapter 7) Sichuan was a staunch advocate of the commune movement during 1958, whereas Guizhou at least was not, it seems reasonable to suggest that it was Sichuan's leaders who advocated joint publication ahead of the Beidaihe resolution.

A second example concerns only Sichuan and Guizhou. During the commune movement, Sichuan had advocated and created urban as well as rural people's communes in the autumn and winter of 1958.[24] Although also established in Henan at the same time the creation of urban people's communes did not become national policy until 1960,[25] and according to Vogel did not exist to any large extent outside these two provinces before the later date.[26] Guizhou later claimed that its first urban communes had been established during March 1960.[27] However, it is quite clear from the reports of the August–September 1958 commune movement in Guizhou that at first urban people's communes had also been established.[28] Indeed, the second people's commune whose establishment in Guizhou was celebrated in the provincial press was in fact an urban people's commune.[29] It could well be argued that Guizhou's creation of urban in addition to rural people's communes was a function of its leadership's general disarray that so typified the province's reaction to the commune movement. However, given Guizhou's general dependence on Sichuan, and that province's promotion of urban communes, it seems possible that Guizhou could have been influenced by Sichuan.

In sum then, by 1961 the impression of the southwest as a region which emerges is not one of a tightly knit unit of equal provinces with shared prespectives. In the first place, it would appear that Tibet could only be considered part of the Southwest as an administrative convenience. Moreover, the common characteristics of the provinces, particularly poor communications, also hindered regional integration. Secondly, within the region the provinces were clearly not equal. The other provinces relied on Sichuan both economically and to a certain extent for political leadership. In large part the existence of the Southwest Region in functional terms depended on Sichuan, and as a corollary, Sichuan dominated the region. Finally, despite similar general characteristics among the provinces – for example, low levels of urbanization and considerable populations of minority nationalities[30] – the contrast between the attitudes of leaders in Sichuan and Guizhou described in previous chapters would seem to indicate widely differing perspectives on both provincial and national politics.

THE SOUTHWEST BUREAU

Similar patterns of regional interaction appear to characterize the activities of the Southwest Bureau. In the first place, Tibet's involvement before 1966 seems to have been less than that of the other provinces. Thus, for example, although one of the bureau's ten secretaries was Tibet's leading cadre, Zhang Jingwu, Tibet does not appear to have participated in the Southwest Drama Festival of September–October 1965, organized by the bureau. Reports of the festival specifically stated that participants had come to Chengdu from Guizhou and Yunnan, but did not mention Tibet.[31] Moreover, it has only been possible to find reference to one occasion before 1966 when Tibetan affairs were discussed at a meeting organized by the bureau. That was the Conference on Minority Nationalities held in Spring 1962.[32] On the other hand, by 1966, when the bureau was co-ordinating the GPCR in the region, it would seem that Tibet was fully involved in the discussions and decisions.[33]

Secondly, Sichuan's influence over, and leadership of, the Southwest not only increased during 1961–5 but was to a certain extent formalized. Thus, not only was the regional bureau located in Sichuan, but there was considerable overlap between the secretariats of the Sichuan party committee and the Southwest Bureau. Seven of the ten regional secretaries held concurrent leadership positions in Sichuan. Only one of the ten regional secretaries, Zhang Jingwu of Tibet, held a concurrent leadership position outside Sichuan, and neither Guizhou nor Yunnan provided a member of the secretariat. Moreover, of the other two regional party secretaries, both of whom had been appointed to the southwest directly from positions at the centre, one, Yu Jiangzhen had previously worked in Sichuan during the 1950s.[34] Although it would be easy to over-emphasize the extent to which Sichuan's leaders influenced the rest of the region, particularly given that the major sources of information on the southwest bureau's activities are attacks on Li Jingquan who was both the bureau's first secretary and first secretary of Sichuan until 1965, their influence would none the less appear to have been considerable. However, the theme of Sichuan's influence over the region will be developed later in this chapter.

Finally, and more generally, the bureau's activities were clearly limited in terms of direct regional rule. Thus, for example, it would appear to have had no authority in military affairs, nor for that matter with respect to the militia.[35] Moreover, as several GPCR sources made explicit, provincial people's governments reported direct to the centre and not through the regional bureau.[36] On the other hand, the bureau's activities were neither excessively restrained in range nor for that matter ineffectual. In particular, it seems to have been responsible for the coordination and planning of

Table 9 *Meetings organized by the Southwest Bureau, 1961–5[1]*

Date	Meeting	Place	Major item(s) of discussion
April 1961	Rural Work Conference		
October 1961	Rural Work Conference	Nanchong	Commune Organization, Rural Markets
Spring 1962	Conference on Minority Nationalities		
22 May 1962	2nd plenum of bureau		
December 1961	Conference on Agricultural Mechanization		
23 January 1963	Conference on Industry and Communications		
June 1963	3rd plenum of Bureau		The 'Second Ten Points' of the Socialist Education Movement
July 1963	Meeting of the Bureau's economic committee		
January 1964	4th (enlarged) plenum of Bureau		The '2–5 cadre work system'
6 August 1964	Work Conference on the Socialist Education Movement	Guiyang	
December 1964	Planning Conference on Industry and Communications		
January 1965	Plenum of Bureau		The 'Twenty-three Points' of the Socialist Education Movement
July 1965	Meetings of Bureau's construction and planning committees		
1 September – 10 October 1965	Southwest Drama Festival	Chengdu[2]	
December 1965	Rural Work Conference		Rural Industry
December 1965	Plenum of Bureau		Attack on Lo Ruiqing and counter-revolutionaries within the PLA

Sources:
[1]. At least two references from separate sources listed in the Appendix.
[2]. Sichuan Radio, 11 October 1965.

Table 10 *Organs of the Southwest Bureau, 1961–5*[1]

Secretariat	General Office	
	Control Commission	
	Finance and Trade Office	
	Industry and Communications Office	
	Departments	*Committees*
Standing Committee	Propaganda	Construction
	United Front Work	Economic
	Organization	Planning
Plenum		

[1]. Identification of each unit is based on at least two entirely separate references in the sources listed in the Appendix.

economic policy for the region; and to have been the main body responsible for party affairs within the region. This latter function was particularly important (even though the evidence is by no means reliable or clear-cut) for it gave the bureau not only control of appointments within the region, but also direction of the Socialist Education Movement and of associated events that led directly to the GPCR.

An attempt has been made to obtain a guide to the structure and functions of the Southwest Bureau through an examination of the attacks made on the southwest's leaders during the GPCR. The results are partially listed in Tables 9 and 10. Table 9 provides a list of meetings of, and organized by the bureau, and of any known details of those meetings. Table 10 lists the known organizational structure of the bureau. In both cases the information is unlikely to be comprehensive, given the nature of the process of data-gathering. However, they do provide a useful guide to the bureau's activities.

In addition, it is possible to obtain information on the areas of the bureau's activities by considering the content of the GPCR accusations levelled at the Southwest's leaders. For example, one criticism of Li Jingquan stated

At the beginning of 1965 the Sichuan provincial Xinhua Bookstore, in accordance with the demands of the masses, applied to print 800,000 copies of Chairman Mao's 'Four Works of Philosophy'. The Southwest Bureau, under the control of Li Jingquan, ignored the application. After a struggle they were only allowed to print 90,000 copies. Obviously, the black regulations were mainly for restricting the printing of Chairman Mao's works.[37]

Regardless of the validity of the accusation, it would appear that the Southwest Bureau, presumably through its propaganda department, supervised the publishing network in the southwest. Indeed, the same GPCR source provides the information that for different sizes of a single publication's print-run permission was necessary at various levels up to and including the Southwest Bureau. Thus, a print-run of up to 50,000 copies had to be approved by the local cultural bureau; of up to 100,000 copies by the propaganda department of the relevant provincial party committee; and over 100,000 copies by the Southwest Bureau. In a similar manner it would appear that the Bureau also had at least supervisory authority over the provinces with respect to the content of their newspapers, journals and publications in general;[38] capital construction; heavy, light and local industry; the development of communications;[39] financial and commercial affairs;[40] higher education;[41] agricultural production;[42] political education in general;[43] personal assignments;[44] and the Socialist Education Movement.[45] Moreover, it would appear that the Bureau was initially responsible for the instigation and management of the GPCR during 1966 in the southwest.[46]

From the available evidence it would seem that the Bureau had wide-ranging co-ordinative and supervisory functions. In particular, it would appear that the provinces' economic development was not only coordinated but also determined to some extent regionally. The Bureau was, in other words, responsible for regional economic policy. However, there is no evidence that the Bureau was responsible for the implementation of that policy or was directly involved in economic management. There are no records of regional budgets detailing expenditure and income such as exist at provincial level, nor for that matter is it known how the Bureau's administration was financed. On the other hand, the Bureau was able to, and did, become directly involved in provincial politics as a result of its responsiblities for party affairs in general, and of all appointments. Thus, for example, in 1962, it was the Bureau's control commission, and not the Sichuan party committee or the provincial organization department, which re-organized the Yibin party committee.[47] Again, the Southwest Bureau, as has already been noted, was instrumental in the implementation of the Socialist Education Movement in Guizhou.[48]

It would thus seem reasonable to suggest that the Southwest Bureau acted in many ways as a regional party committee. The

Bureau could operate at three levels, in full plenum, standing committee, and secretariat; and (assuming the list of departments provided in Table 10 is incomplete) had the usual complement of organizations and departments for a local party committee. However, the Bureau would also seem to have been integrated into the state as well as the party *apparat*. An unusual feature of the bureau's structure was that it contained organizations more usually found in the state *apparat*. Thus, the Bureau had at least two offices, one for finance and trade, the other for industry and communications, whose equivalents (as far as is known) existed neither under the central committee of the CCP nor the provincial party committee, but at the centre within the State Council's organization.[49] Similarly, at local level, committees for construction and planning, were more normally part of, or subordinate to, provincial people's governments rather than the relevant party committees. It is thus likely that those particular organizations resulted from the bureau's regional coordinative functions: the former for liaison with the State Council, the latter with the provincial people's government.

The Southwest Bureau's activities are thus of more than passing significance to any consideration of the relationship between centre and province. Apart from anything else, this necessarily brief description highlights the potential for the regional bureau to become a political actor in its own right. In abstract it might be argued that the bureau filled any one of a number of roles with respect to both the centre and the province within the region. For example, at one extreme it is possible that the bureau acted as a check on the relative autonomy of the provinces within the region. At the other, the bureau might have acted as an institution for, in some manner, the aggregation of the demands of the subordinate provinces. However, given the pattern of interaction between the provinces in the southwest, the latter seems unlikely to have been a function of the Southwest bureau.

In the Southwest, the essence of regionalization was reflected in the control of the Bureau's activities by Sichuan's leaders. As a result, the Bureau had a different relationship to at least Guizhou and Yunnan than it did to Sichuan. In the former case, it would appear that the Bureau did act as a further check on their relative autonomy. In the latter, the Bureau seems largely to have adopted and advocated the policies of Sichuan's leaders. Though Sichuan's ability to dominate the Southwest may have resulted from provincial conditions, the specific content of that domination does not appear to have been similarly determined. The occasions when the Bureau intervened in the affairs of Guizhou and Yunnan, and the policies that the Bureau advocated which might be interpreted as being at variance with national norms were a function of national politics. In short, Sichuan's leaders used the Bureau in an attempt to influence not only the other provinces in the region (where they were successful) but also national politics (where they were not).

THE REGIONAL CIRCULATION OF ELITES

An important power exercised by the Southwest Bureau, through its organization department was its control of cadres, in particular their appointment and removal. It was this power which after all had enabled the bureau to bring Guizhou's leadership to heel during the Socialist Education Movement. Moreover, it was probably reference to that function which lay behind the criticisms voiced in the GPCR that regional first secretary Li Jingquan had 'turned the Southwest into a watertight independent kingdom ... [and] put his own people in positions of power throughout the Southwest'[50] – or at least to the extent that there was any truth in the accusation.

Certainly, an examination of the appointments made to leadership[51] positions within the Southwest during 1961–5 appears to support the suggestion that Li Jingquan had provided 'jobs for the boys'. Not only were the majority of appointments made within the region, but an even greater proportion of those appointed had worked in the Southwest during the early 1950s. 41 appointments were made to leadership positions within the southwest during 1961–65 (Table 11). Of those 41 appointments, 32 were of cadres not already holding similar positions within the southwest. Table 12 lists appointments to the appropriate level according to work-place immediately before appointment; and Table 13 according to workplace during 1950–2. 61% of the appointments made during 1961–5 were of cadres from within the southwest region. Comparative data are not yet available for other regions. In any case, that is clearly a higher proportion than one would expect randomly. Moreover, 85% of the appointments were of individuals who had been working in the Southwest during 1950–2. There would therefore seem to be some evidence to suggest a regional base for the circulation of cadres. Even if one excludes the 9 appointments of cadres already holding leadership positions within

Table 11 *Appointments to leadership positions within the Southwest Region,*
1961–5

Regional/Provincial Level[1]	Name	Immediate previous work-place	Provincial work location in 1950–2
Southwest			
Bureau	Chen Gang	Centre	Sichuan
	Cheng Zihua	Centre	Shanxi
	*Li Dazhang	Sichuan	Sichuan
	*Li Jingquan	Sichuan	Sichuan
	*Liao Zhigao	Sichuan	Xikang
	Ren Baige	Sichuan	Sichuan
	*Xu Mengxia	Sichuan	Sichuan
	*Yan Xiufeng	Sichuan	Sichuan
	Yu Jiangzhen	Centre	Sichuan
	*Zhang Jingwu	Tibet	Tibet
Sichuan	*Liao Zhigao	Sichuan	Xikang
	Jia Qiyun	Centre	Sichuan
	Yang Chao	Sichuan	Sichuan
	Yang Wanxuan	Sichuan	Xikang
	Zhang Huchen	Sichuan	Sichuan
	Zhang Lixing	Sichuan	Sichuan
	Zhang Weiqiong	Sichuan	Xikang
Guizhou	Zhen Dingyou		
	Cheng Hongyi	Beijing	Beijing
	Chen Tie	Guizhou	Guizhou
	Hu Jiayi		
	*Jia Qiyun	Sichuan	Sichuan
	*Li Dazhang	Sichuan	Sichuan
	Li Li	Central-South Bureau	Jiangxi
	Luo Jijing		
	Qian Ying	Centre	Guangdong
	Tian Junliang	Guizhou	Guizhou
	Wu Rongzheng		
	Yao Fengshi		
Yunnan	Zhao Jianmin	Shandong	Sichuan
	Zhang Tianfang	Yunnan	Yunnan
	Gao Zhiguo	Yunnan	Sichuan
	Li Chengfang	Wuhan Military Region	Yunnan
	Liu Linyuan	Yunnan	Yunnan
	Shi Huaibi	Centre	Centre
	Wang Shaoyan	Yunnan	Yunnan
	Zhou Xing	Shandong	Sichuan
Tibet	Hao Jiannan	Inner Mongolia	

Table 11 (*cont.*)

Ma Guishu	Shanxi	
Ren Mingdao	Sichuan	Xikang
Xia Furen	Centre	

* indicates an individual already held a leadership position within the Southwest Region.
¹. PLA appointments are included at the appropriate level. As far as is known there were no new appointments to Kunming Military Region during this period.

Table 12 *Appointments to leadership positions within the Southwest, 1961–5: work-place immediately before appointment*

	Sichuan	Other provinces in the Southwest	Provinces and Regions outside the Southwest	Centre	Unknown	Total
Regional/provincial level						
Bureau	6	1	–	3	–	10
Sichuan	6	–	–	1	–	7
Guizhou	2	2	2	1	5	12
Yunnan	–	4	3	1	–	8
Tibet	1	–	2	1	–	4
Total	15	7	7	7	5	41
% of those whose immediate pre-appointment work-place is known	42%	19%	19%	19%		99%

the region, the proportions are still 50% for those who were appointed from within the region, and 79% for those who had been working within the region during 1950–2.

Sichuan's role at the centre of this regional circulation of cadres is clearly indicated in both Tables 12 and 13. In particular, its role as a feeder province for the Southwest is emphasized in Table 13, especially if one excludes those already holding leadership posts within the Southwest Region. 50% of the 32 individuals newly appointed without already holding a similar position within the

Table 13 *Appointments to leadership positions within the Southwest 1961–5; work-place during 1950–2*

	Sichuan	Other provinces in the Southwest	Provinces Centre and Regions outside the Southwest		Unknown	Total
Regional/provincial level						
Bureau	8	1	1	–	–	10
Sichuan (including Xikang)	7	–	–	–	–	7
Guizhou	2	2	3	–	5	12
Yunnan	3	4	–	1	–	8
Tibet	1	–	–	–	3	4
Total	21	7	4	1	8	41
% of those whose work-place during 1950–1952 is known	64%	21%	12%	3%		100%

Southwest had been working in Sichuan during 1950–2. However, it should be pointed out that Sichuan's central role does not necessarily indicate a conscious attempt to colonize or subordinate the neighbouring provinces. Before 1956, Sichuan comprised five provincial-level units and consequently had a surplus of higher graded cadres for transfer and appointment elsewhere once the province was re-united and Xikang incorporated. On the other hand, Sichuan does appear in general to have dominated the other provinces. In this context, it is interesting to note that during the GLF when the attack was first launched against the leaders of both the Southwest Bureau and Sichuan, the 'rebels' had to go to Guiyang and Kunming to find the necessary support.[52]

SICHUAN AND THE REGIONALIZATION OF POLITICS

As has been previously indicated, it would be easy to overstate the extent to which Sichuan's leaders dominated the Southwest through the regional bureau, since this was a major criticism levelled against them during the GPCR.[53] Clearly, despite that criticism, 1961–5 was not a period of direct regional rule, and the Southwest Bureau did not constantly intervene in provincial affairs. On the other hand, the Bureau not only had a policy-making function for the whole region, but did have the authority to act within the Southwest's provinces. Moreover, it does seem likely that the bureau's activities were heavily influenced by Sichuan's leaders, if indeed the two are distinguishable.

On at least four particular occasions the Southwest Bureau seems to have acted in ways which could be interpreted as being at odds with either central directives or national norms. All but one of those were concerned with the development of the Socialist Education Movement and would appear to bear the mark of Sichuan's influence. In June 1963, the 3rd plenum of the Southwest Bureau adopted the 'Second Ten Points' of the Socialist Education Movement,[54] in advance of their national acceptance in September 1963.[55] There is no evidence that in the autumn–winter of 1964 the 'Revised Second Ten Points',[56] promoted by Liu Shaoqi were ever discussed by the Southwest Bureau let alone implemented in the Southwest. Whereas other developments in the Socialist Education Movement were discussed at plenums and work conferences of the southwest bureau, at least as far as can be ascertained from GPCR sources, the 'Revised Second Ten Points' appear to have been ignored. In January 1965, a plenum of the Southwest Bureau not only discussed the 'Twenty-Three Points' of the Socialist Education Movement, but also agreed on their implementation. In particular, it followed Mao's call to rectify 'Party powerholders who take the capitalist road',[57] a policy which seems to have been ignored outside the Southwest.[58] Finally, at a plenum of the bureau in December 1965, an attack was launched against Lo Ruiqing as a 'counter-revolutionary within the PLA'.[59] This last was unusual because though Lo Ruiqing had first come under attack in early December 1965,[60] he was not in fact officially condemned until March–April 1966.[61] Thus, the Southwest bureau would appear to have been considerably in advance of national developments. However, this instance of variation from central policy may well only reflect an *ex-post facto* rationalization of events on the part of the sources from which it is drawn.

By far the most spectacular and important of these instances would appear to have been the January 1965 plenum's implementation of

Mao's 'Twenty-Three Points' in the Socialist Education Movement. This was important not only because of the role in national politics but also because it led to the Southwest Bureau's intervention in Yunnan and Guizhou. According to Baum, a decisive turning point in the development of the Socialist Education Movement and in the events that eventually led to the GPCR occurred between September 1964 and January 1965. Basically debate polarized between Liu Shaoqi, who advocated the rectification of basic-level cadres in his 'Revised Second Ten Points'; and Mao, who became more concerned with rectifying 'Party powerholders who take the capitalist road', in his 'Twenty-Three Points'. However, in general Mao was unsuccessful in his attempt to have this policy adopted.[62] As has already been noted, at the same time that he outlined his 'Twenty-Three Points', Mao even criticized several provinces by name and those included Yunnan and Guizhou. However, the Southwest would appear to have been the only region where Mao's call for the rectification of the provincial leadership actually took place. At its plenum in January 1965, the Southwest Bureau decided to reorganize the leaderships of those two provinces.[63] In February, Zhou Lin, the first party secretary and governor of Guizhou was replaced; and Yu Yichuan, the governor of Yunnan, was similarly removed. In both cases, several new provincial leaders were appointed, and the execution of the Socialist Education Movement became the responsibilty of the Southwest Bureau.[64]

It could be argued that the Southwest Bureau had no choice but to act as it did with respect to Yunnan and Guizhou given Mao's explicit criticism. However, the fact remains that the other provinces named by Mao, and provinces in general, were able to resist rectification and reorganization.[65] It thus seems reasonable to argue that in this case, as in the other instances of the Bureau's apparent deviations from central policies, the Bureau's policy resulted from the 'special relationship' which existed between Mao and Sichuan's leaders. Although it is not known how the Sichuan party committee reacted to the question of Lo Ruiqing's condemnation, the policies adopted by the bureau with regard to the Socialist Education Movement were identical to those of Sichuan's leaders.

Much of this chapter has of necessity been conjecture. It has been suggested that the Southwest Regional Bureau acted in many ways like a regional party committee, and that local politics were regionalized to a certain extent during 1961–5. The existence of a regiona-

PROVINCIAL POWER, CENTRAL AUTHORITY

In general, the central concern of this book has been the interaction between centre and province in the decision-making process of the PRC. Against the background of a possible shift in the balance of power from centre to province during the late 1950s, it has sought to define the dimensions of the provincial role in national politics. To that end it has examined that role from the provincial perspective during the decade before the GPCR. In particular, it has concentrated on the two southwestern provinces of Sichuan and Guizhou. An essential part of the exercise has been an investigation of three hypotheses which taken together might indicate that the balance of power did indeed move from centre to province. The first is that China's political traditions of provincial autonomy became increasingly relevant after the early 1950s. The second is that provincial flexibility in the policy process came to serve local interests disproportionately. The third is that the decentralization measures of 1957–8 resulted from and aided demands for increased provincial autonomy.

POLITICAL TRADITIONS AND CENTRIFUGAL TENDENCIES

The hypothesis that China's political traditions contributed to the tendency for power to become decentralized is relatively accessible. China's size and diversity historically created centrifugal political tendencies which found their expression, particularly during the twentieth century, in movements for provincial autonomy. The objections are relatively obvious. There is no necessary reason to suppose that each province either did traditionally tend to autarky; or even if it did that such autonomy found its expression at the provincial level; or that the conditions which had led to its political traditions at any time before 1949, remained constant after.

In this case, Sichuan and Guizhou had historically different relations with the centre and their political traditions in general were almost worlds apart. Although both could be said to have had traditions of separateness, they were of very different kinds. Guizhou traditionally was first a border, and then an internal colony, unintegrated not only with China as a whole but also in itself. For the most part under the Empire it was regarded as a buffer zone between China and Southeast Asia. In so far as the province could be said to have a tradition of autonomy, this applied to the various groups of largely self-governing non-Han peoples who lived within and across its boundaries, and was far from being expressed at provincial level. Thus, even if it could be shown that Guizhou's leaders had either before 1958 desired or after 1957 gained a greater degree of autonomy it could hardly be argued that this had arisen from or been reinforced by the province's political traditions.

Sichuan, on the other hand, is a different matter entirely. It did have a tradition of provincial autonomy before 1949 although during the Republican period that had not resulted in a united province. However, Sichuan's independence occurred historically under very specific circumstances. When, and only when, central authority broke down then Sichuan did tend to become a separate state-within-a-state. The basic determinant of Sichuan's independence was thus not the province's strength but the centre's weakness. Moreover, the legitimacy for Sichuan's independence was rarely vested in the province rather than in China as a whole. Sichuan, unlike Guizhou, was an integral part of China politically and culturally, and it was that interrelationship rather than Sichuan's separateness which explains its political traditions. Thus, independence when it occurred was seen as a necessary but temporary expedient pending the restoration of central authority. In addition, Sichuan traditionally served as a refugee for the ruler in times of national disorder; and the southwest's political, economic and cultural centre.

There can be little doubt that the conditions which had historically encouraged Sichuan's separatist tendencies did not exist after 1949. Although central authority had been weak during the first half of the twentieth century, Sichuan was rapidly re-integrated into the Chinese polity. Thus, land reform, which had never been attempted before in Sichuan was implemented speedily and completed by May 1952. There was now a strong centre with a firm guiding hand able to carry out policies through the CCP. Although it can be argued that the centre was increasingly divided after 1955, Sichuan's leaders reacted not by withdrawing from national politics but, as has already been suggested, by becoming a leading radical province in that debate. Moreover, their perspectives on the province's development not only changed with national demands but also reflected the interdependence of province and nation. Thus, Sichuan's agricultural wealth became and remained an important national resource. Throughout the decade before the GPCR, a constant theme emphasized by Sichuan's leaders was the need to increase agricultural output, not just for internal use but for export to both agriculturally deficient provinces and the large urban centres. To this end, transport facilities were not only improved within the province, but the physical barriers that had separated Sichuan from the rest of China were overcome. Navigation on the Yangtze was improved; railways and highways constructed, linking Sichuan not only with Yunnan, Guizhou and Tibet, but with the north and east of China. For its part, Sichuan was dependent on the centre and the rest of China for aid and investment both to develop communications and industry and for the supply of important items, such as cotton, that it did not sufficiently produce. That dependence on the centre was explicitly recognized by Li Jingquan in his speech to the 8th Party Congress, when he asked for greater central investment in Sichuan and did not, unlike other provincial leaders, request greater control over provincial resources. Moreover, even after 1957, when central aid for industrial development was forthcoming, the emphasis was on Sichuan's development as the regional economic base. That was a role it continued to occupy throughout the early 1960s. Although it could be argued that Sichuan's development before the GPCR enhanced its importance and the influence of its leaders nationally it can hardly be argued that their perspectives were reinforced by the provincial tradition of separatism. A symptom and symbol of Sichuan's role as an integral part of the PRC was Li Jingquan's elevation to the Politburo in 1958. Although Li was not a native Sichuanese, the province had historically not produced military or civilian leaders of national standing.

On the other hand, there is considerable evidence that provincial leaders were well aware of provincial traditions. Indeed it would be more surprising if they had not been. Thus, for example, in Sichuan particularly when the province was being urged to produce more grain in order to aid the cities and grain deficit areas, reference was frequently made to Sichuan's reputation as 'The Storehouse of

Heaven'. Similarly, in Guizhou when urging the need for economic development and transformation, Zhou Lin, in particular, often referred to the province as 'The Mountain Land'. However, in general, such traditions and local customs, as for example Sichuan Opera and those of the minority nationalities, were used as integrative devices rather than expressions of a desire for provincial separatism. China's re-integration after 1949 can after all be seen as inherently a two-stage process. First there was integration into the locality; then the locality's integration into the state.[1] In the case of Guizhou, which had never really been under Guiyang's central control before, this was clearly more important than in Sichuan. None the less a similar process occurred in both provinces. The creation, or re-creation of a provincial identity was thus an important part of the extension and maintenance of CCP authority.

Moreover, political traditions do help explain the behaviour of provincial leaders. Though they were clearly not the sole determinant, certain of the circumstances which had led to those traditions historically remained or were reinforced after 1949. As a result the perspectives of provincial leaders – as political middlemen – could not but be at least partially influenced by those circumstances. Thus, Guizhou's traditional status as an internal colony, dependent on Yunnan and particularly Sichuan, remained a constant theme in its development before the GPCR. Despite Guizhou's leaders' emphasis on integration and economic development, particularly during the early part of the GLF, the economic crisis in and after 1959 rendered their attempts ineffectual. Indeed, it can be argued that Zhou Lin's dismissal in 1965, ostensibly for failure to implement the Socialist Education Movement, resulted largely from the provincial leadership's more general inability to integrate Guizhou adequately in itself. The existence of a strong centre reinforced not only Sichuan's political but also its economic integration into China as a whole. Moreover, other of Sichuan's political traditions were also relevant. In particular, Sichuan's role as the southwest's political and economic centre was deliberately encouraged by the centre after 1957, and for largely similar reasons as had emerged historically. Sichuan was strategically located and had a high and stable agricultural output, whereas the other provinces in the region were economically undeveloped and politically potentially unstable. In terms of their preoccupations and responses to national politics it is thus hardly surprising that Sichuan's leaders should be more active in national politics whereas Guizhou's leaders were more concerned with the problems they faced within the province.

PROVINCIAL VARIATIONS AND PROVINCIAL AUTONOMY

Provincial leaders do participate in the formulation and implementation of policy not only with respect to their own provinces but also on a national level. The national decision-making process not only institutionalized the participation of provincial leaders through their attendance at various central meetings, notably enlarged Politburo meetings, central work conferences, and the frequent conferences of provincial first party secretaries, but also utilized their role as political middlemen. Provincial leaders were thus the major channel for both the transmission of central directives downwards and the monitoring of the implementation of those directives. National decision-making was frequently an incremental process involving provincial experimentation before a final decision was reached. In that process, provincial variations were bound to occur.

In considering the interaction between centre and province in the national decision-making process, notably whether political power was generally more centralized or decentralized, it was thus proposed that the relative autonomy of provincial leaders be examined through an analysis of provincial variations. In consequence, the behaviour of provincial leaders in the formulation and implementation of policy has been examined in order to identify any apparent local variations from national norms or central directives. Moreover, an attempt has been made to determine whether those apparent provincial variations are better explained by reference to national politics or provincial conditions.

In terms of central attitudes and provincial response it has proved possible to identify five basic types of provincial variation. In the first place, there were clearly occasions when provincial leaders were explicitly and temporarily exempted from the implementation of certain aspects of national policy by the centre. The best example was that in Sichuan co-operativization in the province's national minority areas was not started until 1958, whereas it had been completed throughout the rest of the province by the end of 1956. Interestingly, however, Guizhou's minority nationalities had been co-operativized at the same time as the rest of the province during 1955–6. This difference is presumably explained by the different conditions in the two provinces. Sichuan's national minorities were not only a small proportion of the population, but had also been subject to various degrees of slavery before 1949. In the first instance the abolition of slavery and consequent problems was considered nationally more important than other issues. In Guizhou, on the other hand, minority nationalities were a much larger proportion of the population. Although, national minority areas of Guizhou had been exempted from immediate land reform at the start of the 1950s, by late 1955 the integration of the whole province had became a major problem facing its leadership, and co-operativization had seemed like a useful means to that end.

Secondly, there were occasions when provincial leaders were explicitly encouraged to experiment and participate in the formulation of national policy. This was particularly the case during the GLF. As the development of rural people's communes in both Sichuan and Guizhou indicates there could be considerable variations in both policy formulation and implementation. However, such provincial variations are not strictly speaking variations from central directives but from national norms. Central policy was largely undefined and dependent on the process of provincial experimentation.

Thirdly, there were provincial variations from central policy which resulted from political debate at the centre, and in particular Mao's influence. The most obvious example of this type of provincial variation was the 'High Tide' of agricultural co-operativization during 1955–6. In general, such variations are more to be found in Sichuan's development than that of Guizhou. Throughout this study, it has been suggested that a major determinant of the perspectives of Sichuan's leaders was their 'special relationship' with Mao. Although the evidence for that relationship can only be circumstantial, there are so many instances suggestive of an alliance that coincidence seems less likely. For example, Sichuan's leaders attempted to accelerate the implementation of the first five year plan during late 1955 and the first half of 1956; they supported Mao's call for, and views on, rectification during 1956–7; they advocated and praised Mao's Twelve Year Plan during its national eclipse; they promoted the commune movement during 1958; and even the province's slow but uncensured collectivization during 1956 has been related to that relationship. Of even greater importance in the context of the widening rift within the centre, it has been argued that Sichuan's leaders, through the Southwest Bureau, not only supported but implemented Mao's 'Twenty-three points' in the Socialist Education Movement, including his injunction to rectify 'Party powerholders taking the capitalist road'. All these were examples of variations from either central policy or national norms, and all can be regarded as evidence of a positive response to Mao by Sichuan's leaders.

Fourthly, in Guizhou there was one example of provincial leaders delaying implementation of a central directive. During 1957, Guizhou did not start its rectification campaign in response to the late April directive until early August. On one level this is not a variation from the central directive since the provincial leadership did eventually comply. However, given the importance of the issue in national politics, and the form the rectification campaign eventually took – largely identical with the anti-rightist movement and aimed at the minority nationalities – it seems reasonable to consider Guizhou's delayed reaction as a provincial variation. On the other hand that delayed action does not seem to indicate outright opposition to the centre, particularly given Zhou Lin's outspoken political support for rectification nationally. Rather it seems to have resulted from Guizhou's preoccupation with the serious problem of flood control at the time.

Finally, there were occasions when provincial leaders did not implement central policies. Two examples of this are of help in reaching an understanding of the relationship between centre and province. The first was Guizhou's non-implementation of the Socialist Education Movement before February 1965. The evidence on this is clearly largely inferential, however, it seems unlikely that Guizhou's non-compliance resulted from decentralized political power at provincial level. Rather it has been suggested that Guizhou's leaders lost their ability to adequately control the province in the wake of the GLF. The result was the reorganization of the provincial leadership, and the removal of Zhou Lin, the provincial first secretary. Zhou, in other words, was removed not simply because he had succumbed to provincial political traditions but because he had failed as a political middleman. The second example was Sichuan's apparent non-implementation of the 'Revised Second Ten Points' in the Socialist Education Movement. This was clearly a very different kind of non-implementation to that which occurred in Guizhou. The 'Revised Second Ten Points' and the 'Twenty-three points' represented alternative strategies in the Socialist Education Movement between September 1964 and January 1965. Sichuan's leaders, as had already been suggested, supported Mao and the latter in the growing inner-party debate. In a sense then, their non-implementation of the 'Revised Second Ten Points' is best understood in terms of the third type of provincial variation – namely that which resulted from divisions at the centre, and Mao's influence.

There is thus little to suggest that provincial variations from central policy or national norms occurred because of provincial political power. All but one of the instances of provincial variation it has proved possible to identify cannot in any sense be interpreted as anti-centre acts. On the contrary, variation was either allowed, explicitly encouraged, or resulted from central debates. Almost all the variations identified fall into the last two categories, and should thus be seen more accurately as a function of the national decision-making process. It is thus suggested that the power to allow or encourage provincial initiative resided at the centre, and was used to widen the sphere of conflict or discussion. Sometimes this power was exercised by the central leadership as a whole, sometimes by Mao alone. Moreover, this suggestion is reinforced by the one example of resistance to the centre (albeit by default) where the result was a reorganization of the provincial leadership. The evidence of these provincial variations would thus seem to indicate that the major divisions within Chinese politics were not between centre and provinces but within the national leadership, of which the provincial leaders were a part. It would seem likely that these divisions within the leadership led to relations between central and provincial leaders based on a mixture of principles, self-interest, and personal ties. It is certainly clear that the importance of such relationships should not be underestimated. For example, it would be difficult to explain how Sichuan's leaders escaped retribution for their promotion of the 'large co-operative' during 1956 if support had not been forthcoming from elsewhere.

On the other hand, this is not to say that provincial leaders had equal room for manoeuvre with respect to either national or provincial politics, or that they were not necessarily influenced by provincial conditions. Indeed, a comparison of provincial variations in Sichuan and Guizhou reveals two interesting contrasts. The first is that Sichuan's leaders clearly had a greater degree of political manoeuvrability than did Guizhou's. In general, Sichuan's variations on national themes tended to run ahead of national political developments. Thus, for example, Sichuan was one of the first provinces to announce its intention to bring forward completion of the first five year plan in late 1955; it was in the forefront of the commune movement; and its leaders had adopted the 'Second Ten Points' of the Socialist Education Movement before those proposals became national policy. Moreover, at times of central debate Sichuan's leaders were able to take a more isolated stand, as for example in their advocacy of the Twelve Year Plan throughout 1956–7 and the 'Twenty-three points' in 1965. By contrast, Guizhou's leaders were clearly more constrained. When experimentation equalled compliance to central directives as during the GLF, or when other provincial leaders reacted positively to Mao's initiatives they followed suit, but in general they were more concerned with continuing provincial problems. Moreover, it has been suggested that Guizhou's leaders' relative autonomy was subject not only to the centre but also to Sichuan's growing influence in the province. The second contrast is that whereas it has been suggested that Sichuan's variations in the formulation and implementation of policy were largely determined by national political considerations (notably its leaders' 'special relationship' to Mao) and did not arise from local circumstances, Guizhou's variations from central policy and national norms would all seem to have resulted from provincial conditions. Thus, for example, it has been suggested that its slow start to rectification during 1957 resulted from its leaders' major concern with flood control; the development of its policy towards communes was determined by local conditions; and the non-implementation of the Socialist Education Movement resulted from problems of political control. Somewhat paradoxically these two contrasts would seem to suggest that provincial conditions as well as the strength of any alliance with other leaders are important to an understanding of the relationship between centre and province. It is, for example, barely conceivable that Sichuan's leaders would have had the degree of manoeuvrability both nationally and regionally that they did had they been faced by the same problems as Guizhou's leaders.

DECENTRALIZATION AND 1957–8

The third hypothesis under investigation was that the centralization measures of 1957–8 mark a turning point in relations between centre and province. In that context, those decentralization measures appear to have accepted and supported the demands for greater provincial autonomy for which provincial leaders had campaigned. The evidence from this examination of Sichuan and Guizhou is that 1957–8 did mark a turning point in the relationship between centre and province, but not in a manner which necessarily resulted from or contributed to greater provincial autonomy.

In the first place, it is clear that not all provincial leaders – and certainly not those in Sichuan and Guizhou – had actively campaigned for, or even desired, decentralization to the provincial level. In the second place, provincial leaders had participated in the national policy process during 1955–7 in ways that were identical to those that existed after 1957. Sometimes their participation was indirect, through their control of policy implementation, as generally during the 'High Tide' of agricultural co-operativization: sometimes it was direct, through attendance at various central meetings of the CCP. Although provincial leaders clearly did have greater degrees of freedom within their own provinces during the GLF this resulted from deliberate central policy designed to encourage experiment and debate. In that context the decentralization measures of 1957–8 became a misleading indicator of political relationships. Far from creating provincial economic bases for political power, the effect of the decentralization measures on both Sichuan and Guizhou was to make them both more, not less, dependent on the centre. Thus after 1958 a higher and substantial proportion of both provinces' budgetary income was from the central exchequer than previously. Certainly the evidence of provincial variations in both Sichuan and Guizhou after the GLF would seem to indicate that in general political initiative remained at the centre.

On the other hand, 1957–8 did mark a turning point in the relationship between centre and province. It seems likely that the real significance of the 1957–8 decentralization measures was not that they provided the provinces with greater political power but that they were symptomatic of the break with the previous economic and political line followed under the First Five Year Plan. At first the abandonment of the Soviet model led to the experiment and debate of the GLF. However, in the longer term, the experience of the Southwest would seem to suggest that the change in line led to the partial regionalization of politics and economics. As Chapter 8 indicates that regionalization under Sichuan's leadership and domination had already started to appear during the mid-fifties, and was also a feature of the GLF. From the available evidence, its institutionalization during the early 1960 did not imply that political power had been decentralized, but rather that the co-ordination of local initiative and central direction was concentrated at the regional level rather than as previously at the provincial. As a result, for provincial leaders the relationship with the region became at least as important as that with the centre. In other words, in the southwest at least, one result of 1957–8 was that the centre-province relationship to some extent became one of centre-region-province, though differently for different provinces.

Understandably, 1957–8 seems to have proved a different kind of turning point for the leaders of Sichuan and Guizhou. In Sichuan it is clear that the change in line had long been advocated and suitable preparations made administratively. Dual rule had been proposed and partially implemented following the 8th Party Congress in September 1956. Politically, its leaders had actively supported Mao's policy initiatives from 1955 up to and including the launch of the GLF. In that sense, the period after 1957 did not mark a turning point. Moreover, the period after 1957 did not see an increase in its leaders' ability to promote policy initiatives against national norms. If anything it could be argued that Sichuan's leaders were more isolated in the initiatives they promoted before 1958 than later, as for example in their promotion of the 'large co-operative' and Mao's 'Twelve Year Plan'. On the other hand, too much should not be made of this essentially quantitative argument since they did appear to support Mao's 'Twenty-three points' in perhaps the most important inner-party wrangle before the GPCR. However, 1957–8 did increase Sichuan's leaders' room for political manoeuvre in one important respect – namely by increasing their influence within the Southwest. At first this influence appears to have been very indirect, as for example in the launching of the commune movement and the promotion of urban communes. But by the mid-sixties their influence was both direct and institutionalized through the activities of the Southwest Bureau, which they dominated.

In contrast, for Guizhou's leaders 1957–8 represented almost the exact opposite; further restrictions on their room for manoeuvre. At first, during the GLF this was not immediately apparent. Thus, although Guizhou did not gain as many decentralized economic functions (as for example control of coal mines) as most other provinces, it was able to determine its own policy on communes, albeit with a little help (ignored in the medium run) from Sichuan. However, from a wider perspective, the change in line further limited Guizhou's leaders, quite apart from the active involvement of the Southwest Bureau. This becomes apparent through a comparison of their reactions to provincial conditions and higher-level attitudes to their behaviour both before and after the GLF. In general, the major preoccupations of Guizhou's leaders during 1955–7 and 1961–5 were broadly similar, namely problems of 'local nationalism' and economic development. If anything, provincial conditions were worse in the sixties than the mid-fifties. Whereas in the earlier period agricultural output had risen (although by no means put on a stable foundation) and, at least partially as a result, progress made in integrating the province politically, after 1959 it would seem that economic conditions were so bad that the gains of the fifties had been reversed both economically and politically. In the period before 1958 Guizhou's leaders had concentrated on these problems to the exclusion of all else. For example, it has been suggested that it was for this reason that Guizhou did not participate in any attempt to accelerate the completion of the first five year plan and delayed the start of rectification during 1957. By and large such attempts to 'Do the best according to local conditions' appear not to have met with the disapproval of the centre. Guizhou's leaders were not unduly censured, criticized or removed from office during this period for their attention to provincial affairs. (The exception that proves the rule is vice governor Ou Baichuan, dismissed precisely because he was a Miao.) On the other hand, during the first half of the 1960s when the size of the problems facing Guizhou's leaders was much greater and had to a large extent resulted from the change in line of 1957, a preoccupation with solving local problems first was not enough to save them from censure. Though it has been suggested that Guizhou's leadership was reorganized in 1965 at least partially in order to prove a point in the national political debate of the time, none the less the non-implementation of the Socialist Education Movement appears from the available evidence to have been real enough. The result was not just Mao's criticism of the leadership as 'rotten', but Zhou Lin's removal and the direction of the Socialist Education Movement in Guizhou largely under the Southwest Bureau.

CENTRE, PROVINCE AND DECISION-MAKING

Even within the limits of decision-making in the PRC there is thus little evidence of a shift in the balance of power from centre to province (either generally, or specifically to Sichuan or Guizhou) during the decade before the GPCR. None the less, the leaders of both Sichuan and Guizhou did participate in the national decision-making process. As indicated in the Introduction, provincial political power must by definition be a relative and not an absolute concept. Its conceptualization depends on its context in the analysis of politics in the PRC. Thus, for example, here it has been suggested that the national decision-making process is not one in which the political initiative resides in the provinces as opposed to the centre, nor where policy is generally determined by the interaction of provincial power bases. On the other hand, it has been suggested that the manner in which the leaders of Sichuan and Guizhou participated in national politics was related to (even though it may not have been totally determined by) provincial conditions.

To a large extent, the dimensions of provincial power in national politics result from the nature of the decision-making process, and in particular the role of provincial leaders as political middlemen. Although this book has provided an essentially 'provincial-eye' view of politics in the PRC, it has also highlighted political divisions within the national leadership and the diffuse nature of the decision-making process during the decade before the GPCR. National policy was rarely, if ever, determined solely by central leaders, let alone by Politburo members meeting in smoke-filled seclusion. On the contrary, decision-making was not only a frequently long-drawn-out process involving experimentation before policy was finalized, but also one that institutionalized the participation of provincial leaders as such.

Others have argued that decision-making was an incremental process during the 'consolidation' phases (for example, the early 1960s), as opposed to the 'transformation' phases (for example, the GLF), in the now widely accepted cyclical explanations of politics in the PRC.[2] However, it would appear that national decision-making was almost inherently an incremental process. Even during the GLF, policy was initially formulated very generally, then executed and the implications of its implementation discussed again centrally (sometimes more than once) before its final form and details were determined. Quite sensibly, in terms of effectiveness, national decision-making consistently involved those responsible for implementing, co-ordinating and supervising policy in the process of initial formulation, assessment, re-assessment, and finalization. Thus, although during the decade before the GPCR provincial leaders increasingly became members of the Politburo and central committee, their role in national decision-making was institutionalized through their attendance at the various formal and informal meetings that process comprised.[3]

One dimension of provincial political power is thus relatively clear. The incremental nature of decision-making not only gave provincial leaders the powers of delay and interpretation in implementing policy (which Guizhou's attitude to rectification during 1957 amply demonstrates) but also the ability to influence that process in line with their own provincial conditions. Provincial leaders, in particular the party first secretary, not only passed down policy from the centre to the province they were also the channel for assessment of that policy's implementation from the province back to the centre. Because of the provincial leaders' role as political middlemen, the interaction between centre and province (in terms of territory rather than just leadership) was thus an inherent part of the decision-making process. On no occasion was that interaction, or the influence of provincial conditions on national policy, so clearly expressed as in the evolution of national policy towards the rural people's communes during 1958–62.

However, that is not to argue that even during periods of experimentation provincial leaders' attitudes in debates were necessarily determined by conditions in their own provinces. A second dimension of provincial political power is that some provinces, as for example in this case Sichuan, had a greater ability than others to experiment in their implementation of policies in order to influence debate because of provincial conditions (for example, wealth, the strength of political integration under the CCP's leadership, etc.) but that the content of their specific experiments was not necessarily derived from provincial conditions. The explanation of that phenomenon may also be found in the nature of the decision-making process. To work backwards, although provincial leaders participated in that process they did so not as representatives of their provinces, but as political middlemen. Of necessity they had two constituencies to satisfy – the province and the centre. However, the latter was not a single actor but several, including provincial leaders, with different perspectives and attitudes. Policy initiatives were launched and given test runs not only by the implementors of policy but also by central leaders, in order to influence (and to some extent to pre-empt) the decision-making process. Sometimes this occurred once the centre had laid down the basic guidelines of policy, but sometimes too that tactic was employed to move central policy more generally in new directions. Particularly during 1955–60 the latter was a practice favoured by Mao. Thus, for example, towards the end of 1955, Mao with the aid of several provinces, launched a movement to complete the First Five Year Plan a year ahead of time, which was adopted as national policy at the end of 1955. Again, during the first few months of 1958 Mao encouraged the creation of people's communes (if not always by that name) in several provinces, and effectively determined the national decision taken later that year. Although it is obviously easier to identify Mao's initiatives in that respect, it would appear to have been a more general practice. Thus, for example, it would seem that Pheng Zhen and Deng Xiaoping enlisted Li Jingquan's aid in a similar manner during 1963 with a trial implementation of the 'Second Ten points' of the Socialist Education Movement.'

In general then, informal alliances sometimes developed between a central leader and one or more provincial leaders whereby a policy initiative could be put into practice on a trial run. For the central leader, the choice of province, or provinces, was obviously an extremely important political decision if the initiative was to influence other decision-makers successfully. To some extent choice was determined by the nature and content of the initiative. However, it also depended on the perceived relative importance of the province, and its leaders' ability to achieve the desired results in any experiment or from any particular policy initiative. Thus, a province with relatively few political, social, and economic problems internally (such as Sichuan) was rather more in demand for such purposes than one faced by severe internal difficulties (such as Guizhou). As a corollary, whereas the leaders of the former had greater leeway in the national decision-making process the content of their initiatives and experiments resulted not only from provincial conditions but also from the relationships they had established with central leaders and which to a large extent underwrote their political manoeuvrability. On the other hand, the leaders of the latter were likely to be more constrained in national politics, and when they did participate to be preoccupied with their own province's problems.

Despite the incremental nature of decision-making and the participation of provincial leaders in that process, a third dimension of provincial political power is that it was extremely limited. The centre, either in whole or in part, carefully guarded provincial participation in national decision-making. It could allow a high degree of provincial relative autonomy, as in the evolution of policy on the rural people's communes. However, it was also able, both before and after the decentralization measures of 1957–8, not only to restrict the participation of provincial leaders in national politics but also to ensure compliance from those that erred. Thus, for example, Sichuan's experiments with 'large co-operatives' during the first half of 1956 were quickly suppressed; and Guizhou's non-implementation of the Socialist Education Movement was met by the ultimate deterrent, a reorganization of the provincial leadership. In general, there is little evidence that the political initiative was not retained by the centre in its relations with the provinces. Though there were manifestations of provincial political power on the national stage, they were relatively restricted. Moreover, as had already been indicated, such manifestations were either allowed or encouraged by the centre, or were an integral part of debates at the centre.

A fourth and final dimension of provincial power in national politics that must of necessity follow from the previous discussion of the decision-making process is its variability. A constant theme throughout this book has been the contrast between Sichuan and Guizhou in terms of their relationship to the centre. Generalizing from that contrast would seem to indicate that there are at least two variants of the relationship between centre and province in the decision-making process. Guizhou's experience would seem to suggest that the poorer the province economically and the less integrated internally, the less potential its leaders have for political manoeuvre in national politics, but the more the perspectives of its leaders are shaped by provincial conditions. On the other hand, the case of Sichuan suggests that the wealthier and more integrated the province, the greater potential its leaders have for political manoeuvre in national decision-making, but the less the perspectives of its leaders are determined by provincial conditions. However, an examination of two provinces cannot expect to uncover more than a few of the variables that might contribute to, or help to explain, the role of a province (or rather its leaders) in national politics. Economic wealth, internal integration, intra-regional economic and political relationships, and the nature of informal alliances between central and provincial leaders have been suggested as some of the more significant potential determinants of provincial political power. In addition, it would seem likely that distance from Beijing (both geographical and political); the internal structure of the provincial economy; the presence of military forces and the pattern of military organization might also be significant factors.

Obviously, a study of two southwestern provinces during the decade before the GPCR might provide conclusions that are severely limited in both time and space. However, on balance it would seem that the nature of national decision-making and the interaction of centre and province in that process described here continued not only after 1966, but also after Mao's death in 1976. Certainly, it would appear that during the last decade of Mao's life, decision-making remained an incremental process in which provincial leaders participated and in which not only informal but also more formal alliances between central and provincial leaders played no small part.[4] Indeed, one of the more remarkable aspects of decision-making during the early 1970s was the way Jiang Qing and Shanghai's leaders were prepared to promote policy initiatives in that city in the attempt to influence national politics.[5] It was remarkable not only because of the frequency with which that tactic was used to force (though not always successfully) the national decision-making process, but also because most of the policy initiatives promoted were not drawn from local conditions, and some at least encountered considerable local resistance.

Although Mao's death has clearly removed a radicalizing and mercurial element from politics in the PRC, there is as yet little evidence that the decision-making process and its spatial dimensions have been fundamentally altered. The national decision-making process, as with other aspects of political life, may have become more routinized. However, it still appears to be much the same as that described in the preceding pages. If anything, it could probably be argued that the routinization of politics that has occurred during the past few years has institutionalized the previously less formally accepted patterns of national decision-making that evolved during the preceding twenty-seven years. Certainly, that would appear to be the case with respect to its provincial dimension. Strange to relate, during the late 1970s and early 1980s the PRC media provided considerable publicity for Zhao Ziyang's 'Sichuan experiment'. That became the collective title applied to a whole series of economic reforms, in particular of enterprise management, popularized by the current Premier when he was provincial first party secretary in Sichuan (1976–1980).[6] The coincidence of Sichuan is strange enough. However, what makes it stranger still is that Zhao's 'Sichuan experiment' contains essentially the same proposals for reform suggested by Li Jingquan at the 8th Party Congress in 1956.[7] Authority may reside at the centre, but there could well be an institutional memory (or indeed memories) in the provinces, of considerable power and influence.

APPENDIX

GPCR sources providing information on the Southwest Regional Bureau, CCP Central Committee, and its activities during 1961–5

Date	Source	Author	Title
1967			
3 June	Guizhou Radio	*New Guizhou Daily* (editorial)	'Down with Jia Qiyun!'
4 June	Guizhou Radio	Proletarian Revolutionaries of the *New Guizhou Daily*	'The crimes of the biggest office-holder in the Southwest'
16 June	Guizhou Radio	Wu Xingwu	'A look at the wolfish ambition of Jia Qiyun to restore capitalism in the countryside'
17 June	Guizhou Radio	Liu Jieting	'Li Jingquan is the Khrushchev of the Great Southwest'
22 June	Guizhou Radio	*New Guizhou Daily* (editorial)	'More on knocking down Li Jingquan'
22 June	Guizhou Radio	Mao Zedong Thought Red Revolutionaries of the Guizhou Provincial Broadcasting Administration	'Resolutely knock down Li Jingquan – defend Mao Zedong Thought to the death!'
23 June	Guizhou Radio	Zhang Xiting	'Defend Chairman Mao to the death'
25 June	Guizhou Radio	Li Li	'Li Jingquan is the deadly enemy of the people of the Southwest'
28 June	Guizhou Radio	Zunyi Conference Battle Corps in Defence of Mao Zedong Thought	'Remove the outrageous crimes of the counter-revolutionary revisionist Li Jingquan in restoring capitalism in the rural areas of the Southwest'
3 July	Guizhou Radio	Red Guards of the Land Fossils Research Institute of the Chinese Academy of Science	'Li Jingquan is the arch-criminal in sabotaging the Great Proletarian Cultural Revolution in the Southwest'
7 July	Guizhou Radio	Yan He	'Knock down Li Jingquan, defend proletarian dictatorship!'

8 July	Guizhou Radio	Lin Dezhong	'Vehement denunciation of the outrageous counter-revolutionary crimes committed by Jia Qiyun in the rural "Four clean-ups"'
12 July	Guizhou Radio	Ye Qingchuan	'Denounce Li Jingquan!'
13 July	Guizhou Radio	–	'Cut off Li Jingquan's black arms that have been stretched to various places in the Southwest'
18 July	Guizhou Radio	Red Rebel Joint HQ of Sichuan Provincial Offices	'Tear the mask off Li Jingquan, the local emperor'
20 July	Guizhou Radio	Changying Red Literature and Art Rebellion Group	'Recapture the culture and education battle positions from the hands of Li Jingquan and his gang'
20 July	Guizhou Radio	Red Battle Squad in Defence of Mao Zedong Thought of the former Guizhou provincial party committee's Industry and Communications Political Departments	'Cut off the devilish paws stretched to Guizhou by Li Jingquan'
23 July	Guizhou Radio	Li Zhengfang	Report of Kunming Military Region Conference to denounce Li Jingquan
25 July	*Down with Li Jingquan* No. 6	Chongqing University Red Guards	'Smash the Li Family's "black shop" – exterminate the band of scoundrels'
4 Aug.	Yunnan Radio	–	Report of Struggle Meeting against Yan Hongyan
17 Aug.	Guizhou Radio	–	Report of 11 August Struggle Meeting against Jia Qiyun
31 Aug.	Sichuan Radio	Li Dazhang	'Vehement denunciation of the outrageous anti-party, anti-Socialist and anti-Mao Zedong Thought crimes of the counter-revolutionary revisionist Li Jingquan'
6, 7 Sept.	Sichuan Radio	Fei Hongzhuan	'Vehement denunciation of the anti-party, anti-Socialist, and anti-Mao Zedong Thought crimes of the counter-revolutionary revisionist Li Jingquan' (Parts I and II)
12 Sept.	Sichuan Radio	Fei Hongzhuan	'The towering crimes of the counter-revolutionary revisionist Li Jingquan in pursuing a restoration of capitalism in finance and trade work'

15 Sept.	Sichuan Radio	*Sichuan Daily* (Editorial)	'Mobilize! Unite! Down with Li Jingquan!'
19 Sept.	Sichuan Radio	–	Report of 17 September Struggle Meeting against Li Jingquan
22 Sept.	Sichuan Radio	–	Report of 15 September Struggle Meeting against Li Jingquan
23 Sept.	Sichuan Radio	Proletarian Revolutionaries of the Southwest Bureau Offices	'The counter-revolutionary revisionist Li Jingquan and the anti-party element, great schemer, careerist and warlord Peng Dehuai'
23 Sept.	Sichuan Radio	–	Report of 20 September Struggle Meeting against Li Jingquan
25 Sept.	Sichuan Radio	Proletarian Revolutionaries of the Sichuan Philosophy and Social Science Research Institute	'The counter-revolutionary revisionist Li Jingquan's proposition that "The whole party is of the same mind, strength, and kind" was for the purpose of restoring capitalism'
29 Sept.	Sichuan Radio	–	Report of 27 September Struggle Meeting against Li Jingquan
6 Oct.	Sichuan Radio	–	Report of 6th Struggle Meeting (29 September) against Li Jingquan
7 Oct.	Sichuan Radio	Tian Bao	'The counter-revolutionary revisionist Li Jingquan's towering crimes in nationality work in Sichuan'
9 Oct.	Guizhou Radio	–	Report of Struggle Meeting against Jia Qiyun and Zhou Lin
13 Oct.	Sichuan Radio	Proletarian Revolutionaries of the Sichuan Provincial Economic Commission	'Cut off the counter-revolutionary black hands stretched out by Li Jingquan to the industry and communication fronts'
13 Oct.	Sichuan Radio	–	Report of the 7th Struggle Meeting (5 October) against Li Jingquan
19, 22 Oct.	Sichuan Radio	Proletarian Revolutionaries of the former Sichuan party committee's industry and communications political departments	'The harm of the "Five-Act Sichuan Opera" pushed through by Li Jingquan in industry, communications, and capital construction was that it took the capitalist road' (Parts I and II)
26 Oct.	Sichuan Radio	*Sichuan Daily*, editorial, 21 October	'Totally smash the Li dynasty'
26 Oct.	Sichuan Radio	Southwest Bureau cadres	'Thoroughly expose and denounce the towering crimes of the counter-revolutionary revisionist Li Jingquan in organizing an anti-party, anti-Socialist, and anti-Mao Zedong Thought Independent Kingdom'

28 Oct.	Guizhou Radio	Revolutionary Rebels HQ of Southwest Bureau Offices	'We must settle accounts for Li Jingquan's towering crimes in finance and trade'
4 Nov.	Sichuan Radio	Revolutionary Rebels HQ of Southwest Bureau Offices	'Settle accounts with the local emperor Li Jingquan for his crimes of negating class struggle, restoring capitalism, and exercising bourgeois dictatorship'
11 Nov.	Sichuan Radio	–	Report of 8th Struggle Meeting against Li Jingquan
25 Nov.	Sichuan Radio	The Culture and Education Red HQ	'Utterly purge the poison spread by Li Jingquan and his revisionist line in education'
7 Dec.	Sichuan Radio	Long Chen and Wu Lian	'Thoroughly settle accounts with Li Jingquan for the counter-revolutionary revisionist crimes he committed in the rural areas'
23 Dec.	Sichuan Radio	–	Report of 20 December Struggle Meeting against Li Jingquan
23 Dec.	Guizhou Radio	Revolutionary Rebels of Southwest Bureau Offices	'Look at Li Jingquan's counter-revolutionary double-dealing features'
29 Dec.	Sichuan Radio	Shen Shihong	'Totally settle accounts for Li Jingquan's towering crimes in sabotaging the printing and distribution of Chairman Mao's Works'
1968			
13 Feb.	Sichuan Radio	–	'The "Meishan 2–5 system" and planting of experimental plots, thrown up by Li Jingquan, were black examples of revisionism'
8 Apr.	Sichuan Radio	Red Rebellion Joint HQ of Provincial Offices	'Totally settle accounts for the crimes of Liao Zhigao'
6 June	Guizhou Radio	–	Report of Struggle Meeting against Jia Qiyun
15 Sept.	Sichuan Radio	You Bin	'Refute Li Jingquan's absurd theory that "Without Sichuan, there would be no China"'

NOTES

1 Those decentralization measures have been discussed in detail elsewhere, and it is not intended to repeat that exercise here. In particular, see: H. F. Schurmann *Ideology and Organization in Communist China* University of California Press, Berkeley, 1968 (2nd edn.) especially Ch. 3, p. 173ff. A. Donnithorne *China's Economic System* George Allen & Unwin, London, 1967. N. Lardy *Economic Growth and Distribution in China* Cambridge University Press, Cambridge, 1978, especially Ch. 3, p. 90ff.

2 For a detailed account of both the debate within the CCP's leadership and the party congress, see R. MacFarquhar *The Origins of the Cultural Revolution*, Vol. 1: *Contradictions Among the People 1956–1957* Oxford University Press, London, 1974.

3 The text of the 'Resolution on certain questions in the history of our party since the founding of the People's Republic of China' adopted by the 6th plenum of the 11 central committee of the CCP, see *Beijing Review* No. 27, 6 July 1981. For comment, see *inter alia* D. S. G. Goodman 'The Sixth Plenum of the 11th Central Committee of the CCP: Look Back in Anger?' in *The China Quarterly* (CQ) No. 84, September 1981, p. 518.

4 Perhaps the best known contemporary statement to that effect is contained in Mao Zedong's 'On the Ten Major Relationships' of 25 April 1956, in *Selected Works of Mao Tsetung* Volume v (SW5), Foreign Languages Press, Peking, 1977, Section V 'The relationship between the central and the local authorities', p. 292ff.

5 'Province' here, and throughout, is used in the specific sense of provincial-level to refer to China's provinces, municipalities, and autonomous regions, which after 1954 were the immediate sub-central level in the political and administrative hierarchy.

6 For a useful discussion of this and other problems, see N. Furniss 'The Practical Significance of Decentralization' in *Journal of Politics* Vol. 36 (1964), p. 958.

7 J. Gottmann 'The Political Partitioning of Our World: An Attempt at Analysis', in *World Politics* Vol. iv (1952) p. 512.

8 J. B. R. Whitney *China: Area, Administration and Nation Building* University of Chicago, Department of Geography, Research Paper No. 123, 1970, especially p. 41ff.

9 See, for example: S. M. Lipset and S. Rokkan 'Cleavage structure, party systems and voter alignment: an introduction' in S. M. Lipset and S. Rokkan (eds) *Party Systems and Voter Alignments: Cross-National Perspectives* New York, 1967, p. 1.

10 R. Hartshorne 'The Functional Approach in Political Geography' in *Association of American Geographers, Annals* Vol. XL (1950) p. 110.

11 F. C. Teiwes 'The Purge of Provincial Leaders, 1957–58' in CQ No. 24, p. 32.
12 A. D. Barnett *Cadres, Bureaucracy and Political Power in Communist China* Columbia University Press, New York, 1967, p. 7.
13 'Regional' here and throughout refers to the six large Regions above the provinces in the political and administrative hierarchy, which existed 1949–54, and during 1960–7. During the 1960s these large Regions were bureaux of the CCP's central committee and units of party organization only.
14 A. Donnithorne 'Central Economic Control in China' in R. Adan (ed) *Contemporary China* Peter Owen, London, 1969, p. 151.
15 A. Donnithorne *China's Economic System*, p. 461.
16 A. Donnithorne 'Central Economic Control in China', p. 160.
17 P. Chang 'Research notes on the changing loci of decision making in the CCP' in CQ No. 44, p. 175–6.
18 A. D. Barnett *Cadres, Bureaucracy and Political Power in Communist China*, p. 112.
19 A. Donnithorne *China's Economic System*, p. 161–2.
20 W. Whitson 'The Field Army in Chinese Communist Military Politics' in CQ No. 37, p. 12–13.
21 The various statistics are adapted from D. Klein 'The State Council and the Cultural Revolution' in CQ No. 35, p. 87; P. Chang 'Provincial Party Leaders' Strategies for Survival During the Cultural Revolution' in R. Scalapino (ed) *Elites in the People's Republic of China* University of Washington Press, London, 1972, p. 501; F. C. Teiwes *Provincial Party Personnel in Mainland China, 1956–1966* Paper of the East Asian Institute, Columbia University, New York, 1967, p. 5; and from my own data.
22 See, for example: A. Donnithorne 'China's cellular economy: trends since the Cultural Revolution' in CQ No. 52, p. 616–17.
23 Such is very much the case presented by Schurmann, when he says 'Local power meant party power' in *Ideology and Organization in Communist China*, p. 362.
24 For an excellent account of such behaviour, see P. Moody 'Policy and Power: The Career of T'ao Chu, 1956–66' in CQ No. 54, p. 267.
25 Mao Zedong 'Talks at the Nanning Conference – I' 11 January 1958, in Mao Zedong *Sixiang Wansui* (1969), p. 148; translated in *Miscellany of Mao Tse-tung Thought* US Joint Publications Research Services (JPRS) No. 61269–1, p. 79.
26 *Mao Zedong Sixiang Wansui* (1969) 'Reading notes on the Soviet Union's "Political Economics"', p. 378; translated in *Miscellany of Mao Tse-tung Thought* JPRS No. 61269–2, p. 296.
27 *Renmin ribao* (RMRB) 25 June 1958, p. 1.
28 Two notable examples are: V. C. Falkenheim 'Provincial Leadership in Fukien, 1949–66', and L. T. White III 'Leadership in Shanghai, 1955–69' both in R. Scalapino (ed) *Elites in the People's Republic of China* op. cit., p. 199 and p. 302 respectively.
29 See, for example: B. Ahn *Chinese Politics and the Cultural Revolution* University of Washington Press, London, 1976, especially p. 233 where he suggests that decision-making was incremental only during 'consolidation' phases, as opposed to 'transformation' phases, in a cyclical explanation of PRC politics.
30 The recent history of the PRC would seem to indicate that the promotion of the Dazhai production brigade after 1963 was a moot case in point.
31 See chapters by Gluckman, Swatz and Tinker in M. Swatz (ed.) *Local-Level Politics*

University of London Press, London, 1968. For further discussion of the role of provincial party secretaries as 'political middlemen' and its consequences, see Goodman 'Provincial Party First Secretaries in National Politics' in D. S. G. Goodman (ed) *Groups and Politics in the People's Republic of China* University College Cardiff Press, 1984, p. 68ff.

32 A. Donnithorne *China's Economic System* George Allen & Unwin, London, 1967; and *The Budget and the Plan in China* Contemporary China Papers No. 3, Australian National University, Canberra, 1972. N. Lardy *Economic Growth and Distribution in China* Cambridge University Press, 1978, especially Chapter 3, p. 90ff. K. Walker *Food Grain Procurement and Consumption in China* Cambridge University Press, 1984.

33 I am grateful to Prof. Walker (SOAS) for this information.

34 R. MacFarquhar *The Origins of the Cultural Revolution* Vol. 1: *Contradictions Among the People 1956–1967*, pp. 26–32.

35 For example: Wang Xiaochuan, 'Guizhou shows that the changes in Man produce changes in heaven and on earth' in RMRB 23 November 1958.

36 See, for example: S. Shapiro *Experiment in Sichuan* New World Press, Beijing, 1981.

37 This notion is developed further in Goodman 'Guizhou and the People's Republic of China: The Development of an Internal Colony' in D. Drakakis-Smith and S. Williams (ed) *Internal Colonialism* Institute of British Geographers, Edinburgh University, 1983, p. 107.

I POLITICAL TRADITIONS AND THE CONSOLIDATION OF RULE

1 F. von Richthofen *Tagebücher aus China* Dietrich Reiner, Berlin, 1907, Vol. 2, p. 265.

2 A. Little, Introduction to Hosie's *Three Years in Western China* George Philip & Son, London, 1890, p. xxxii.

3 Li Dazhang 'Report on the work of the provincial people's council to the 5th session of the provincial people's congress' in *Sichuan ribao* (SCRB) 22 August 1957, p. 4, and *Chengdu ribao* (CDRB) 23 August 1957, p. 1.

4 Little, Introduction to Hosie, *Three Years in Western China*, p. xiv.

5 SCMP No. 4181, 20 May 1968, p. 1 – 'Important speeches by central leaders on March 15th', from an undated, unattributable tabloid-size Red Guard paper.

6 Supplement to SCMP (SCMP(S)) No. 225, 19 June 1968, p. 1 – 'Important speeches by central leaders on March 15th', from *Jinggangshan*, Beijing, 21 March 1968.

7 For Liu Xiang and Tan Mouxin's *Joint Declaration of Independence* and comments thereon, see R. A. Kapp *Szechwanese Provincial Militarism and Central Power in Republican China* Ph.D. Thesis, Yale University, 1970; University Microfilms, Ann Arbor, Michigan. A much abbreviated version of this thesis has been published as *Szechwan and the Chinese Republic: Provincial Militarism and Central Power, 1911–1938* Yale University Press, New Haven, 1973.

8 Ch'u T'ung-tsu *Local Government in China under the Ch'ing* Stanford University Press, 1969, p. 6. The other two were Zhili and Gansu. According to Hosie in *Three Years in Western China*, p. 85, only Zhili was in similar position.

9 A. Hosie, *Three Years in Western China*, p. 209.

10 A. D. Barnett *China on the Eve of Communist Takeover* Praeger, New York, 1963, p. 103.

11 G. B. Cressey *China's Geographic Foundations* McGraw Hill, New York, 1934, p. 300.

12 A. Hosie *Three Years in Western China*, p. 208.

13 R. A. Kapp *Szechwanese Provincial Militarism and Central Power in Republican China*, p. 116.

14 Sun Jingzhi et al., *Xinan diqu jingji dili* Science Publishing House, Beijing, 1960, p. 63. The few poor highways that existed were short and unconnected around Chengdu, Jianyang, Suinang and Chongqing.

15 A. Hosie *Szechwan; its products, industries and resources* Kelly & Walsh, Shanghai, 1922, p. 3.

16 A. Barnett, *China on the Eve of Communist Takeover* p. 105.

17 Except for the 'n' sound which is pronounced as an 'l', the syllables are theoretically identical in pronunciation.

18 R. A. Kapp *Szechwanese Provincial Militarism and Central Power in Republican China*, p. 1). *Xinan diqu jingji dili*, p. 12. After the Qin invasion '10,000 Qin households moved in', and in the early Qing there was an importation of people from Hunan and Guangdong.

19 A. Hosie *Szechwan; its products, industries and resources* op.cit., p. 15.

20 Chi Ch'ao-ting *Key Economic Areas in Chinese History* George Allen & Unwin, London, 1936, p. 96.

21 Particularly by the CCP, as for example in the title of national minorities' 'Autonomous Regions' – *xiaoshu minzu zizhi diqu*.

22 Allen to Eashington, 7 April 1922, State Department Papers 893.00/4405, quoted in R. A. Kapp *Szechwanese Provincial Militarism and Central Power in Republican China*, p. 46.

23 ibid., p. 44. Fan Ch'ung-shih '1920–2 ti Ssu-chuan chun-fa k'un-shan' from *Chin-tai shih tzu-liao* No. 4 (1962), p. 3.

24 R. Hartshorne 'The functional approach in political geography' in *Annals of the Association of American Geographers* Vol. 40 (1950) p. 110–13.

25 R. A. Kapp *Szechwanese Provincial Militarism and Central Power in Republican China*, p. 78.

26 ibid., p. 116.

27 *Xinan diqu jingji dili* p. 6.

28 J. B. R. Whitney *China; Area, Administration and Nation Building* University of Chicago, Department of Geography, Research Paper No. 123, 1970, pp. 42–3.

29 *Xinan diqu jingji dili*, p. 7.

30 R. A. Kapp *Szechwanese Provincial Militarism and Central Power in Republican China*, p. 5.

31 This typology has been rather loosely adapted from Kapp, *Szechwanese Provincial Militarism and Central Power in Republican China*, p. 6ff.

32 For the history of the incorporation of the Southwestern provinces see Stanford China Project *South West China* Human Relations Area Files Inc., New Haven, 1956, p. 26ff.

33 A. Hosie *Three Years in Western China*, p. 207.

34 A. Hosie *Szechwan; its products, industries, and resources*, p. 15.

35 A. Hosie *Three Years in Western China*, p. 209.

36 ibid., p. 14.

37 *Xinan diqu jingji dili*, p. 57.

38 ibid., p. 22.

39 R. A. Kapp *Szechwanese Provincial Militarism and Central Power in Republican China*, p. 9.

40 A. Hosie *Three Years in Western China*, p. 86.

41 ibid., p. 13.

42 R. A Kapp *Szechwan and the Chinese Republic: Provincial Militarism and Central Power, 1911–1938*.

43 For example, see J. B. R. Whitney *China: Area, Administration and Nation Building*, p. 84 and p. 166/7, who claims that traditional provincial separatism as manifested by warlordism in the 1920s reasserted itself in the second half of the 1950s.

44 R. A. Kapp *Szechwan and the Chinese Republic: Provincial Militarism and Central Power, 1911–1938*, p. 34ff.

45 ibid., p. 43ff.

46 For example, Introduction to Zhang Xiaomei *Guizhou jingji* Southwest Economy Reprint No. 2, Republic of China Economic Research Institute, 1939.

47 A. Hosie *Three Years in Western China*, p. 206.

48 For example, Zhang Xiaomei *Guizhou jingji* op. cit., p. 1; section on Guizhou in *Zhonghua renmin gongheguo fensheng jingtu* 7th edition, Map Publishing House, Shanghai, 1953, n.p.; and speech by Wang Xiaochuan, director Guizhou CCP Propaganda Department in RMRB 23 November 1958.

49 Zhou Lin 'Strive to develop production and change the face of the "mountain land"' in *Xinhua banyuekan* (XHBYK) No. 21, 1956 (General No. 95), p. 178.

50 A. Hosie *Three Years in Western China*, p. 207.

51 *Baron von Richthofen's Letters, 1870–1872* North China Herald, Shanghai, 1873, p. 201.

52 RMRB 23 November 1958.

53 *Xinan diqu jingji dili*, p. 100.

54 G. B. Cressey *Land of the Five Hundred Million* McGraw-Hill, New York, 1955, p. 223.

55 ibid., p. 226.

56 Stanford China Project, *South West China*, p. 174.

57 G. B. Cressey *China's Geographic Foundations* McGraw-Hill, New York, 1934, p. 376.

58 *Xinan diqu jingji dili*, p. 101.

59 ibid., p. 102.

60 Hung-mao Tien *Government and Politics in Kuomintang China 1927–1937* Stanford University Press, 1972, p. 189–94.

61 A. Hosie *Three Years in Western China*, p. 32.

62 *Xinan diqu jingji dili*, p. 101.

63 Stanford China Project *South West China*, p. 26. On the *tu si* system in general see, She Yize *Zhongguo tusi zhidu*, China Publishers, Shanghai, 1947.

64 Fei Xiaotong 'Minority Groups in Guizhou Province' in *Zhongguo yuekan*, Shanghai, December 1951, p. 2.

65 Inez de Beauclair *Tribunal Cultures of South West China* Sun Yatsen University, Taipei, 1970, p. 33.

66 The following outline is taken from *Xinan diqu jingji dili*, p. 101.

67 Fei Xiaotong 'Minority Groups in Guizhou Province', p. 3.

68 ibid., p. 5.

69 ibid., p. 6.

70 *Baron von Richthofen's Letters, 1870–1872*, p. 201.

71 ibid., p. 200.

72 *Xinan diqu jingji dili*, p. 124.

73 F. von Richthofen *Tagebücher aus China*, p. 312.

74 Useful accounts of Guizhou during the 1911 Revolution and the Republican period are to be found in J. E. Spencer 'Kueichou: An internal Chinese colony' in *Pacific Affairs* Vol. 13, No. 2 (1940) pp. 162–72; and Zhang Pengnian 'Guizhou at the time of the 1911 revolution' in *Xinhai geming huiyi lu* China Publishers, Beijing, 1962, Vol. 3, pp. 439–52.

75 Quotation from Zhu De's notes in Agnes Smedley *The Great Road: The Life and Times of Chu Teh* Monthly Review Press, London, 1972, p. 315.

76 He Qiwu *Shinianlai zhi Guizhousheng jianshe* Nanjing Publishing House, Nanjing, 1947.

77 See p. 31.

78 A. Hosie *Three Years in Western China*, p. 207.

79 *Current Background* (CB) US Consulate-General Hong Kong, No. 170, 8 April 1952, 'Pattern of Control: The Regional Organization of Communist China' and No. 245, 25 May 1953, 'Regional Administration in Communist China'.

80 SCRB 1 September 1952 and *Xinhua ribao* (XHRB) Chongqing, 18 November 1952, p. 1 and 4.

81 T. Shabad *China's Changing Map* Praeger, New York, 1972, p. 26.

82 Liao Kai-hung *From Yenan to Peking* Foreign Languages Press, Peking, 1954, p. 108–9.

83 Lo Ruiqing 'The mighty movement for the suppression of counter-revolutionaries' in RMRB 11 October 1951.

84 D. J. Solinger *Regional Government and Political Integration in Southwest China, 1949–1954* University of California Press, Berkeley, 1977, p. 173–80.

85 XHRB 23 November 1952.

86 Radio Chongqing, 23 May 1952.

87 In *Zhengfu gongzuo baogao huibian 1950* Beijing, 1951, p. 991. Rebellion did in fact break out in Kunming led by Li Mi and Yu Chengwan and troops had to be sent from South Guangxi.

88 XHRB 23 October 1952. Report by Yu Jiangzhen, director, Organization Department, Southwest Bureau, CCP.

89 D. J. Solinger estimates that of 180,000 cadres in the Southwest, only 30,000 were party members, whereas approximately a half were former Nationalist-regime personnel. In *Regional Government and Political Integration: the case of Southwest China* Stanford Ph.D., 1975, University Microfilms, Ann Arbor, Michigan, p. 130.

90 XHRB 18 October 1952, 'Southwest Bureau notice on developing and strengthening the work of establishing the Party'.

91 XHRB 22 November 1952, p. 1.

92 XHRB 3 September 1952, p. 2.

93 RMRB 30 June 1954, p. 3.

94 XHRB 13 November 1952, p. 1.

95 XHRB 22 November 1952, p. 1.

96 XHRB 11 August 1954, p. 1.

97 NCNA Chengdu, 22 May 1955, p. 1.

98 *Xinqian ribao* (XQRB) 25 March 1955, p. 1.

99 See Zhang Jichun's speech to the Southwest Bureau's Rural Work Conference, 'On the mutual aid movement in the Southwest', XHRB 18 December 1952, p. 2.

100 Sichuan party membership was 0.71% and Guizhou 1.22% of their provincial populations; the comparative figure for Hebei was 3.18%. See CB, No. 411, 27 September 1956.
101 XHRB 10 May 1952, p. 1.
102 XHRB 28 September 1952, p. 1.
103 *Xinan diqu jingji dili*, p. 14 and p. 102–3.
104 For example, with respect to land reform see XHRB 28 September 1952, p. 1.
105 SCRB 7 January 1953, p. 1.
106 ibid., p. 6 and p. 99.
107 *Xinan diqu jingji dili*, p. 13 and p. 18.
108 ibid., p. 13.
109 ibid., p. 36.
110 Nai-ruenn Chen *Chinese Economic Statistics* Edinburgh University Press, Edinburgh, 1967, p. 361, Table 5.90.
111 *Xinan diqu jingji dili*, p. 33.
112 SCRB 19 January 1955, p. 1 and 3 – 'Report on the conditions of important work in Sichuan province during the last five months, and industrial and agricultural production tasks for 1955'. Report to 2nd Session, 1st Provincial People's Congress.
113 *Xinan diqu jingji dili*, p. 13.
114 See, for example, Chang Yiu-sung '13 years in Chungking' in *China Reconstructs* No. 3, 1952, p. 46.
115 *Xinan diqu jingji dili*, p. 52.
116 See, for example, section on Sichuan in *Zhonghua renmin gongheguo fensheng jingtu* 7th edition, 1953.
117 *Xinan diqu jingji dili*, p. 63.
118 ibid., pp. 66–8.
119 'First trains in Sichuan' in *China Reconstructs* No. 2, 1952, p. 32.
120 'Chungking–Chengtu Railway Completed' in *China Reconstructs* No. 5, 1952, p. 19.
121 *Xinan diqu jingji dili*, p. 105.
122 Radio Beijing, 6 October 1956.
123 *New China News Agency* (NCNA) Guiyang, 26 August 1955.
124 *Xinan diqu jingji dili*, p. 105–6.
125 Zhou Lin, 'Strive to develop production and change the face of the "mountain land"' in XHBYK NO. 21, 1956, p. 178.
126 *Xinan diqu jingji dili*, p. 106.
127 See, for example, Radio Chongqing on agriculture in Guizhou, 21 February 1952.
128 Radio Beijing, 17 October 1953.
129 Radio Beijing, 14 October 1962.
130 *Xinan diqu jingji dili*, pp. 128–9.
131 ibid., p. 106.
132 Stanford China Project *South West China* op. cit., p. 896.
133 Radio Chongqing, 27 February 1952.

2. 1955–7: THE END OF THE SOVIET MODEL

1 R. MacFarquhar *The Origins of the Cultural Revolution*, Vol. I: *Contradictions among the people, 1956–1957* Oxford University Press, London, 1974, is the most detailed

account of the period available, and has been used as a guide to national politics and the divisions within the leadership during 1955–7. The following brief account is thus based on that source. However, as will become apparent, this study differs from MacFarquhar's account on several points of detail, particularly with reference to the actions and attitudes of Sichuan and Guizhou leaders. Three other important sources which have also been used as a guide to this period are S. R. Schram 'The Cultural Revolution in Historical Perspective' in S. R. Schram (ed.) *Authority, Participation and Cultural Changes in China* Cambridge University Press, Cambridge, 1973, especially p. 38–51; H. F. Schurmann *Ideology and Organization in Communist China* op. cit., p. 73ff. and p. 195ff. and R. Solomon *Mao's Revolution and the Chinese Political Culture* University of California Press, Berkeley, 1971, p. 259–329.

2 R. MacFarquhar *The Origins of the Cultural Revolution*, Vol. I: *Contradictions among the people, 1956–1957*, p. 293ff.

3 SCRB 19 January 1955.

4 *Chongqing ribao* (CQRB) 2 December 1955; by Yan Xiufeng, Chairman of the Provincial Planning Committee to the 3rd session of the 1st PPC on 28 November 1955.

5 *Chengdu ribao* (CDRB) 23 August 1957, Li Dazhang's Government Work Report to the 5th session of the 1st PPC.

6 Zhang Huchen '1956 Final Account and 1957 Budget' presented to the 5th session of the 1st PPC, in SCRB 24 August 1957, p. 2.

7 Report of Provincial People's Council 87th Administrative Meeting in SCRB 18 August 1957, p. 2.

8 'The province's cotton producing areas strengthen and expedite cotton shipments in SCRB 3 October 1957, p. 1.

9 NCNA 28 November 1955. See R. MacFarquhar *The Origins of the Cultural Revolution*, Vol. 1, p. 28.

10 SCRB 26 April 1956, p. 1. Report of the 13th meeting of the Provincial People's Council. In his presentation of the 1956 revised plan, Yan Xiufeng pointed out that the original provincial five year plan was now completed. Later statements proved otherwise. For example in SCRB 16 April 1957, p. 3, an editorial stated: 'In 1957 we must ensure the victorious completion of the First Five Year Plan.'

11 CQRB 2 December 1955, in Yan Xiufeng's report on the provincial five year plan, section 2. Yan's report was delivered on 28 November 1955, the same day that other provinces announced similar advancements of their five year plan targets.

12 SCRB 22 November 1956 p. 1, 'Sichuan grain output passes five year plan target'.

13 A notable exception is Zhang Huchen's statement in his budgetary report of 1957 to the PPC that the grain target for 1957 was 47,600 mn *jin* – even higher than the figure revised in late 1955; in SCRB 24 August 1957, p. 3.

14 SCRB 24 August 1957, Zhang Huchen 'Report on Sichuan's 1956 Budget and 1957 Draft Budget', p. 2.

15 See for example, Li Dazhang's Government Work Reports to the 4th (SCRB 23 November 1956, p. 2) and 5th (CDRB 23 August 1957, p. 1) sessions of the 1st PPC.

16 *Xinan diqu jingji dili* Science Publishing House, Beijing, 1960, p. 63ff.

17 SCRB 23 November 1956, p. 2.

18 SCRB 16 October 1956, p. 1, report of the 17th session of the Provincial People's

Council, 15 October 1956. In his Government Work Report of November 1956, Li Dazhang claimed that there was more than 100,000 tons of equipment and daily necessities waiting to be brought into the province.

19 SCRB 24 October 1956, p. 2.

20 SCRB 20 September 1956, p. 1, 'The tense conditions for transporting material resources into Sichuan are about to be moderated'.

21 SCRB 25 September 1956, p. 1.

22 SCRB 27 September 1956, p. 1, 'Material resources brought into Sichuan by Bao-Cheng railway'.

23 According to *Jane's Fighting Ships, 1956*, there were only 18 boats which could possibly have qualified as 'warships': 1 light cruiser, 12 frigates, 3 gunboats, and 2 destroyers.

24 SCRB 28 September 1956, p. 4, 'Two warships fully laden with material resources arrive in Chongqing'. Also articles and pictures in SCRB 5 and 6, October 1956.

25 For a report of one such meeting, in Chongqing, see SCRB 13 October 1956, p. 1. Chongqing's Brick and Tile Plant which had stopped production because there was no oil to drive its generators, was able to obtain 60 tons of unneeded oil from the machine-building factories' system.

26 SCRB 24 August 1957, p. 2, Zhang Huchen 'Report on Sichuan's 1956 Budget and 1957 Draft Budget'.

27 SCRB 21 October 1956, p. 1, editorial 'Fully utilize popular transport capacity'.

28 SCRB 12 October 1956, p. 1.

29 SCRB 18 October 1956, p. 1, 'Strive to make appropriate reforms in agricultural techniques'.

30 SCRB 18 August 1957, p. 2. Editorial 'A large cotton harvest, a faster cotton harvest', reported the failure of the 1956 plan.

31 *Xinan diqu jingji dili*, p. 61.

32 SCRB 23 November 1956, p. 2, Li Dazhang's report to the PPC; the only exceptions were tea and dried tobacco.

33 SCRB 21 September 1956, p. 3, Li Jingquan's speech to the 8th National Party Congress, where he pointed out that the total value of sideline production had fallen by 5–15%.

34 SCRB 10 December 1956, p. 1, editorial, 'Manage State Grain Markets properly'.

35 SCRB 3 December 1956, p. 1, editorial, which stated: 'Procurements have not advanced, but sales have, and there is still much more grain which has not been sold.'

36 SCRB 23 November 1956, Li Dazhang's Government Work Report.

37 ibid., section on commercial work.

38 SCRB 16 October 1956, p. 1, resolution of the Sichuan Provincial People's Council.

39 SCRB 6 October 1950, p. 1.

40 SCRB 4 October 1956, p. 1, 'This province unites to form socialist markets'.

41 SCRB 23 November 1956, p. 2.

42 XHBYK No. 15, 1956 (General no. 89) p. 39. Li Dazhang's speech to the 3rd session of the 1st NPC.

43 SCRB 24 August 1957, Zhang Huchen 'Report on Sichuan's 1956 Budget and 1957 Draft Budget', p. 2.

44 Planning and Statistics Section of Jiangjian *xian*, 'Survey of the present develop-

ment of rural sideline industry' in *Tongji gongzuo tongxun* No. 17 (14 September 1956), p. 28.

45 SCRB 12 October 1956, p. 1; and SCRB 9 March 1957, p. 1.

46 For example, SCRB 12 April 1956, p. 3 article on Neijiang Special District.

47 CQRB 31 July 1956.

48 SCRB 21 September 1956, p. 3.

49 According to F. C. Teiwes 'Provincial Politics in China, Themes and Variations' in J. M. Lindbeck (ed.) *China: Management of a Revolutionary Society* University of Washington Press, Seattle, 1971, p. 118–19, government work reports, as opposed to those delivered to party congresses are almost exclusively confined to discussions of economic and administrative affairs. When political work is discussed it is usually only in the broadest and very general terms, and even then they are concerned with the organization and specific political campaigns, such as those against counter-revolutionaries, rather than with problems of political ideology. This work report is clearly an exception, and indeed there is nothing similar in other available government work reports for either Sichuan or Guizhou.

50 SCRB 23 November 1956, part 4. 'Oppose bureaucratization, improve leadership style'.

51 A cause célèbre in Sichuan during 1956 was the unrestrained growth of the provincial agricultural department. In 1954 the department had one office, eight sections and a total of 124 work personnel; but by the end of 1956 it had grown to two offices, six bureaux, and four sections, with 403 personnel, not including its field agents. At least two of the bureaux had been set up without official permission, and they now each had three to six sections. In 1955 its Grain Crops Section had 18 work personnel; but by 1956 this had become a Grain Crops Bureau, without official sanction, with five sections and 48 people, although its work load had not expanded. SCRB 8 December 1956, p. 1.

52 These were outlined by Li Dazhang in detail later in his 1956 Government Work Report. See n. 49.

53 SCRB 11 December 1956, p. 1. Report of the 2nd plenum of Sichuan party committee.

54 R. MacFarquhar *The Origins of the Cultural Revolution*, Vol. 1, p. 253–5. The CCP directive of 27 April 1957 is in RMRB 1 May 1957, p. 1.

55 MacFarquhar's argument is that lack of positive evidence in the national press is actually negative evidence. However, since it is more than a provincial leader's desire that determines national-level coverage (i.e. who controls the media and their relationship, political and personal, with an individual provincial leader) then it can be argued that the intensity of publicity within the province is at least equally as good an indicator. All four of MacFarquhar's indicators of a pro-Mao stance received considerable publicity in the provincial media. Moreover, there is a simple explanation of the discrepancy between MacFarquhar's finding and this study. His source for Sichuan's attitude to the rectification directive (and all his sources for all provinces) actually pre-dates Sichuan's detailed response. That appeared on 22 May 1957, whereas MacFarquhar's source is dated 10 May 1957 and is a very brief NCNA report of 5 May 1957 (SCMP 1527, p. 26/7) that was not carried by the *Sichuan Daily*.

56 SCRB 22 May 1957, p. 1, 'Sichuan CCP Committee Plenum formulates plan for implementing the party centre's directive on rectification'.

57 SCRB 11 December 1956, p. 1, 'Next year the whole province will unfold an increased production and economy movement'.

58 SCRB 25 October 1957, p. 1, 'On the basis of the decisive victory achieved in the anti-rightists' struggle, the rectification movement in provincial-level organizations enters the important stage of transformation'.

59 SCRB 28 May 1957, p. 1, 'First Provincial Secretary Comrade Li Jingquan & co. go down to the villages to investigate, research, and to participate in manual labour'. SCRB 23 May 1957, p. 2, 'Provincial level leadership comrades participate in manual labour'.

60 For example, Li Jingquan's speech on 22 October 1957, in SCRB 25 October 1957.

61 For example, SCRB 22 August 1957, p. 1, '5th Session of 1st Provincial People's Congress Opens'.

62 *Chongqing gongshang* No. 3, 1 February 1958, p. 7.

63 H. F. Schurmann *Ideology and Organization in Communist China*, University of California Press, Berkeley, 1968, p. 195.

64 CQRB 31 July 1956, p. 1.

65 SCRB 23 November 1956, p. 4.

66 SCRB 24 August 1957, p. 4.

67 SCRB 25 October 1957, p. 1, report of enlarged meeting of Sichuan Party Committee, 15–19 October 1957.

68 Ou Baichuan, a Miao and Vice Governor, was removed during the provincial 'anti-rightists movement' in November 1957, for having conspired to create a 'five province local empire' based on 'local nationalism' (i.e. the national minorities); in GZRB 15 November 1957, p. 3. Later in 1958, when trying to restore harmony between the national minorities and the Chinese in Guizhou, Zhou Lin mentioned that certain cadres had made mistakes in their management of policy towards the national minorities and that their cases had been handled appropriately; in GZRB 25 September 1958. Since both Zhang Song and Zhang Shenru had both been concerned with national minority affairs, and neither appeared in provincial politics after 1958, it is reasonable to infer that they were either the guilty cadres or the sacrificial lambs.

69 F. C. Teiwes 'The Purge of Provincial Leaders, 1957–1958' CQ, no. 27, July 1966.

70 NCNA Guiyang, 28 September 1955.

71 GZRB 15 August 1957, p. 3, in Xu Jiansheng's 'Report on the 1956 Budget and the 1957 Draft Budget'.

72 GZRB 25 September 1958, p. 5 in Xu Jiansheng's 'Report on the 1957 Budget and the 1958 Draft Budget'.

73 *Xinan diqu jingji dili*, p. 4 and p. 106.

74 XQRB 23 November 1955, p. 1.

75 NCNA, Guiyang 26 August 1955, 'Guizhou changes from a grain deficit into a grain surplus area'.

76 GZRB 14 August 1957, p. 1, Zhou Lin's opening address to the 5th session of the 1st PPC.

77 *Zhongguo qingnian* No. 1, 1 January 1960, Zhou Lin 'Construction of Guizhou – "The Mountain Land"', p. 17.

78 GZRB 6 August 1957, p. 1, 'Transport speeded up'.

79 GZRB 4 August 1957, p. 2, 'Our province's river navigation has developed considerably'.

80 NCNA, Guiyang 12 December 1955, 'New passenger coach routes open this year'.

81 GZRB 11 August 1957, p. 2, 'The whole province has established a communications network'.

82 GZRB 29 August 1957, p. 1.

83 *Xinan diqu jingji dili*, p. 106–8. On the other hand the increase in grain output 1955–7 was not inconsiderable at 10%, GZRB 15 August 1957, p. 3. The obsession of Guizhou's leadership with grain output (almost to the exclusion of all else) and the province's dubious statistical procedures are reflected in Zhou Lin's assertion (in his 1958 Government Work Report) that grain output 1955–7 had increased 36.5%; in GZRB 25 September 1958.

84 Zhou Lin 'Strive to develop production and change the face of the "mountain land"' in XHBYK No. 21, 1956 (General No. 95) p. 178.

85 XQRB 21 July 1956, p. 1, 'Urgent notice of Prov. Office for Flood Prevention'.

86 GZRB 14 July 1957, p. 1, Provincial People's Council Directive on helping disaster areas.

87 'Strive to develop production and change the face of the "mountain land"' in XHBYK No. 21, 1956 (General No. 95) p. 178–80.

88 GZRB 15 August 1957, p. 2 in Xu Jiansheng's 'Report on the 1956 Budget and 1957 Draft Budget'.

89 GZRB 25 September 1958, p. 5 in Xu Jiansheng's 'Report on the 1957 Budget and 1958 Draft Budget'.

90 For example, see GZRB 31 January 1957, p. 1, Editorial 'In order to advance'. Interestingly, the main emphasis was on local organization in order to defeat natural disasters. Unlike elsewhere, as for example Sichuan, neither cadres' work-style nor other politico-administrative problems were major concerns of the campaigns to combat economic problems.

91 GZRB 20 February 1957, p. 1. Report of 3rd plenum (enlarged) of Guizhou CCP Committee.

92 XQRB 15 May 1956, p. 1, 'Our province completes the first five year plan target for forestry'.

93 GZRB 8 August 1957, p. 1, 'Our province's most important agricultural products complete the five year plan in four years' (sic).

94 GZRB 31 July 1957, p. 1, 'Help the peasants of the flooded areas solve their difficulties'. The floods affected 20 of the province's 79 *xian*.

95 GZRB 1 June 1957, p. 1. Guizhou party committee directive on the rectification campaign. At this stage rectification was limited to provincial-level organizations and institutes of higher education in Guizhou. As required by the central directive on rectification, a 'small group' had been established to direct rectification. However, neither at that time nor later was either Zhou Lin's leadership of the rectification campaign or his participation in manual labour, publicized through the provincial media. This latter is surprising not least because throughout 1955–7 Guizhou's media relied heavily on national sources and Zhou Lin did receive national-level publicity for both these activities, see RMRB 19 May 1957, p. 4.

96 GZRB 15 August 1957, p. 2; and GZRB 25 September 1958, p. 5.

97 Radio Beijing, 4 January 1956.

98 Radio Beijing, 15 January 1957.

99 See p. 71.
100 GZRB 10 March 1957, p. 1, 'Higher Stage Collectivization is basically realized throughout the province'. Moreover, during collectivization there had been some indication that there were difficulties in national minority areas: 'In the movement for the co-operativization of agriculture, consideration paid to the characteristics of the minority peoples was inadequate' – from NCNA Guiyang 14 August 1956, in SCMP No. 1362, 'Guizhou examines implementation of nationalities policy', p. 19.
101 Several articles in GZRB between 6 and 9 August 1957 dealt with the importance of refuting 'rightist' attacks and stressed the extent of improved conditions, particularly in national minority areas, as a result of collectivization. See also GZRB 6 August 1957, p. 1, 'Qiandongnan Miao-Tong Autonomous *zhou* opens 1st session of Party Congress'; and GZRB 13 August 1957, p. 1, editorial 'Oppose the demons in the villages'.
102 For example: XQRB 11 May 1956, p. 1, Editorial 'The way to deal with counter-revolutionaries'; and GZRB 30 January 1957, p. 1, 'Report on provincial public security department's 14th public security meeting'.
103 See, for example, Zhou Lin's 1958 Government Work Report, part 1, in GZRB 25 September 1958, p. 1.
104 For example, GZRB 30 January 1957, p. 1, 'Provincial Public Security Department holds 14th provincial Public Security meeting'; and GZRB 1 March 1957, p. 1, 'Almost 8,000 provincial cadres go down to the basic level'.
105 RMRB 10 May 1957, p. 4.
106 SCRB 16 April 1957, p. 1, Editorial, 'The democratic life of the new high tide', commentary on a meeting held to discuss 'On the correct handling of contradictions among the people'.
107 GZRB 11 August 1957, p. 1, 'Representatives denounce the absurd statements of the rightists and firmly support the party's leadership along the socialist road', report on preparatory meetings for the PPC.
108 GZRB 25 September 1958, p. 1.
109 For example, GZRB 29 April 1958, p. 1, 'Decision of the 5th plenum of Guizhou CCP Committee on the expulsion of Kang Jian from the Party'.
110 For example, GZRB 15 December 1957, p. 1, 'Report of 36th meeting of provincial people's council on the administrative consequences of the draft provincial agricultural plan'.
111 GZRB 7 December 1957, p. 1. 'Final report to conference of cadres from four levels within the party, "Local Nationalism must be seriously criticized"'.

3 AGRICULTURAL CO-OPERATIVIZATION

1 P. Chang 'Research notes on the changing loci of decision making in the CCP' op. cit., especially p. 173ff.
2 K. Lieberthal *A Research Guide to Central Party and Government Meetings in China 1949–1975* International Arts and Science Press, White Plains, New York, 1976, especially p. 18ff.
3 For example, Mao's speeches 'On the question of agricultural co-operation'', and 'On the ten major relationships' were delivered to two such meetings; 31 July–1 August 1955, and 25–8 April 1956, respectively. For further details see K.

Lieberthal *A Research Guide to Central Party and Government Meetings in China 1949–1975*, p. 72 and pp. 81–2.

4 SCRB 19 October 1956, p. 2 'Neijang Special District realizes higher stage collectivization'.

5 NCNA Guiyang, 14 October 1957, report on Tongshan collective, in SCMP 1640, p. 24.

6 A more detailed discussion of policy implementation and in particular its experimental phase may be found in V. C. Falkenheim 'Provincial Leadership in Fukien: 1949–66' in R. Scalapino (ed.), *Elites in the People's Republic of China* University of Washington Press, London, 1972, pp. 218–22.

7 The model for the commune was the Weixing Joint Co-operative in Henan, which was formed in April 1958. See Wu Zhipu 'From Agricultural Producer Cooperative to People's Commune' in *Hongqi* (HQ) No. 8, 16 September 1958; and H. F. Schurmann *Ideology and Organization in Communist China* University of California Press, Berkeley, 1968, p. 474–478.

8 V. C. Falkenheim *Interview Protocol No. 56* Hong Kong 3 April 1969, Centre for Chinese Documentation, Columbia University.

9 The major sources on agricultural co-operativization and collectivization are: Shi Jingtang et al. (ed.) *Zhongguo nongye hezuohua yundong shiliao* (ZNHYS) 2 vols. Sanlian Shudian, Beijing, 1959; The General Office of the Central Committee of the CCP *Zhongguo nongcun de shehuizhuyi gaochao* 3 vols, People's Publishing House, Beijing, 1956 (a one-volume edited version of which was also published and this appeared in English as *Socialist Upsurge in China's Countryside* Foreign Language Press, Peking, 1957); Chao kuo-chun *Agrarian Policy of the Chinese Communist Party, 1921–59* Asia Publishing House, London, 1960; K. R. Walker 'Collectivization in retrospect: The "Socialist High Tide" of Autumn 1955–Spring 1956', in CQ 26, p. 1; and CB No. 373, 20 January 1956, *Agricultural Co-operativization in Communist China*.

10 P. Chang 'Research notes on the changing loci of decision making in the CCP' CQ 44, pp. 173–6; and *Power and Policy in China* Pennsylvania State University Press, University Park, Pa, 1978, p. 14 and p. 52.

11 H. F. Schurmann *Ideology and Organization in Communist China*, p. 195ff.

12 CB 373, op. cit., p. 9.

13 'Report on the First Five Year Plan for Development of the National Economy of the People's Republic of China in 1953–1957', reprinted in R. R. Bowie and J. K. Fairbank (eds.) *Communist China 1955–1959* Harvard University Press, Cambridge (Mass.), 1965, p. 55. Li Fuchun's speech and report were originally published in RMRB 27 July 1955.

14 *Renmin Shouce 1956*, p. 80.

15 'On the question of agricultural co-operation' has been reprinted as 'On the co-operative transformation of agriculture' in *Selected Works of Mao Tsetung* vol. v (SW5) Foreign Languages Press, Peking, 1977, p. 184–207. Under the previous title it appeared in *Selected Readings from the Works of Mao Tsetung* Foreign Languages Press, Peking, 1971, p. 389–420. References are to *Selected Works*, vol. v; here p. 184.

16 ibid., p. 187.

17 ibid., p. 202–3.

18 CB 373, op. cit., p. 14/15 lists targets by province.

19 *Decision on Agricultural Co-operation* Foreign Languages Press, Peking, 1956, p. 29–30.

20 CB 373, op. cit., pp. 19–20 for provincial targets after the 6th plenum.

21 ibid., pp. 21–4.

22 *1956 nian dao 1967 nian zhongguo nongye fazhan gangyao* (The Twelve Year Plan) People's Publishing House, Beijing, 1956, p. 7, presented to Politburo, 23 January 1956.

23 ZNHYS op. cit., p. 991.

24 K. R. Walker 'Collectivization in retrospect: the "Socialist High Tide" of Autumn 1955–Spring 1956', op. cit., p. 38.

25 Deng Zihui 'The current situation in agricultural co-operativization', 7 May 1956. For a discussion see Chao Kuo-chun *Agrarian Policy of the Chinese Communist Party, 1921–1959* op. cit., p. 159ff.

26 ZNHYS op. cit., p. 1012 and p. 1019.

27 ibid., p. 1011 and p. 1018.

28 K. R. Walker 'Collectivization in retrospect: The "Socialist High Tide" of Autumn 1955–Spring 1956', op. cit., p. 35.

29 Mao Tsetung 'On the cooperative transformation of agriculture' in SW5, p. 190.

30 See articles in ZNHYS op. cit., p. 888 (Sichuan) and p. 892 (Guizhou).

31 NCNA Guiyang, 28 September 1955, '5th representative conference of Guizhou CCP'.

32 For example, XQRB 17 January 1956, p. 3 'We must strengthen our leadership over the socialist high tide in agriculture'.

33 For example, XQRB, 19 May 1956, p. 1, report of enlarged meeting of Guizhou CCP Committee on co-operativization.

34 XQRB 5 June 1956, p. 1, 'Province achieves rich wheat harvest this year'.

35 GZRB 19 February 1957, p. 2, 'An investigation of the basic economic conditions of six higher stage collectives'.

36 NCNA Guiyang 1 September 1955, 'Guizhou has developed 10,000 Agricultural Producers' Cooperatives'.

37 NCNA Guiyang 20 December 1955.

38 NCNA Guiyang 14 August 1956 'Guizhou examines the implementation of policy towards the minority nationalities'.

39 For example, GZRB 16 January 1957, p. 1, Zhou Lin's speech to the 5th Guizhou Congress of Model Workers in Agriculture, Forestry and Water Conservancy.

40 Yang Li 'Advance by running people's communes well' in *Shangyou* No. 4, 1958, p. 18. *Shangyou* was the Sichuan CCP's theoretical monthly started during the Great Leap Forward.

41 Li Dazhang 'The Conditions of Sichuan's Agricultural Co-operativization Movement' in XHBYK No. 15, 1956 (General No. 89) p. 39.

42 Section 4 of his 1956 Government Work Report in SCRB 23 November 1956. His criticisms were echoed by an article in SCRB 9 October 1956, p. 2, 'Why is it that the activism of co-operative cadres is not high?'

43 NCNA Chengdu, 12 September 1956, 'Elevation of Agricultural Producer Cooperatives to Higher Stage Started in Sichuan'.

44 SCRB 24 September 1956, p. 1, report of conference organized by Sichuan Agricultural Work Department.

45 SCRB 3 October 1956, p. 1, 'More than 13,000 higher stage collectives in the

province'.

46 SCRB 19 October 1956, p. 2, 'Neijang realizes higher stage agricultural collectivization'.

47 SCRB 29 September 1956, p. 1, 'Wanxian meeting on advanced co-operatives'.

48 SCRB 1 November 1956, p. 1, 'Increased production for higher stage collectives, more income for members'.

49 SCRB 29 September 1956, p. 1, 'Wanxian meeting on advanced co-operatives'.

50 *Renmin Shouce* 1957, p. 478.

51 SCRB 19 October 1956, p. 2, provincial directive cited in 'Neijiang realizes higher stage agricultural collectivization'.

52 H. F. Schurmann *Ideology and Organization in Communist China*, p. 473ff.

53 ibid., p. 455.

54 Li Dazhang 'The conditions of Sichuan's Agricultural Co-operativization Movement' in XHBYK No. 15, 1956 (General No. 89) p. 40.

55 SCRB 28 November 1956, p. 3, 'Why at present there is generally an inappropriate management of co-operatives'.

56 see p. 144.

57 SCRB 28 November 1956, p. 3, 'Why at present there is generally an inappropriate management of co-operatives'.

58 SCRB 29 September 1956, p. 1, report of Wanxian meeting on collectivization.

59 SCRB 6 December 1956, p. 2, 'Why it is generally inappropriate at present to run *da she*'.

60 SCRB 13 April 1956, p. 2, 'Unite in production to implement *baogong baochan* and make up lost time'. *Baogong baochan* was 'the system of fixed annual responsibility for certain fields and fixed definite output' introduced in 1954, see RMRB 15 May 1955, p. 2.

61 ZNHYS op. cit., p. 999.

62 *Xinan diqu jingji dili* Science Publishing House, Beijing, 1960, p. 15, Map 2, Density of population and cities in Sichuan.

63 SCRB 19 October 1956, p. 2, 'Neijang realizes higher stage agricultural collectivization'.

64 According to SCRB 30 October 1956, p. 1 'More than 13,000 higher stage collectives in the province', the average size of collectives in the province by mid-September 1956 was 212 peasant households. In Neijang Special District there are eight *xian*. If Neijang *xian*'s 24 APCs of April 1956 had not been reorganized there would have been 5,704 HSCs in the other seven *xian* with an estimated average size of 75.9 peasant households each.

65 SCRB 21 November 1956, p. 2, 'Yibin *xian* achieves higher stage collectivization'.

66 For example, SCRB 6 December 1956, p. 2, 'Why it is generally inappropriate at present to run *da she*'.

67 H. F. Schurmann *Ideology and Organization in Communist China*.

68 Mao Tsetung 'On the co-operative transformation of agriculture', in SW5, p. 199–200.

69 *Xinandiqu jingji dili*, p. 7–8.

70 ZNHYS, p. 1018.

71 ibid., p. 998.

72 F. C. Teiwes *Politics and Purges in China* M. E. Sharpe, New York, 1979, p. 349–64.

73 *Twelve Year Plan* op. cit., Article 1, p. 7.

74 *Socialist Upsurge in China's Countryside* op. cit., p. 460.

75 *Twelve Year Plan* op. cit., p. 7.

76 *Mao Zedong sixiang wansui* (1969), Chengdu Speech of 20 March 1958, p. 166; translated in S. Schram (ed.) *Mao Tse-tung Unrehearsed* Penguin, Harmondsworth, 1974, p. 105.

4 DECENTRALIZATION AND NATIONAL POLITICS: 1955–7

1 See, for example: P. Chang *Power and Policy in China*, p. 14–39, and p. 52.

2 P. Chang 'Research Notes on the changing loci of decision making in the CCP' CQ no. 44, p. 175.

3 Reported by Liao Luyan, Minister of Agriculture and Deputy Director of the Rural Work Department of the CCP, in his presentation of the Twelve Year Plan to the Supreme State Conference of 25 January 1956; in *Zhengzhi xuexi* No. 2, 1956, 'An explanation of the 1956–1967 Outline for National Agricultural Development', p. 12. See also Mao Zedong 'Request for opinions on the seventeen-article document concerning agriculture' in SW5, op.cit., p. 277.

4 R. MacFarquhar *The Origins of the Cultural Revolution*, Vol. 1, Part Two, The CCP's Eighth Party Congress, especially p. 126–33.

5 For example, those of 25–28 April 1956 (when Mao talked 'On the ten major relationships'); 4–6 January 1957; and government meetings in China, 1949–1976, International Arts and Science Press, White Plains, New York, 1976, p. 81, p. 91, and p. 98, respectively.

6 R. MacFarquhar *The Origins of the Cultural Revolution*, Vol. 1, p. 329, note 11.

7 Liao Luyan 'An explanation of the 1956–1967 Outline for National Agricultural Development' in *Zhengzhi xuexi* No. 2, 1956, p. 12. This version of the Twelve Year Plan was published as *1956 nian dao 1967 nian quanguo nongye fazhan gangyao (caoan)* People's Publishing House, Beijing, 1956, and includes a summary by Mao, and a subtitle to the effect that it was adopted by the Politburo on 23 January 1956.

8 The revised version of the Twelve Year Plan is reprinted in XHBYK No. 22, 1957, p. 127–32.

9 Chao Kuo-chun *Agrarian Policy of the Chinese Communist Party, 1921–59*, op. cit., p. 159; and R. MacFarquhar *The Origins of The Cultural Revolution*, Vol. 1, p. 90.

10 R. MacFarquhar *The Origins of the Cultural Revolution*, Vol. 1, p. 26ff.

11 ibid., pp. 86–8.

12 H. F. Schurmann *Ideology and Organization in Communist China* University of California Press, Berkeley, 1968, p. 202.

13 *Eighth National Congress of the Communist Party in China* 3 vols., Foreign Languages Press, Peking, 1956, Vol. 1, p. 274.

14 ibid., p. 46.

15 Speeches at the 8th Party Congress are reprinted in XHBYK No. 20 and No. 21, 1956 (General Nos. 94 and 95). The eight who referred to the Twelve Year Plan were from Anhui (XHBYK 20, p. 60), and XHBYK 21, p. 194); Fujian (XHBYK 21, p. 164 and p. 201); Guizhou (XHBYK 21, p. 178); Hunan (XHBYK 21, p. 196); Jiangsu (XHBYK 212, p. 174); and Sichuan (XHBYK 20, p. 52).

16 XHBYK 21, p. 201.

17 GZRB 25 February 1957, p. 1.

18 XHBYK 21, 1956 (General No. 95) p. 178.

19 SCRB 26 October 1956, p. 2 'Experiments with "Sichuan Large Rice" are a success'. It should perhaps be pointed out that the target of 800 *jin* of grain per *mou* was not generally applicable. The Twelve Year Plan explicitly promoted different targets dependent on local conditions.

20 SCRB 7 April 1958, p. 1 'Chairman Mao at Hongguang'. A picture of Mao visiting Hongguang, as well as an article, appears in *Sichuan nongmin ribao* 17 May 1958, p. 1.

21 SCRB 27 December 1958, p. 2 'Jiaotong APC realizes "1,000 *jin* grain, 1,000 *jin* sugar cane" plan'.

22 SCRB 2 January 1957, p. 1 'Natural village higher stage collectivization is basically realized'.

23 XHBYK 15, 1956 (General No. 89) p. 40.

24 SCRB 23 November 1956, p. 2.

25 XHBYK 20, 1956, p. 52; and SCRB 21 September 1956, p. 3.

26 Provincial leaders' speeches to the 8th Party Congress are reprinted in XHBYK 20 and 21, 1956 (General nos. 94 and 95).

27 SCRB 23 November 1956, p. 4.

28 SCRB 16 January 1957, p. 11 'By 1967 the per *mou* output of grain can reach 800 *jin*'.

29 GZRB 6 December 1957, p. 1, report on party congress; also GZRB 25 November 1957, p. 1, 'Guiyang people warmly welcome and discuss agricultural development outline'.

30 GZRB 20 December 1957, p. 1 'The 1956–1967 Draft Outline Plan on Guizhou's Agriculture'.

31 SCRB 16 November 1957, p. 1.

32 SCRB 5 December 1957, p. 1 'Sichuan realizes the concise plan of the 1956–1967 Outline on National Agriculture Development'.

33 SW5, pp. 292–5, Section V – the relationship between the central and the local authorities.

34 NCNA 30 June 1956, 'Premier Chou En-Lai on government work at concluding session of NPC, 30 June', in CB 398, 12 July 1956, p. 9.

35 H. F. Schurmann *Ideology and Organization in Communist China*, p. 176.

36 XHBYK 21, 1956 (General No. 95) p. 68.

37 ibid., p. 183.

38 XHBYK 20, 1956 (General No. 94) p. 64.

39 XHBYK 21, 1956 (General No. 95) p. 198.

40 ibid., p. 201.

41 'Strive to develop production and change the face of the "Mountain Land"' in XHBYK 21, 1956 (General No. 95) p. 178–80.

42 'The uninterrupted improvement of relations between the state and the peasants' in XHBYK 20, 1956 (General No. 94) p. 52–4; and SCRB 21 September 1956, p. 3.

43 According to Liao Luyan (see footnote 2) the first secretary of inner Mongolia participated. A reasonable assumption would be that those first secretaries who attempted to accelerate the implementation of the first five year plan in late November 1955 also participated. In addition to Li Jingquan, they were the first secretaries of Shanxi, Jiangxi, and Shandong. None of these advocated provincial-level decentralization at the 8th party congress.

44 For example, according to R. MacFarquhar *The Origins of the Cultural Revolution*,

Vol. 1, Liu Shaoqi supported Mao on the Twelve Year Plan (p. 125), but not on
rectification (pp. 189–99, especially p. 191).

45 Mao, as early as his speech 'On the cooperative transformation of agriculture' in
SW5, op.cit., had criticized 'some comrades' who 'tottering along like a woman
with bound feet, are complaining all the time, "You're going too fast, much too
fast"', (p. 184) and later 'their idea of moving at a snail's pace' (p. 198).

46 Zhou Enlai in his report on the Second Five Year Plan to the 8th Party Congress (in
Zhongguo gongchandang dibaci quanguo daibiao dahui wenxian, Zhonggong zhongyang
bangongtingbian, 1957) commented that 'In implementing the first five year ...
Our achievements are tremendous but we have also had some defects and errors in
our work' (p. 111) and that '... in certain sectors of the national economy there has
been a tendency to rash advance' (p. 118). Similar expressions and arguments that
the speed of development should be more gradual were articulated by other
speakers at the Congress. For example, see the speeches by Deng Zihui in Foreign
Languages Press, *Eighth National Congress of the Communist Party of China*, Vol. II,
p. 177ff; and Jiang Weiqing, first secretary of Jiangsu, in XHBYK 21, 1956
(General No. 95) p. 174–178. Mao, speaking to provincial leaders in January 1957,
('Talks at a conference of secretaries of provincial, municipal and autonomous
region party committees' in SW5 op.cit.) criticized not only 'defeatism' in general,
but also the accusations of 'rash advance' made during 1956 (p. 351).

47 R. MacFarquhar 'Communist China's Intraparty Dispute' in *Pacific Affaris* Vol.
31, No. 4 (December 1958) p. 325.

48 *Mao Zedong sixiang wansui (1969)*, Mao's speech of 22 March 1958, p. 179. This was
almost an exact repetition of what he had said at the Nanning Conference on 12
January 1958, ibid., p. 151. The former is translated in S. Schram (ed.) *Mao
Tse-tung Unrehearsed* Penguin, Harmondsworth, Middx. 1974, p. 122; the latter in
Miscellany of Mao Tse-tung Thought JPRS No. 61269–1, p. 83.

49 'Be Activists in Promoting the Revolution', in SW5 op.cit., p. 491–2.

50 R. MacFarquhar *The Origins of the Cultural Revolution*, Vol. 1, p. 30 (and n.42)
considers the exegeses of the slogan.

51 SCRB 23 November 1956, p. 2.

52 SCRB 2 December 1956, p. 1 'Iron and Steel, Coal, and Five Systems produce
7,000 tons of material resources in first nine months'.

53 In April, when others were already having second thoughts about the accelerated
speed of development, (see R. MacFarquhar *The Origins of the Cultural Revolution*,
Vol. 1, p. 59ff.) Sichuan published a revised provincial plan for 1956 (SCRB 26
April 1956 p. 1).

54 Li Dazhang's Work Report in SCRB 23 November 1956, section 4, and Li
Jingquan's speech of 22 October 1957, in SCRB 25 October 1957, p. 1 'Provincial-
level organization's rectification movement enters the important transformation
stage on the basis of the decisive victory achieved in the anti-rightist's struggle',
both make it clear that rectification was intended to, and did, start in November
1956. At the national-level a rectification movement had been planned for the
future. Of the national leadership, it was Mao who was impatient to start
rectification earlier rather than later.

55 *Mao Zedong sixiang wansui (1969)*, p. 173; translated in s. Schram (ed.) *Mao Tse-tung
Unrehearsed* op.cit., p. 114.

56 *Renmin Shouce* 1959, p. 32.

57 For example, Li Dazhang in his 1957 provincial government work report stressed '... the peasants of our province have supplied a large quantity of good grains to aid the disaster-stricken areas and the industrial and mining cities', in CDRB 23 August 1957, p. 2. It was reported that during the period of the First Five Year Plan, Sichuan supplied 21 provinces with 14,900 million *jin* of grain, representing an average 7% of its own yield p.a., in Ye.A. Afanas'yeakiy, *Szechwan*, Publishing House of Oriental Literature, Moscow, 1962, translated in *Joint Publications Research Services* (JPRS) No. 15,308, 17 September 1962.

5. 1958–60: THE GREAT LEAP FORWARD

1 The major source on which this account of national-level politics has been based is K. Lieberthal *Research Guide to Central Policy and Government Meetings in China, 1949–1975*, International Arts and Science Press, White Plains, New York, 1976. Other useful sources in whole or in part, which have been consulted include Bill Brugger, *Contemporary China* Croom Helm, London, 1977, p. 149–280; P. Moody *The Politics of the Eighth Central Committee of the Communist Party of China* The Shoe String Press, Connecticut, 1973; F. C. Teiwes *Politics and Purges in China* Dawson, Folkstone, 1979, pp. 333–600; B. Ahn *Chinese Politics and the Cultural Revolution* University of Washington Press, London, 1976, pp. 31–181; S. Schram 'The Cultural Revolution in Historical Perspective' in S. R. Schram (ed.) *Authority, Participation and Cultural Change in China*, Cambridge University Press, Cambridge, 1973, especially p. 51–85; and R. Baum *Prelude to Revolution* Columbia University Press, London, 1975.

2 This study ends with 1965 rather than the Enlarged Politburo Meeting of May 1966, because by then the issues and politics of the GPCR were already beginning to influence the centre-province relationship in new ways outside the scope of this study.

3 See p. 31.

4 'Resolution of the 2nd session of the 8th National Congress of the CCP on the report on the work of the central committee' 23 May 1958, in *Documents of the Chinese Communist Party Central Committee, September 1956–April 1969* 2 vols. Union Research Institute, Hong Kong, 1971, Vol. 1, p. 87.

5 Certainly this was the case in Sichuan and Guizhou. The relevant data for other provinces are not as readily available as during the 'High Tide'. However, the evidence of other studies would seem to confirm those general trends. Cf. for example, E. Vogel *Canton under Communism* Harper & Row, New York, 1969, p. 227–66.

6 Mao Zedong 'Speeches at the Nanning Conference', 11 and 12 January 1958, in *Mao Zedong sixiang wansui (1969)* p. 145–54; and 'Sixty Work Methods' in CB, 21 October 1969, p. 1–14. The former is translated in *Miscellany of Mao Tse-tung Thought* JPRS No. 61269–1, p. 77–84.

7 'Speech at the Supreme State Conference', 28 January 1958, in S. Schram (ed.) *Mao Tse-tung Unrehearsed* Penguin, Harmondsworth, Midx, 1974, p. 91–5.

8 First used in an RMRB editorial on 14 January 1958.

9 Mao Zedong 'Speech at the 6th Plenum of the 8th Central Committee', 19 December 1958, in *Mao Zedong sixiang wansui (1969)*, p. 260; translated in *Miscellany of Mao Tse-tung Thought* JPRS No. 61269–1, p. 141.

10 Liu Shaoqi 'Report on the Work of the Central Committee of the Communist Party of China to the Second Session of the Eighth Party Congress', 5 May 1958 in Bowie and Fairbank (eds.) *Communist China 1955–1959* Harvard University Press, Cambridge (Mass.) 1962, p. 417–38.

11 H. F. Schurmann *Ideology and Organization in Communist China* University of California Press, Berkeley, 1968, pp. 472ff; and K. Walker 'Organization of Agricultural Production', in Eckstein, Galenson and Liu (eds.) *Economic Trends in Communist China* Aldine, Chicago, 1968, pp. 440ff.

12 *Mao Zedong sixiang wansui (1969)*, p. 228.

13 Mao's revised attitude to the GLF comes through clearly in his 'Conversations with the Directors of the Coordinating Regions' November/December 1958 in *Mao Zedong sixiang wansui (1969)*, p. 251–8, where *inter alia* he mentions that he had been over-optimistic at the Beidahe meeting in August. However, he argued that given China's problems and backwardness the strategy of the GLF would work, although it might take longer, and should be persevered with for at least another year. Translated in *Miscellany of Mao Tse-tung Thought* JPRS No. 61269–1, pp. 133–9.

14 'Communiqué of the 6th Plenary Session of the Eighth Central Committee' 17 December 1958, in Bowie and Fairbank (eds.) *Communist China 1955–1959*, p. 483–6.

15 Much has been written about the Lushan Conference and the Mao–Peng divide. Useful accounts are F. C. Teiwes *Politics and Purges in China* Dawson, Folkestone, 1979, Ch. 9, pp. 384–440; and J. D. Simmonds 'P'eng Te-huai: A Chronological Reexamination', in CQ No. 37, p. 120–38.

16 'Communiqué of the 8th Plenary Session of the 8th Central Committee of the CCP' 16 August 1959, in *Documents of Chinese Communist Party Central Committee*, Vol. 1, pp. 51–6.

17 The later slogan first appeared in RMRB on 21 November 1958, p. 2, and it is reasonable to assume that it arose from the discussions leading to the 6th plenum in Wuchang during late November, when a note of caution was first introduced.

18 As far as can be ascertained, the first mention of the Second Five Year Plan after 1957 was in the communiqué of the 8th plenum (cited in n. 16). For example, Liu Shaoqi did not refer to it in his report to the 2nd session of the 8th party congress (cited in no. 10). Although the communiqué of the 8th plenum refers to both the Second Five Year Plan and the slogan of 'catching up with Britain within fifteen years', it is the former which is emphasized. By way of comparison, the communiqué of the 7th plenum (April 1959) in *Documents of Chinese Communist Party Central Committee* op. cit., Vol. 1, pp. 149–50, stresses the GLF but does not mention the Second Five Year Plan.

19 K. Lieberthal *A Research Guide to Central Party and Government Meetings in China, 1949–1975*, pp. 160–1.

20 It should perhaps be emphasized that in the Chinese context 'light industry' refers to agriculture-based or agriculture-supporting industry.

21 23 July 1959 in *The Case of Peng Teh-huai, 1959–1966* Union Research Institute, Hong Kong, 1968, p. 23.

22 The other two provinces were Henan and Hubei. Interestingly, even after 1960, when a rectification campaign against the 'leftist excesses' of the GLF was launched, none of the leading cadres of these three provinces was purged. Li Jingquan remained a politburo member until the GPCR; first provincial party secretary until 1965; and became first secretary of the Southwest Region Bureau

when it was formally established, having previously been the director of the Southwest Co-ordinating Region. Wang Renzhong remained first party secretary of Hubei until the start of the GPCR. Wu Zhipu, famed as the originator of the people's commune, ceased to be Henan's first party secretary in 1960, but he retained his position as provincial governor, and became a secretary of the Central-South Regional Bureau when that was formally established after the 9th plenum in January 1961.

23 P. Moody *The Politics of the Eighth Central Committee of the Communist Party of China,* pp. 136–50.

24 The provincial media were generally reluctant to admit that there was any problem. In his government work reports of both 1959 (SCRB 24 June 1959) and 1960 (SCRB 26 May 1960) Li Dazhang mentioned that (to quote his 1960 report): 'Despite the expansion of production the supply of some commodities has fallen below market demand instead of exceeding it.' However, his emphasis was on the fact that the GLF had increased consumption and demand, rather than causing shortages directly.

25 SCRB 7 May 1958, p. 1. Report of 2nd session of 1st provincial party congress, 11–15 April 1958.

26 SCRB 16 November 1957, p. 1, report of 28th meeting of provincial people's council.

27 Several articles during the first three months of 1958 in SCRB stressed the twelve year plan's early realization. For example, SCRB 17 January 1958, p. 1, 'Use the marching step of the Great Leap Forward to realize and advance the 40 articles by 10 years'.

28 SCRB 29 October 1957, p. 1, 'Every area leaps into a "High Tide" of winter water conservation'.

29 SCRB 5 November 1957, p. 3, 'Implement and realize the draft agricultural development plan'.

30 SCRB 16 November 1957, p. 1.

31 SCRB 28 November 1957, p. 1, 'The all-round development of water conservancy construction projects in Nanchong'.

32 SCRB 26 December 1957, p. 1, editorial 'Decisively organize a great leap forward in agricultural production'.

33 SCRB 5 January 1958, p. 1, editorial 'Overcome conservative ideology, achieve production tasks, strengthen technical leadership'.

34 SCRB 21 January 1958, p. 1, 'Winter production enters a new high tide throughout the province', and Comment, 'Organize a competition to bring forward the realization of the agricultural development outline'.

35 SCRB 15 December 1957, p. 2, 'Irrigation projects completed'.

36 SCRB 26 December 1957, p. 2, 'Realize a Great Leap Forward in agricultural production – make an effort to develop "Two Quarters" rice'.

37 SCRB 3 July 1958, p. 2. Provincial Government Work Report of 26 June 1958.

38 SCRB 22 November 1957, p. 2.

39 NCNA Chengdu 22 November 1957 in SCMP 1666, p. 41.

40 NCNA in English, Peking, 29 January 1958, in SCMP 1705, p. 34.

41 *Xinan diqu jingji dili,* p. 56.

42 SCRB 8 February 1958, p. 2, 'The whole province's handicraft industry actively organizes a leap forward'.

43 As far as can be ascertained that slogan was first used in Sichuan in SCRB 4 December 1957, p. 1, 'Chengdu workers resolve to realize the party's slogan to construct the nation through struggle, diligently and frugally, and to catch up and surpass Britain within 15 years'.

44 SCRB 28 March 1958, p. 1, 'Continue the technical revolution'.

45 SCRB 22 January 1958, p. 2, 'Provincial Coal Industry determines on an advanced plan'.

46 NCNA in English, Chengdu, 23 February 1958, in SCMP 1721, p. 42, 'Szechwan rich in mineral deposits'.

47 SCRB 19 March 1958, p. 1, 'China's largest modernized precision instruments and tools manufacturing plant'.

48 SCRB 19 December 1957, p. 1, 'Communications and Transport Departments realize a new high tide in production'.

49 NCNA, Chungking, 6 February 1958 in SCMP 1716, p. 29.

50 NCNA in English, Chungking, 6 March 1958 in SCMP 1729, p. 29.

51 SCRB 3 July 1958, p. 2. 1958 provincial government work report.

52 SCRB 2 November 1957, p. 1, 'Improve the backward condition of agricultural production in mountain areas'. Report of meeting held on 31 October.

53 SCRB 6 November 1957, p. 3, 'We must generally and firmly create an increased agricultural production new high tide'.

54 SCRB 23 December 1957, p. 1. Report of meeting on 20–1 December.

55 SCRB 18 December 1957, p. 1. Report of Chongqing party committee's 8th enlarged plenum.

56 The most notable victims were Li Chunzheng, the vice chairman of the provincial political and legal office (SCRB 20 January 1958); Xie Wenbing, vice president of Sichuan University; and Ye Shi, Mayor of Chengdu and director of propaganda of Chengdu party committee (CDRB 3 April 1958).

57 SCRB 28 February 1958, p. 1, 'Millions in basic-level units throughout the province enter rectification'.

58 SCRB 18 February 1958 pp. 2–3, 'Use the revolutionary temperament to advance the realization of the 40 articles of the agricultural development outline'.

59 SCRB 25 October 1957, p. 1, Report of Sichuan party committee enlarged plenum, 15–19 October.

60 SCRB 23 December 1957, p. 1.

61 SCRB 22 February 1958, p. 3, 'Provincial-level organs' revolutionary energy overflows'.

62 SCRB 7 May 1958, p. 1, 'Sichuan provincial Communist party holds the second session of its first congress'. The session met from 16–21 April.

63 SCRB 20 May 1958, p. 1, 'Firmly grasp the general line of socialist construction'. This article contains a fuller report of the 2nd session of the 1st provincial party congress than that in the previous note.

64 SCRB 21 March 1958, p. 2, 'How to use the double-wheeled double-bladed plough'. According to this article the plough had been in use in Shuangliu since 1954.

65 Article 3, Point 8; in CB 892, p. 2.

66 Ye. A. Afanas'yeakiy *Szechuan*, p. 98. This emphasis is even more remarkable since Sichuan's agricultural output represented about 12% of China's total during the first five year plan.

67 Zhang Huchen 'The great achievements of fiscal administration in Sichuan during the past decade' in *Caizheng* No. 19, 1959 (General No. 49) 9 October 1959, p. 24.

68 Based on figures taken from SCRB 1 October 1959 and SCRB 5 October 1959, and subject to the same restraints that apply to all statistics during the GLF.

69 Ye. A. Afanas'yeakiy *Szechuan* Publishing House of Oriental Literature, Moscow, 1962 op. cit., p. 114.

70 *Xinan diqu jingji dili* Science Publishing House, Beijing, 1960, p. 52.

71 ibid., Foreword and Introduction.

72 Ye. A Afanas'yeakiy *Szechuan* op. cit., p. 102.

73 'Nanchong region's good effort' in HQ No. 4, 1958, 16 July 1958, pp. 38–41.

74 Zhang Huchen 'The great achievements of fiscal administration in Sichuan during the past decade', p. 24.

75 Po I-po 'China's Economic Plan for 1958' in *People's China* March 1958, p. 8.

76 Li Bin 'Draft 1959 Economic Plan for Sichuan' in SCRB 25 June 1959, p. 2.

77 SCRB 20 September 1959, p. 1, 'Capital Construction in Sichuan'.

78 Li Bin 'Report on the draft national economic plan for Sichuan during 1960' in SCRB 27 May 1960, p. 2.

79 Peking Radio, 22 November 1958.

80 SCRB 21 June 1958, p. 1, 'Look! Weiyuan produces steel!'

81 SCRB 21 November 1959, p. 1, 'Second Bridge over Changjiang completed'.

82 SCRB 20 May 1958, p. 1, 'Firmly grasp the General Line of Socialist Construction'.

83 SCRB 24 June 1959, p. 2, Li Dazhang's provincial government work report.

84 Sichuan Radio, 26 September 1973. By 1973 it was said that the Twelve Year Plan had only been completed in 28 of the province's *xian*.

85 SCRB 24 June 1959, p. 2. Li Dazhang's 1959 provincial government work report. Comparing the revised figures for output in 1958 with those for 1957's output, it would appear that the disparity was even greater. Based on the figures in Table 5, steel output only rose 4% and coal 76%; on the other hand grain output rose 40% and cotton 63%.

86 See Table 5.

87 SCRB 25 June 1959, p. 2. Li Bin's report on the draft 1959 economic plan for Sichuan.

88 SCRB 27 May 1960, p. 2. Li Bin's report on the draft 1960 economic plan for Sichuan; and p. 3 Zhang Huchen's report on the final budget for 1959 and the draft budget for 1960 in Sichuan.

89 Zhang Huchen 'The great achievements of fiscal administration in Sichuan during the past decade' in *Cai Zheng (Financial Administration)* No. 19, 9 Oct. 1959, p. 24.

90 SCRB 13 September 1958, p. 1, 'Start a Communist Education and Propaganda Movement'.

91 Criticisms were first voiced at the Zhengzhou Conference of 2–10 November 1958. See K. Lieberthal, *A Research guide to central party and government meetings in China, 1949–1975*, pp. 123–4.

92 SCRB 4 March 1960, p. 2.

93 SCRB 26 May 1960, p. 3.

94 SCRB 20 August 1958, p. 1, 'The whole province's theoretical work looks completely different'.

95 'Educate the new generation with Mao Zedong Thought' in *Zhongguo qingnian bao*

p. 1, 22 December 1960; and SCRB 30 October 1960, p. 1, 'Advance under the fluttering banner of Mao Zedong Thought'.

96 SCRB 1 February 1960, p. 1, Editorial 'Create an upsurge in the movement to study Mao Zedong Thought'.

97 Wu Li 'It is necessary to place politics in command of labour training' in SCRB 27 January 1960, p. 2.

98 SCRB 6 December 1960, p. 1, 'Sichuan's cadres transferred downwards create great achievements'.

99 SCRB 22 January 1960, p. 1, 'Greet the Sichuan provincial congress of militiamen'.

100 SCRB 1 July 1959, p. 1. Editorial on Party Day.

101 SCRB 1 July 1960, p. 1. Editorial on Party Day.

102 The estimate is based on CQRB's editorial on party day, 1960. This stated that the Chongqing party membership was 125,000 and that its 11,000 new recruits represented 10% of provincial recruits over the same period (the first half of 1960). The estimate is based on the assumption that Chongqing's party membership is approximately 10% of the province's and that Sichuan's population in 1960 was 68 million.

103 SCRB 16 September 1960, p. 1. Report of conference of 15 September.

104 GZRB 6 December 1957, p. 1.

105 Several areas were publicized for their achievement of the generalized targets of the twelve year plan, for example, Zhengan *xian* in GZRB 14 December 1957, p. 1, '*Xiang* and APCs in advance of the targets of the Agricultural Development Outline'. Similarly, the 2nd session of the 1st Guiyang city party congress called for a new 'high tide' in production in GZRB 23 December 1957, p. 1.

106 GZRB 24 December 1957, p. 1 'Strive to develop local industry to support agricultural advance'. The meeting was held from 10–23 December.

107 GZRB 31 January 1958, p. 1, 'Our province decides to increase water conservation constructions tasks'.

108 GZRB 3 January 1958, p. 2, 'Propagandize to advance the speed of the "high tide" in industrial production'.

109 GZRB 14 January 1958, p. 1. It was claimed that since the turn of the year the construction of new plants or mines had been started daily.

110 GZRB 5 January 1958, p. 1. Report of provincial meeting of 1000 about to *xiafang* cadres.

111 GZRB 17 January 1958, p. 1, 'Give a good send-off to the pioneering cadres and specialists going "up to the mountains"'.

112 GZRB 16 February 1958, p. 1, 'Guizhou party committee indicates the all-round aims of struggle in the Great Leap Forward'.

113 See Table 8.

114 GZRB 6 March 1958, p. 1, 'Advance the socialist education movement'.

115 GZRB 23 May 1958, p. 1, 'An inspection army of 600,000 is formed'.

116 GZRB 25 September 1958, p. 2. Zhou Lin's provincial government work report.

117 RMRB 23 November 1958, p. 5, Wang Xiaochuan 'Guizhou province shows that changes in man determine changes in the world'. Interestingly, and a clear indicator of the confusion that must have existed even within Guizhou's leadership during the GLF, Zhou Lin had an article in the same issue of *People's Daily* in which he repeated his claim that the irrigated area was only 9 million *mou*.

118 GZRB 25 September 1958, p. 2. Zhou Lin's provincial government work report.
119 ibid.
120 GZRB 11 June 1958, p. 1, 'Develop the campaign to eliminate the "Four Pests"'.
121 GZRB 25 September 1958, p. 2.
122 GZRB 30 September 1959, p. 3. Report on the work of the Guizhou Higher People's Court.
123 GZRB 15 January 1960, p. 1, 'Peasants study theory: ideology liberates greatly'.
124 GZRB 4 July 1960, p. 1. Editorial 'Carry out well the work of granting full membership to candidate party members'.
125 GZRB 23 February 1960, p. 1. Report of Militia Work Conference held 15–21 February.
126 GZRB 27 January 1960, p. 1. Jiang He and Sun Zhengshi 'More than 75,000 cadres return to the office after participating in physical labour in factories and communes'.
127 GZRB 9 April 1960, p. 1, 'Cadres go to the front line of production'.
128 GZRB 12 September 1958, p. 1, 'Cultural revolution's great victory'.
129 GZRB 7 January 1958, p. 2. Report of provincial education work conference.
130 D. Lampton 'Performance and the Chinese Political System: A preliminary assessment of education and health policies' in CQ No. 75, p. 518 and 521.
131 Radio Beijing, 4 February 1958.
132 GZRB 25 September 1958, p. 2. Provincial government work report.
133 Zhou Lin 'Construction of Guizhou – the Mountain Land' *Zhongguo qingnian* No. 1, 1960, p. 18. As might be expected, higher education was at an even lower level. Guizhou University only started to take students in 1958. By 1960 there were 15 institutes of higher education in Guizhou with a total enrolment of 3,365 students; GZRB 26 June 1960, p. 1, 'Regulations on enrolment of new students in higher education institutes, Summer 1960'.
134 GZRB 12 September 1958, p. 1, 'Cultural Revolution's great victory'.
135 Jen Hai 'Report from Kweichow: New Life in a Hill Region', in *Peking Review* No. 43, 1960 (25 October 1960), p. 16. The original article from which this report is taken appeared in *Zhongguo qingnian* No. 16, 16 August 1960, and concerns Changshi Commune.
136 RMRB 23 November 1958, p. 5, 'Guizhou province shows that changes in man determine changes in the world'.
137 GZRB 4 May 1960, p. 1, 'Premier Zhou inspects the Guiyang Iron and Steel Works'.
138 GZRB 3 October 1959, p. 2, Zhang Ping 'Report on the provincial 1958 budget and draft budget for 1959'.
139 GZRB 24 April 1959, p. 1, 'Coal production leaps forward'.
140 GZRB 21 August 1959, p. 1; and GZRB 7 February 1959, p. 1; on the Sichuan–Guizhou railway and the Guangxi–Guizhou–Yunnan railway respectively. Work started on both in 1958.
141 GZRB 4 January 1960, p. 1, 'Guiyang Iron and Steel Plant Opens'. Construction started in April 1958, and the first phase was completed at the end of 1959.
142 GZRB 19 April 1958, p. 1. Construction started 17 April and was scheduled for completion in 1961.

143 GZRB 3 July 1958, p. 1. Report of 41st meeting of provincial people's council.

144 GZRB 8 July 1958, p. 1, 'Guizhou welcomes builders from outside areas to help this province build industry'.

145 GZRB 22 August 1959, p. 1, 'The whole province's Great Leap Forward increases daily'.

146 GZRB 5 May 1958, p. 1. Report of provincial planning committee.

147 See Table 8.

148 RMRB 23 November 1958, p. 5.

149 See Table 8.

150 GZRB 4 January 1960, p. 1, 'Guiyang Iron and Steel Plant Opens'.

151 GZRB 9 January 1959, p. 1. Report of 8th plenum of Guizhou Provincial Party Committee.

152 See Table 8.

153 Zhou Lin 'Construction of Guizhou – the Mountain Land' in *Zhongguo qingnian* No. 1, 1960, p. 17.

154 GZRB 30 September 1959, p. 2.

155 GZRB 8 October 1959, p. 1.

156 GZRB 6 January 1960, p. 1, 'Agricultural Production in 1959 and tasks for 1960'.

157 GZRB 12 December 1960, p. 2. Provincial Government Work Report, delivered by Chen Puru.

158 SCRB 14 March 1958, p. 1, 'Longanshi oil prospecting area'.

159 SCRB 16 March 1958, p. 1, 'Central Sichuan is our country's new oil-field' and SCRB 18 March 1958, p. 1, 'Third victory message of Central Sichuan Oil prospecting field'.

160 SCRB 16 March 1958, p. 1, 'Central Sichuan is our country's new oil-field'.

161 SCRB 30 March 1958, p. 1, 'Central Sichuan's Oil-field's 4th Victory Message'; and SCRB 31 March 1958, p. 1, 'Central Sichuan Oil-field constructs oil-refineries'.

162 NCNA in English, Yunan, 4 April 1958, 'Oil Specialists to help Szechuan', in SCMP 1749, p. 28.

163 SCRB 16 April 1958, p. 1, 'Refineries for new oil field in Nanchong'.

164 SCRB 4 June 1958, p. 1, 'Sichuan's Petroleum Industry'.

165 SCRB 3 July 1958, p. 1, 'More oil gushers in Central Sichuan oilfield'.

166 GZRB 14 August 1959, p. 1.

167 GZRB 30 September 1959, p. 3.

168 GZRB 8 April 1960, p. 2.

169 Zhou Lin 'Struggle between the new and old forces in the Great Leap Forward' in RMRB 31 December 1959.

170 For example, Zhou Fulin 'Refute the absurd conclusion that the Great Leap Forward is the cause of market tension', in *Sichuan daxue xuebao: shehui kexue* No. 5, 1959, p. 3; and Yang Kejiang 'Refute the right opportunist elements' foul slanders that "the communes were set up too early and too fast and are in a mess"', in *Sichuan daxue xuebao: shehui kexue* No. 4, 1959, p. 19.

171 Chen Puru, Guizhou provincial government work report in GZRB 12 December 1960, pp. 1–3.

172 Li Dazhang, Sichuan provincial government work report in SCRB 24 May 1960, pp. 2–3.

6. 1961–5: THE PRELUDE TO THE CULTURAL REVOLUTION

1 Chou En-lai 'Government Work Report' delivered to the 1st session of the 3rd NPC, 21 and 22 December 1964, in *Peking Review* No. 1, 1965, p. 7.

2 For example, on Guizhou see RMRB 16 December 1965, 'Southwest China province casts off traditional poverty' in SCMP 3602, p. 18 that states: 'Traditionally considered one of the poorest provinces in China ... [Guizhou] has taken considerable giant strides in the past 16 years.'

3 R. Baum and F. C. Teiwes *Ssu-Ch'ing: The Socialist Education Movement of 1962–1966* University of California Centre for Chinese Studies, Berkeley, 1968.

4 At a central work conference in December 1964, Mao criticized several provinces for being either 'rotten' or 'leftist'. These were Anhui, Qinghai, Guizhou, Gansu, Yunnan, and Henan; in *Mao Zedong sixiang wansui (1969)*, p. 583; translated in *Miscellany of Mao Tse-tung Thought* JPRS No. 61269–2, p. 412.

5 K. Lieberthal *Research Guide to Central Party and Government Meetings in China 1949–1966* International Arts and Science Press, White Plains, New York, 1976, pp. 160–1 and 175–7.

6 'Communiqué of the 9th Plenary Session of the CCP 8th Central Committee' 14–18 January 1961, in *Documents of Chinese Communist Party Central Committee 1956–1969* 2 vols. Union Research Institute, Hongkong, 1971, p. 173–8.

7 K. Lieberthal *Research Guide to Central Party and Government Meetings in China 1949–1975* op.cit., pp. 171–2.

8 ibid., pp. 179–81. For Mao's speech see S. Schram (ed.) *Mao Tse-tung Unrehearsed* Penguin, Harmondsworth, Middx., 1974, especially pp. 182–7 in the context of the contemporary debate.

9 'Communiqué of the 10th Plenary Session of the CCP 8th Central Committee' 24–7 September 1962, in *Documents of Chinese Communist Party Central Committee 1956–1969*, pp. 185–92.

10 R. Baum *Prelude to Revolution* Columbia University Press, London, 1975, pp. 11ff.

11 In *Mao Zedong sixiang wansui (1969)* op.cit., p. 430–436; translated in S. Schram *Mao Tse-tung Unrehearsed* op.cit., p. 188–196.

12 R. Baum *Prelude to Revolution* details the development of the Socialist Education Movement. On the drastic transformation wrought by Mao's 'Twenty-three points' see especially p. 127ff.

13 F. C. Teiwes *Politics and Purges in China* Dawson, Folkestone, 1979, pp. 572–600.

14 L. W. Snow *China on Stage* Random House, New York, 1972, p. 21.

15 Using sources emanating from the GPCR is obviously a process fraught with problems. Here and throughout, the rule of thumb employed in dealing with such sources is that all interpretable information has been regarded sceptically and factual information only accepted when there is consistency among the differing accounts from separate sources.

16 V. Nee *The Cultural Revolution at Peking University* Monthly Review Press, New York, 1969, especially pp. 49ff.

17 J. Gray and P. Cavendish *Chinese Communism in Crisis* Praeger, London, 1968, especially pp. 81ff; and J. R. Pusey *Wu Han: Attacking the Present through the Past* East Asian Research Centre, Harvard University, Cambridge (Mass.) 1969.

18 SCRB 5 July 1961, p. 1. 'The provincial coal industry department brings forward and completes the first half of the year's capital construction plan'.

19 SCRB 2 August 1961, p. 1, provides both the text of the party committee's directive and Li Dazhang's speech of 29 July.

20 SCRB 1 August 1961, p. 3. Huang Xinting 'Develop our army's glorious tradition of bitter struggle, unity with the people and the government'.

21 SCRB 7 August 1961, p. 1. 'Industrial production's priority is to supply the villages'.

22 For example, SCRB 24 September 1961, p. 1. Editorial 'Actively increase production of light material goods to supply the villages'; SCRB 18 September 1961, p. 1, 'Regard grain as the key link and actively develop the production of oil-bearing crops'; and SCRB 9 October 1961, p. 1, 'Li Dazhang's speech to the provincial people's council on the autumn harvest and rural sideline industry.'

23 SCRB 29 August 1961, p. 3. 'PLA units stationed in this province are prominent in resisting disaster and aiding production'.

24 SCRB 15 September 1961, p. 1. 'The provincial public security department is prominent in raising pigs and growing vegetables'.

25 SCRB 11 October 1961. Report of the meeting of 10 October, p. 1. Full text of speech, p. 3.

26 SCRB 2 September 1961, p. 1. 'Production brigades strengthen leadership all round – procurement work is "More, faster, better and more economical"'.

27 SCRB 19 August 1962, p. 1, 'Provincial handicraft industry advances "More, faster, better, and more economical"'. That is in the period before the 10th plenum. The slogan was only out of use provincially during 1963. By 1964, its usage was well-established once again; as for example, *Chengdu wanbao* 17 April 1964, p. 1 'Sizhou factory develops the progressive experience of "More, faster, better and more economical"'.

28 *Da gong bao* Beijing, 23 April 1960, p. 2.

29 For example SCRB 28 July 1962, p. 1. Report of the 28th meeting of provincial people's council.

30 On the 1961 and 1962 'Patriotic grain procurement campaigns' see SCRB 30 August 1961, p. 1 and SCRB 20 January 1963, p. 1, respectively. The same concern was reflected in the 1963 grain procurement campaign (SCRB 13 November 1961, p. 1) and Li Dazhang's reports to the several meetings of the PPC.

31 Chou En-lai 'Government Work Report', 21 and 22 December 1964, p. 7.

32 Li Dazhang's provincial government work reports for 1959 and 1960 in SCRB 24 June 1959 and SCRB 26 May 1960.

33 RMRB 12 September 1963, p. 2, '1st session of 3rd Sichuan Provincial People's Congress'.

34 SCRB 14 August 1962, p. 3. Party life No. 2 – 'Correctly treat majorities and minorities'.

35 Beijing Home Service Radio Broadcast, 9 April 1962. 60 of the province's *xian* centring on Leshan, Mianyang, Jiangjin, Yaan and Neijang, were affected by the drought.

36 SCRB 20 January 1962, p. 1. 'The province completes its 1962 grain procurement target'.

37 SCRB 12 January 1962, p. 1. 'Wanxian has repeatedly completed its grain transfer targets every year of the last twelve'.

38 SCRB 17 April 1964, p. 1, 'Our province's victory in successfully completing the sugar-cane cultivation plan'.

39 *Xinan diqu jingji dili*, Science Publishing House, Beijing, 1960, p. 38.
40 The figure of rice output in 1965 is an estimate based on figures broadcast in 1966 when it was claimed that output had risen 1.5 million tons in 1966 over 1965 (Sichuan Radio, 6 December 1966) and by 10% for the same period (Sichuan Radio, 14 December 1966). The figures for 1957 can be found in *Xinan diqu jingji dili*, p. 18.
41 SCRB 2 August 1961, p. 1. Provincial party committee directive of 30 July.
42 For examples see SCRB 1 December 1961, p. 1. 'Unified regulation and distribution of material resources speeds production'; SCRB 21 August 1962, p. 2, 'Liangzhong opens a material resources exchange conference'; and SCRB 20 October 1963, p. 2, 'Our province pursues the holding of "3-kinds-material resources" exchange meetings'.
43 'Local transport networks – "walking on two legs",' in *Peking Review* No. 45, 1961 (10 November 1961), p. 11.
44 SCRB 22 February 1963, p. 1. Article on work of provincial communications department.
45 SCRB 21 November 1963, p. 2. 'The price of the chemical industry's products in the province has fallen'.
46 For example, Fei Hongzhuan 'Vehement denunciation of the anti-party, anti-socialist, and anti-Mao Zedong Thought crimes of the counter-revolutionary revisionist Li Jingquan', broadcast by Sichuan Radio 6 September 1967, claimed *inter alia*: 'In agriculture Li agitated for a policy of "going-it alone" to sabotage the socialist collective economy. He advocated ... the setting of production quotas for individual households; and disbanded production teams.'
47 SCRB 10 March 1963, p. 1, 'The province's 63 key-point cotton and grain *xian* hurry to complete ploughing'.
48 SCRB 13 November 1963, p. 1, 'Our province brings forward and surpasses the grain procurement target for the whole year'.
49 For example, SCRB 3 February 1964, p. 1. Editorial 'Do a good job of all-round agricultural production'.
50 For example, SCRB 20 November 1963, p. 1, Editorial 'Industry has a glorious task to support the technical transformation of agriculture'; and Sichuan Radio, 27 October 1965, which reported that 18 medium and small-scale hydro-electric power stations were built between 1963 and 1965 on the Fujiang river, with a combined capacity of 12,000 kws, able to irrigate 33,000 hectares.
51 After the original experimental units at Xibu Commune, founded in 1963, (NCNA in English, Chengdu, 4 February 1966 in SCMP 3634, p. 16) and Huohua Commune, founded in 1964, Political and Technical Advancement Centres were established at a further 140 communes during 1964 and 1965 (Peking Radio, 24 July 1965).
52 Sichuan Radio, 19 November 1967, Agricultural and Forestry Political Department and office of the former Sichuan provincial CCP committee, 'The "Political and Technical Advancement Centre" is a test for restoring capitalism'.
53 Peking Radio NCNA International Service (in English), 24 July 1965, 'Szechwan Commune establishes "Political and Technical Advancement Centre"'.
54 SCRB 8 December 1963, p. 1. 'The province's No. 1 hydro-electric rural construction project at Luosi dam'.
55 Fei Hongzhuan, 'Vehement denunciation ... of Li Jingquan'.

56 NCNA, Chengdu 27 February 1966, 'Sichuan makes further farming gains by eliminating complacency', in JPRS 36342, p. 8.

57 Sichuan Radio, 15 April 1965.

58 For example, SCRB 6 November 1961, p. 1, 'Unfold socialist education and increase production'.

59 In general, this account of the Socialist Education Movement in Sichuan uses R. Baum *Prelude to Revolution* as its guide to the national development of the movement. The 'First Ten Points' were adopted in May 1963. The 'First Ten Points', the 'Second Ten Points' and the 'Revised Second Ten Points', are often referred to as the 'Early Ten Points', the 'Later Ten Points', and the 'Revised Later Ten Points', respectively. This account follows Baum in using the former terminology.

60 For example, SCRB 14 August 1962, p. 3, 'Have a close relationship with the masses and serve the people totally – that is a CCP member's natural duty'.

61 This is really no surprise. If Sichuan's leaders had implemented all the directives of the Socialist Education Movement from 1962 on in detail at every stage of its development, they would have achieved what probably no other provincial leadership did. In general, as previously indicated, however, one interprets the years 1961–5, provincial leaders were almost certainly somewhere along the way bound to be out of line.

62 For an example of that claim, see Zhang Xiting 'Vehement denunciation of Li Jingquan's outrageous crimes' in Guizhou Radio broadcast of 23 June 1967. Zhang, together with her husband, Liu Jieting, Yan He, Wang Maoqu and Guo Lichuan, had formed the secretariat of the Ibin party committee removed in 1962. According to their account given during the GPCR they had earlier defended the GLF and Mao against Li Jingquan and been removed to a psychiatric hospital for their pains. Unsurprisingly, they were the first local cadres in Sichuan to respond to Mao's call 'To rebel is justified' at the start of the GPCR. As of July 1978, Zhang and her husband had been returned to psychiatric care after a public denunciation (Associated Press Tokyo, 28 July 1978).

63 R. Baum *Prelude to Revolution*, especially pp. 21ff. and Ch. 3, pp. 63ff. For Baum, the turning point in the evolution of the Socialist Education Movement towards the GPCR came with the 'Dazhai Affair', pp. 117ff.

64 ibid., pp. 24–7.

65 SCRB 6 May 1962, p. 1, 'Thoroughly help production team cadres to raise their leadership level'.

66 SCRB 22 March 1963, p. 2, 'Place the work of production teams under mass control and supervision'.

67 See for example, SCRB 27 March 1963, p. 1, 'Depend on the poor and lower-middle peasants'.

68 SCRB 1 April 1963, p. 1, 'Poor and lower-middle peasant conferences held throughout the province'. The model for such conferences was that held in Fuling.

69 For example SCRB 4 April 1963, p. 1, 'Fully rely on poor and lower-middle peasants to strengthen production team management'.

70 SCRB 5 June 1963, p. 1. Article with same title. See also, SCRB 18 March 1963, p. 1, 'Cadres go deep down to lead spring ploughing production'.

71 For example, SCRB 25 May 1963, p. 1, 'Cadres should participate in production: the form of the leadership production system'.

72 See for example, SCRB 24 July 1962, p. 3 and SCRB 25 July 1962, p. 3, 'From Zunyi to the Huanghe'.

73 For example, SCRB 21 July 1963, p. 1, 'The masses enter the "Three histories" and raise their consciousness to greet the new socialism'.

74 R. Baum *Prelude to Revolution*, pp. 43ff.

75 ibid., pp. 46–8.

76 Fei Hongzhuan, 'Vehement denunciation ... of Li Jingquan'.

77 R. Baum *Prelude to Revolution*, p. 45.

78 ibid., p. 68.

79 SCRB 14 January 1963, p. 1, 'Production Brigades choose "Five-Good" Commune Members monthly'.

80 For example, SCRB 12 June 1963, p. 1, 'Strive hard to study Chairman Mao's works: make oneself a soldier in the fight for the proletarian line'. See also, SCRB 20 June 1963, p. 3, 'Major points in the history of class struggle'.

81 SCRB 12 July 1963, p. 1, 'Use class and class struggle to educate as a principle', includes a report of the provincial party committee's decision to establish work teams to implement the Socialist Education Movement.

82 For example SCRB 15 April 1964, p. 3, 'The history of poor peasant Wang Qiuying's family' which was contrasted with 'The history of despotic landlord Chen Yongqi's family'.

83 For example, Sichuan Radio, broadcast of 19 October 1964, reported the speeches of delegates to the 2nd session of the 3rd PPC concerning the Socialist Education Movement. All placed the importance of the class struggle between the 'two lines' first in their discussions of their own experiences.

84 SCRB 16 April 1964, p. 3, 'Investigate and analyse the "2–5 plan" leadership methods'.

85 NCNA in English, Chengdu, 20 February 1965, 'Cadres in Sichuan persist in manual work' in SCMP 3404, p. 18.

86 As for example in Guangdong. See E. Vogel *Canton under Communism* Harper & Row, New York, 1971, pp. 302–20.

87 Sichuan Radio, 2 May 1964, 'Report of the 6th session of the Sichuan provincial people's council.'

88 Beijing Home Service broadcast 9 October 1964 reported that a further 4,000 educated youth from Chengdu had settled in Liangshan and Xichang special districts in western Sichuan.

89 Yang Chao 'A new thing' in *Red Flag* No. 2, 1965 (27 February 1965), p. 25.

90 SCRB 23 May 1962, p. 1, 'Provincial literary and art workers launch a movement to commemorate the 20th anniversary of the publication of Chairman Mao's "Talks at the Yanan Forum on literature and art"'; and p. 4, 'Art and literature serve workers, peasants and soldiers'.

91 For example, SCRB 14 November 1963, p. 3, 'A talk on how Sichuan Opera demonstrates problems of modern drama'.

92 *Sichuan wenxue* No. 7, 1963, p. 71. Guan Jian 'Some opinions on drama reflecting contemporary life'.

93 *Sichuan wenxue* No. 10, 1964, p. 45, Editorial 'Thoroughly revolutionize Sichuan opera'. This is an excellent example of the provisional leadership's 'no win' position. They could follow Jiang Qing's direction before 1966 and still end up being criticized for 'putting locality before nation'.

94 Beijing Home Service, 11 November 1965, 'Sichuan Art display portrays class struggle'.

95 Sichuan Radio, 9 September 1963.

96 NCNA Chengdu, 23 October 1964, in SCMP 3331, p. 1.

97 Sichuan Radio, 25 November 1965.

98 Sichuan Radio, 5 December 1965.

99 Sichuan Radio, 14 October 1965. The Conference met 9–20 September.

100 Sichuan Radio, 30 August 1965. Report to a meeting of Representatives of Activists in Studying Mao's Work. The meeting was also addressed by Li Dazhang and Liao Zhigao.

101 NCNA Guiyang, 17 October 1964.

102 At a central work conference when outlining the 'Twenty-three points' of the Socialist Education Movement; in *Mao Zedong sixing wansui (1969)* op.cit., p. 583; translated in *Miscellany of Mao Tse-tung Thought* JPRS No. 61269–2, p. 412.

103 The only provinces condemned by Mao and where provincial leaders were removed (a major emphasis of the 'Twenty-three Points') were in the Southwest, namely Guizhou and Yunnan. This phenomenon will be discussed in Chapter 9.

104 NCNA in English, Guiyang, 25 June 1963.

105 United States Consulate-General Hong Kong, *Agricultural Report on Mainland China* Hong Kong, 1967, n.p. According to Zhou Lin in *Zhongguo qingnian* No. 1, 1960, p. 18, 'Construction of Guizhou – the mountain land': 'there is abundant rainfall in Guizhou; the annual average is more than 1,000 millimetres. The many mountains and abundant rainfall give Guizhou a plentiful water supply.' Moreover, in RMRB 12 December 1965, p. 1, 'A visit to Guizhou Province', it was reported that the province had 'only suffered two natural disasters in the last sixteen years'.

106 Guizhou Radio, 28 November 1965.

107 NCNA, Guiyang, 26 August 1963.

108 Guizhou Radio, 20 September 1964.

109 *Xinan diqu jingji dili*, p. 110.

110 Guizhou Radio, 28 November 1965.

111 *Xinan diqu jingji dili*, p. 106.

112 Beijing Radio International Service, 23 October 1963.

113 Beijing Radio, 26 March 1961. It also seems likely that those who *xiafang* were peasants who had drifted townwards during the GLF.

114 For example, Guizhou Radio, 16 June 1967, Wu Xingwu 'A look at the wolfish ambition of Jia Qiyun to restore capitalism in the countryside'.

115 GZRB 24 June 1959, p. 1, 'Arrange production and organize the supply of goods'.

116 NCNA Guiyang, 28 February 1962 in SCMP 2691, p. 22.

117 Guizhou Radio, 4 September 1965.

118 RMRB 12 December 1965, pp. 1–2, 'A Visit to Guizhou province'.

119 Guizhou Radio, 19 December 1967, Wang Dezhou 'Always Follow Chairman Mao and take the socialist road'.

120 Sichuan Radio, 31 August 1967, Li Dazhang 'Vehement denunciation of the outrageous anti-party, anti-socialist and anti-Mao Zedong thought crimes of the counter-revolutionary revisionist Li Jingquan'. Li's denunciation also includes details of the Southwest Bureau's management of the Socialist Education

Movement in Guizhou. Zhou Lin had already lost his place on the Nationalities Committee of the NPC in late 1964.

121 For example, Guizhou Radio 4 June 1967, Proletarian Revolutionaries of the *New Guizhou Daily* 'The crimes of the biggest office-holder in the southwest'.

122 For example, Guizhou Radio 8 July 1967, article by Lin Dezhong of Guizhou Military District Political Department.

123 Guizhou Radio, 12 September 1967.

124 For example, Guizhou Radio 29 June 1967, Tian Qing 'Accounts of the crimes of Jia Qiyun'.

125 Guizhou Radio, 11 September 1965.

126 Guizhou Radio, 3 June 1967, *New Guizhou Daily* Editorial (undated) 'Down with Jia Qiyun!'

127 XHBYK No. 13, 1959, p. 37. Jia himself seems to have had a knack for being in the right place at the wrong time. He became director of the State Statistical Bureau in 1959 only to lose his position in 1961 as a consequence of the reaction to the GLF; first secretary of Guizhou in 1965 only to fall victim to the GPCR; and first secretary of Yunnan in 1975 only to fall again after the arrest of the 'Gang of Four'.

7. RURAL PEOPLE'S COMMUNES

1 The following account of the development of rural people's communes from a national perspective is based on various sources including T. S. Hsia *The Commune in Retreat as Evidenced in Terminology and Semantics*, Studies in Chinese Communist Terminology No. 11, Center for Chinese Studies, Institute of International Studies, University of California, Berkeley, 1964; J. Domes *Socialism in the Chinese Countryside* Hurst, London, 1980, pp. 20–60; F. W. Crook 'The Commune System in the People's Republic of China' in *China: A Reassessment of the Economy*, Report to Joint Economic Committee, 94th US Congress, 1st session, US Government Printing Office, Washington DC, 1975; K. Walker 'Organization of Agricultural Production' Eckstein, Galenson and Liu (eds.) *Economic Trends in Communist China* Aldine Press, Chicago, 1968, p. 440–452; H. F. Schurmann *Ideology and Organization in Communist China* University of California Press, Berkeley, 1968, p. 464–494; C. Chen and C. Ridley, *Rural People's Communes in Lien-chiang* Hoover Institution, Stanford, 1969; and L. Kuo *Agriculture in the PRC: Structural Change and Technical Transformation* Praeger, London, 1976.

2 H. F. Schurmann *Ideology and Organization in Communist China*, p. 474ff.; and K. Walker 'Organization of Agricultural Production', p. 440.

3 Xue Muqiao 'Economic Work Must Grasp the Laws of Economic Development", report to the State Economic Commission's Research Conference on Enterprise Management, 14 March 1979; in B. Szajkowski (ed.) *Documents in Communist Affairs 1980* Macmillan, London, 1981, p. 143.

4 'Resolution of the CCP Central Committee on the Establishment of People's Communes in the Rural Area' in *Documents of Chinese Communist Party Central Committee, 1956–1969* 2 vols, Union Research Institute, Hong Kong, 1971, vol. 1, pp. 299–304.

5 There is an interesting comparison to be made between the accounts of Hsia and Domes written before and after the GPCR respectively. Hsia relates the evolution

of commune policy as it appeared contemporaneously, and thus dates the significant changes by reference to the official media. Domes, with the hindsight of the GPCR goes to the other extreme, sees everything in terms of Mao versus Liu and Deng, and thus dates the significant changes in commune policy according to the start of 'resistance' to Mao's point of view at each specific stage (largely as evidenced by GPCR sources). Both accounts seem too well ordered. It seems more likely that change was more gradual and national leaders less certain than both argue. Certainly both accounts highlight the uneven spatial distribution in the evolution of PCs.

6 Letter of 15 March 1959 from Wuchang, in *Mao Zedong sixiang wansui (1967)*, pp. 106–7; translated in *Miscellany of Mao Tse-tung Thought* JPRS No. 61269–1, p. 166–7.

7 T. S. Hsia *The Commune in Retreat*, pp. 38–9.

8 RMRB 3 September 1958, p. 1. Editorial on Weixing People's Commune, 'Raise high the red flag of the people's communes in the march forward'.

9 S. Schram *The Political Thought of Mao Tse-tung* (2nd edition) Penguin, Harmondsworth, 1969, p. 349–50. RMRB report of 13 August 1958. Moreover, various articles published after the beginning of September 1958 referred to the earlier development of people's communes. Thus, for example, Wu Zhipu, the first secretary of Henan, the man commonly held responsible for the *Weixing* commune, accredited Mao with having stressed that the new rural units should be 'large and communal' (*yi da, er gong*) when visiting that commune; in *Hongqi* No. 8, 6 September 1958, p. 8. On the first anniversary of the Beidaihe resolution (29 August 1959) the *People's Daily* actually said: 'In June the party centre and comrade Mao Zedong chose people's commune as the best name to express the conduct of the organization and that most likely to meet with public acclaim. The name was unanimously adopted at the Beidaihe Conference of the Party in August', p. 2.

10 RMRB 29 August 1958, p. 1, 'Welcome the High Tide of Education in the People's Communes'.

11 *Hongqi* No. 7, 1 September 1958, p. 14. To quote: '... the bud of communism is indeed growing as can be seen in such developments as the system of food supply.'

12 T. Hsia *The Commune in Retreat*, pp. 12ff. Hence too the original intention that the commune would replace the *xiang* as the basic-level of the politico-administrative hierarchy. Although some PCs grew temporarily much larger than a single *xiang*, this design was eventually fulfilled.

13 RMRB 10 September 1958, p. 1.

14 *Dagongbao* 29 September 1958 quoted in Domes *Socialism in the Chinese Countryside*, p. 27.

15 K. Lieberthal *A Research Guide to Central Party and Government Meetings in China* International Arts and Science Press, White Plains, New York, 1976, pp. 123–4.

16 ibid., p. 126.

17 'Resolution on some questions concerning the people's communes' 10 December 1958, in *Documents of Chinese Communist Party Central Committee 1956–1969*, pp. 123–8.

18 Letter of 15 March 1959 from Wuchang in *Mao Zedong sixiang wansui (1967)* pp. 106–107; translated in *Miscellany of Mao Tse-tung Thought* JPRS No. 61269–1, pp. 166–7.

19 K. Lieberthal *A Research Guide to Central Party and Government Meetings in China*, pp. 137–8.

20 Figures based on those quoted in Domes *Socialism in the Chinese Countryside*, p. 48, from *Dagongbao* 17 and 24 September 1964.

21 T. Hsia *The Commune in Retreat*, p. 24.

22 T. Hsia *The Commune in Retreat*, p. 40, analyses the policy adopted by the 8th plenum.

23 T. Hsia *The Commune in Retreat*, pp. 36–9, notes the change in terminology from the 6th to the 8th plenum. In December 1958 the production brigade was known as the *shengchandadui* but by August 1959 it was referred to as the *shengchandui*, whereas between the same dates the production team changed from *shengchandui* to *shengchanxiaodui*, thus indicating the agreement on the production brigade as the major management unit at the later date.

24 RMRB 21 December 1960, p. 1. Editorial 'Three level ownership rests on the brigade as the fundamental institution of the people's commune at the present stage'.

25 Domes *Socialism in the Chinese Countryside*, p. 49.

26 K. Lieberthal *A Research Guide to Central Government and Party Meetings in China*, pp. 168–70.

27 Domes *Socialism in the Chinese Countryside*, p. 49.

28 T. Hsia *The Commune in Retreat*, p. 39.

29 RMRB 30 March 1961, quoted in T. Hsia *The Commune in Retreat*, p. 48.

30 RMRB 29 August 1961, p. 1. Editorial 'Each sharing the responsibility: each displaying their ability'.

31 'Regulations on the work of the rural people's communes (revised draft)' in *Documents of Chinese Communist Party Central Committee 1956–1969*, Vol. 1, pp. 695–725.

32 RMRB 1 January 1962, New Year's Day Editorial, quoted in T. Hsia *The Commune in Retreat*, p. 61.

33 Based on figures quoted in Domes *Socialism in the Chinese Countryside*, p. 48, from *Dagongbao* 17 and 24 September 1964.

34 F. W. Crook 'The Commune System in the People's Republic of China', p. 373.

35 ibid., p. 375.

36 ibid., p. 374.

37 *Hongqi* No. 8, 1958, 16 September 1958, in CB 524 (21 October 1958) p. 16.

38 GZRB 30 September 1958, p. 1, 'Our province realizes communization'.

39 SCRB 27 September 1958, p. 1, 'All the province's *xian* and *shi* are in people's communes'.

40 H. F. Schurmann *Ideology and Organization in Communist China*, pp. 472ff.

41 For example, SCRB 20 April 1958, p. 1, 'To extend public accumulation and assist the leap forward in agriculture, the democratic socialization of pigs increases quickly'.

42 See p. 74.

43 For example, CDRB 24 March 1958, p. 1, 'Faxuan *she* amalgamates the area of dwelling houses and opens new ground'; and CDRB 13 May 1958, p. 1, '253 co-ops amalgamated into 137'.

44 Li Jingquan 'The People's Communes are the inevitable outcome of China's social development', in *Ten Glorious Years* Foreign Languages Press, Peking, 1960, p. 216.

45 H. F. Schurmann *Ideology and Organization in Communist China*, p. 474.

46 H. Johnson *The Upsurge of China* New World Press, Peking, 1961, p. 280.

47 SCRB 7 April 1958, p. 2, 'Chairman Mao at Hongguang'.

48 NCNA 12 April 1948 'Mao's visist to Szechwan', reported that Mao had visited an unspecified APC in West Sichuan on 16 March. Pixian is near Chengdu in what was formerly (before 1952) the West Sichuan Administrative Area.

49 SCRB 13 September 1958, p. 1, 'Sichuan Party Committee's regulations for implementing the party centre's decision on the question of establishing people's communes in the rural areas'.

50 SCRB 24 June 1959, p. 2.

51 SCRB 15 August 1958 p. 1, 'Comrade Mao Zedong at Qiliying people's commune, Xinxiang county Henan'.

52 SCRB 19 August 1958, p. 1, 'Run People's Communes Well'.

53 SCRB 19 September 1958, p. 3.

54 SCRB 27 September 1958, p. 1, 'All the province's rural and urban areas have been communized.

55 GZRB 24 August 1958, p. 1, 'According to Chairman Mao's directive, Dongfeng People's commune is established'.

56 ibid.

57 ibid., p. 2, 'How Dongfeng People's commune came about'.

58 ibid.

59 GZRB 4 September 1958, p. 1, 'Guiyang's villages realize communization'.

60 GZRB 10 September 1958, p. 1, 'Our province also has three counties and one city which have realized communization'.

61 GZRB 19 October 1958, p. 2, 'From this winter to next spring we must resolutely consolidate the rural people's communes'.

62 GZRB 30 September 1959, p. 1.

63 GZRB 8 April 1960, p. 2.

64 GZRB 24 August 1958, p. 2, 'How Dongfeng People's commune came about'.

65 GZRB 2 September 1960, p. 1. Wu Su 'Raise the standard of administration and management of basic-level organizations in rural people's communes to higher levels'. According to this article there were 537 PCs, 19,000 production brigades, and 100,000 production teams.

66 GZRB 25 September 1958, p. 2.

67 GZRB 19 October 1958, p. 2. Report of work conference held 6–11 October.

68 These figures are estimates based on two sources. The first is GZRB 30 September 1958, p. 1, 'Our province realizes communization', which claimed that 87.9% of the province's peasant households were in 231 PCs with an average of 1262 peasant households. It can thus be reasonably estimated that there were 3,272,205 peasant households in the province, which is consistent with known total provincial population at that time. The second is that cited in n. 65 above.

69 GZRB 8 April 1960, p. 2.

70 By February 1959, Guizhou had approximately the same number of production brigades as it had APCs on the eve of communization. By comparison, Sichuan in 1963, when the size of the average provincial PC had been reduced, had 63,000 production brigades as opposed to 160,000 higher stage collectives before communization (F. W. Crooks 'The Commune System in the People's Republic of China', p. 375 and p. 387). A further interesting aspect of Guizhou's communization is that if the province's reported communization before the end of September 1958 was included in the national figure of PCs established in 1958, then the provincial process of consolidation by which 2,389 PCs became 537 in February 1959,

accounted for 72% of the reduction in the number of PCs nationally. According to Jia Qiyun, 26,578 had been established in 1958, and that had been reduced to 24,000 in 1959. ('Superiority of People's Communes' NCNA 25 September 1959 in SCMP 2107, p. 34.)

71 GZRB 24 August 1958, p. 1, 'According to Chairman Mao's directive, Dongfeng People's Commune is established'.

72 GZRB 19 October 1958, p. 2, 'From this winter to next spring we must resolutely consolidate the rural people's communes'.

73 GZRB 13 November 1958, p. 1, 'Comrade Deng Xiaoping in Zunyi'. On his visit to various communes in Zunyi *xian* on 3 November, Deng was reported to have advocated the extension of mess-halls and the free supply system. It was also reported that: 'On hearing this, Comrade Cheng Yaohua [Secretary of Zunyi *xian* party committee] could only smile as he himself had not been able to make such a thorough analysis of the new situation.'

74 GZRB 11 November 1958, p. 1, 'When you eat, eat without paying: Zunyi special district popularizes grain supply system'. This would appear to be the only article of its kind in the *Guizhou Daily* during this period.

75 SCRB 13 September 1958, p. 1.

76 *Hongqi* No. 7, 1958, 1 September 1958, p. 14.

77 GZRB 25 September 1958, p. 2.

78 GZRB 30 September 1959, p. 2.

79 GZRB 8 April 1960, p. 2.

80 Li Jingquan 'The People's Communes are the inevitable outcome of China's social development', p. 210.

81 *Shangyou* No. 4, 1958, p. 20, Yang Li 'Advance by running people's communes well'.

82 *Chongqing gongshang* No. 23–4 23 December 1958, p. 4.

83 For example, *Sichuan daxue xuebao: shehui kexue* No. 4, 1959 (October) Yang Keqiang 'People's communes are the inevitable product of our economic and political development', p. 4.

84 Li Jingquan 'The people's communes are the inevitable outcome of China's social development', p. 216.

85 GZRB 12 December 1960, pp. 1–2.

86 SCRB 26 May 1960, p. 2.

87 SCRB 15 March 1960, p. 1.

88 GZRB 8 April 1960, p. 2. Zhou Lin's report to the 1st session of the 2nd provincial party congress.

89 GZRB 12 December 1960, p. 2. Chen Puru's provincial government work report to the Guizhou PPC.

90 In both cases this contrasted with earlier experiences. In Sichuan, the provincial regulation for establishing PCs (SCRB 13 September 1958) had placed no limit on the proportion of free supply and indeed encouraged experimentation. In Guizhou, during 1959 when communal mess-halls were first popularized on a large scale, the limit was set at 'no more than 40%', in GZRB 26 June 1959, p. 1, Report of the 9th Plenum of the Guizhou provincial party committee.

91 T. Hsia *The Commune in Retreat*, p. 36ff.

92 GZRB 19 October 1958, p. 2, 'From this winter to next spring we must resolutely consolidate the rural people's communes'.

93 SCRB 13 September 1958, p. 1.

94 GZRB 9 January 1959, p. 1. The plenum met 6–7 January and had been preceded by meetings of secretaries at *zhou* level (22–5 December) and *xian* level (26 December–5 January).

95 SCRB 24 June 1959, p. 2.

96 GZRB 30 September 1959, p. 2.

97 GZRB 15 November 1960, p. 1, 'Banjiaquan People's Commune runs industry well'.

98 For example both the 9th plenum of the Guizhou party committee (GZRB 26 June 1959, p. 1) and Dai Xiaodong in his speech to the 1959 Representative Conference of Provincial Advanced Units in Agricultural Socialist Construction (GZRB 6 January 1960, p. 1), addressed themselves mainly to the tasks of management of production brigades.

99 GZRB 2 September 1960, p. 1, Wu Su 'Raise the standards of administration and management of basic-level organizations in rural people's communes to higher levels'.

100 GZRB 14 November 1960, p. 1, 'Guarantee the "four rights" of production teams'.

101 GZRB 14 November 1960, p. 1. Editorial 'Production jobs must be arranged by the teams'.

102 SCRB 2 September 1961, p. 1, 'Production brigades strengthen leadership – procurement work is better and faster'.

103 For example: SCRB 4 November 1961, p. 1. Editorial 'Every production team should implement the "3 fixed" and resolutely realize the guaranteed production and fixed procurement plan'.

104 For example: SCRB 17 November 1961, p. 1. Editorial 'Strengthen production team's financial and management work'.

105 For example: SCRB 13 December 1961, p. 1, 'Sichuan party committee comments on Huohua Commune's report on fixing production contracts'.

106 For example: SCRB 12 January 1963, p. 1. Sichuan party committee and people's council directive on rural construction work; and SCRB 14 January 1963, p. 1, 'Production brigades choose "5-good" commune members each month'.

107 SCRB 28 March 1960, p. 1, 'A report from the party branch of the provincial grain department on the exchange experience conference concerning the successful handling of public mess-halls in Nanchong district'. Amongst other things this account reported that: 'Experience shows that in order to make a success of the public mess-halls, we must bring food grains under the unified control of the basic accounting unit – the production brigade.'

108 For example: GZRB 17 July 1960, p. 1. 'At present our provincial party's most important task is to do a good job of the summer's production'. This article distinguishes between *shengchandui* and *schengchan xiaodui*, thus indicating that the production brigade is the basic level of ownership within the commune.

109 *Tuanjie* No. 12, 1960 (December), pp. 3–5. Editorial 'More on the resolute implementation of the policy of making agriculture the foundation'.

110 GZRB 1 December 1960, p. 1, Wang Xingyuan 'Resolutely implement the policies on people's communes at the present stage'.

111 *Jingji yanjiu* No. 1, 1961, p. 11, 'The superiority of the three level system: Lungmen people's commune, Wusheng county.

112 For example: SCRB 1 July 1962, p. 1. Editorial 'Strengthen collectivist education – alter the difficulties that production teams face'; and SCRB 8 July 1962, p. 1, 'Production team leadership is strong – collective production develops'. There are no provincial newspapers or radio broadcasts available for the first half of 1962. However, it is clear that the production brigade was still regarded as the commune's basic level of ownership at the end of 1961. For example: SCRB 15 December 1961, p. 1. ' "One guarantee, two fixed" is a good method', which described the production contract system between commune and production brigade.

113 See p. 132.

114 GZRB 19 October 1959, p. 1. 'Comrade Zhou Lin on present rural work', report of inspection tour, 14–17 October.

115 SCRB 4 September 1961, p. 1, 'Do a good job of raising pigs'.

116 SCRB 19 March 1963, p. 2. 'Help production teams to develop collective sideline industry'.

117 Thus, for example: NCNA in English, Beijing Radio, 28 September 1963 'Local trade flourishing in Szechwan'; and Beijing Radio, 9 January 1964 'Szechwan living standards improve'; both refer only to pig-raising when mentioning the private portion of peasants' income.

118 F. W. Crook 'The Commune System in the People's Republic of China', pp. 375ff.

119 RMRB 31 December 1959, p. 3, Zhou Lin 'The struggle between the old and the new forces in the Great Leap Forward'.

120 GZRB 2 September 1960, p. 1, Wu Su 'Raise the standard of administration and management of basic-level organizations in rural people's communes to higher levels'. Interestingly, where it was said that the average production team had 30 peasant households, and the smaller 10–20, the larger were reported to have 50–60 peasant households, thus indicating that production teams tended to be smaller rather than larger.

121 In August 1958 there had been c. 20,000 APCs. In December 1960 there were c. 100,000 production teams.

122 Apart from anything else, it was emphasized in Article 17 of the Twelve Year Plan.

123 For example: GZRB 8 April 1960, p. 2, Zhou Lin's report to the provincial party congress, provides several examples of the general exhortation; and GZRB 19 October 1959, p. 1 'Comrade Zhou Lin on Present Rural Work' (which is a report of Zhou Lin's visit to several communes in Jinsha *xian*) includes evidence of both its encouragement and application in mountain areas.

124 For example: GZRB 6 January 1960, p. 1, Dai Xiaodong '1959 Agricultural production conditions and tasks for 1960': 'Some rightists and defeatists have claimed "deep ploughing in mountain areas is too arduous" . . .'.

125 Li Jingquan 'The people's communes are the inevitable outcome of China's social development', p. 212.

126 In 1962, Sichuan had approximately 45,000 production brigades as opposed to 160–170,000 higher stage collectives in the winter of 1957–8. In 1963, the number of communes rose from the 4–5,000 of 1958–9 to 7,000. These latter had c. 63,000 production brigades and c. 427,000 production teams. Sources: F. W. Crook, 'The commune system in the People's Republic of China', p. 375 and 387; RMRB 5 October 1963, p. 2, 'National Day Celebrations held enthusiastically in cities

throughout China'; SCRB 24 June 1959, p. 2, Li Dazhang's 1959 provincial government work report; SCRB 27 September 1958, p. 1, 'All the province's *xian* and *shi* are communized'; *Shangyou* No. 4, 1958, p. 18, Yang Li 'Advance by running people's communes well'.

8 THE SOUTH-WEST REGION AND THE SOUTH-WEST REGIONAL BUREAU

1 These sources are listed in the Appendix. The same rules for interpreting information from those sources, as outlined in Chapter 6, apply here. See p. 226, n.15.

2 'Communique of the 9th plenary session of the CCP 8th Central Committee' 14–18 January 1961, in *Documents of Chinese Communist Party Central Committee, 1956–1969* 2 vols. Union Research Institute, Hong Kong, 1971, Vol. 1, pp. 177–8.

3 P. Chang *Patterns and Processes of Policy-Making in Communist China, 1955–1962: Three Case Studies* Ph.D. dissertation, Columbia University, 1969, p. 269–270.

4 *Xinan diqu jingji dili* Science Publishing House, Beijing, 1960, Foreword.

5 'Talks with the leaders of the co-ordinative regions', 30 November 1958 and 12 December 1958, in *Mao Zedong sixiang wansui (1969)*, pp. 251–8; translated in *Miscellany of Mao Tse-tung Thought* JPRS No. 61269–1, p. 133–9.

6 For example: in his speech to the Chengdu Conference on 20 March 1958, in *Mao Zedong sixiang wansui (1969)*, p. 167, he said: 'Every two months each province, municipality and autonomous region must hold a meeting to make an investigation and sum up the results, a small meeting of from several to a dozen or so people. Co-ordinative Regions must also hold a meeting every two or three months.' Translated in S. Schram (ed.) *Mao Tse-tung Unrehearsed* Penguin, Harmondsworth, Midx., 1974, p. 106. Again in his 'Speech at a meeting of leaders of delegations to the 2nd session of the 8th party congress' on 18 May 1958, in *Mao Zedong sixing wansui (1969)*, p. 224, Mao remarked 'How are the co-operative regions? It is the negation of a negation.' Translated in *Miscellany of Mao Tse-tung Thought* JPRS No. 61269–1, p. 122. A further example may be found in article 31 of Mao's *Sixty Work Articles* of 1958; in CB 892, p. 9.

7 *Xinan diqu jingji dili*, Forword.

8 For example: Yu Dingyi *Xinan liu sheng shehui jingji niaokan* Bank of China, Economic Research Department, 1938, pp. 1ff. points out the inconsistencies in the definition of the southwest region, and that at various time different combinations of Sichuan, Yunnan, Guizhou, Guangdong, Guangxi and Hunan had all been so designated.

9 The following analysis of the southwest region's development before 1954 is based mainly on *Xinan diqu jingji dili* and D. J. Solinger *Regional Government and Political Integration in Southwest China, 1949–1954* University of California Press, Berkeley, 1977.

10 G. W. Skinner 'Regional urbanization in Nineteenth Century China' in G. W. Skinner (ed) *The City in Late Imperial China* Stanford University Press, London, 1976, p. 47.

11 D. J. Solinger *Regional Government and Political Integration in Southwest China, 1949–1954*, especially ch. 6, pp. 164ff.

12 For example, *Xinhua yuebao* No. 11, 1951, p. 114–18.

13 *Xinan diqu jingji dili*, p. 4–5.

14 ibid.

15 Ye A. Afanas'yeakiy *Szechwan* Publishing House of Oriental Literature, Moscow, 1962, p. 299.

16 The following analysis of regional economic development after 1954 is based on *Xinan diqu jingji dili* op. cit., and Ye. A. Afanas'Yeakiy *Szechwan*.

17 *Xinan diqu jingji dili*, p. 3; and SCRB 21 June 1958, p. 1, 'Look! Weiyuan produces steel!'

18 *Xinan diqu jingji dili*, pp. 4–5.

19 ibid. p. 4, p. 54, and p. 124.

20 According to the 1953 census, Sichuan and Xikang had 65.3 million inhabitants, Guizhou 15 million, Yunnan 17.5 million and Tibet 1.2 million.

21 SCRB, GZRB and *Yunnan ribao*, all 19 August 1958, p. 2, NCNA report from Zhengzhou, dated 18 August 1958.

22 SCRB 15 August 1958, p. 1.

23 S. R. Schram *The Political Thought of Mao Tse-tung*, Penguin, Harmondsworth, Midx., 1969, pp. 349–50.

24 For example, SCRB 14 September 1958, p. 2 "People's Communes are fine: production rises with every step". Sichuan's advocacy of urban communes is yet more circumstantial evidence of the suggested alliance with Mao, for in November 1958, he too urged their creation; in "Talks with leaders of the coordinative regions", 30 November 1958, in *Mao Zedong sixiang wansui (1969)* op.cit., p. 252, translated in *Miscellany of Mao Tse-tung Thought* JPRS No. 61269–1, p. 134.

25 D. E. T. Luard 'The Urban Communes' in CQ No. 3, p. 76; and H. F. Schurmann *Ideology and Organization in Communist China* University of California Press, Berkeley, 1968, p. 385.

26 E. Vogel *Canton under Communism* Harper & Row, New York, 1971, p. 267.

27 GZRB 29 March 1960, p. 1, 'Collective life for residents of Guiyang', announced that the province's first urban communes had been established in mid-March.

28 GZRB 30 September 1958, p. 1, 'Our province realized communization', in detailing the number and size of communes established clearly differentiates between urban and rural people's communes.

29 GZRB 31 August 1958, p. 1, 'The province's first urban people's commune established', on 30 August and unoriginally called the *Weixing* people's commune in the Nanming district of Guiyang.

30 In 1957, nationally, 15% of the population lived in urban centres of 20,000 or more inhabitants. In the Southwest the corresponding figures were 12% for Guizhou, 10% for Yunnan, and 9% for Sichuan; source: *Dili zhishi* No. 9, 1957, p. 412. According to the 1953 census, Sichuan had a non-Han population of 1.86 mn., Guizhou 3.75 mn., Yunnan 5.83 mn., and Tibet 1.08 mn.

31 Sichuan Radio 4 September 1965, 'Opening of Southwest Drama Festival'. Li Dazhang in his opening speech welcomed participants from Sichuan, Guizhou, and Yunnan.

32 For example: Guizhou Radio 7 October 1967, Tian Bao 'The counter-revolutionary revisionist Li Jingquan's towering crimes in nationality work in Sichuan'.

33 For example: Guizhou Radio 4 June 1967, Proletarian Revolutionaries of the *New Guizhou Daily* 'The crimes of the biggest office-holder in the Southwest', claimed that at the June 1966 plenum of the Southwest Bureau quotas had been fixed for the removal of 'Those in authority taking the capitalist road' in each of the region's

provinces – not more than 20 in Sichuan, about 10 in Yunnan, not more than 10 in Guizhou, and about 5 in Tibet.

34 *Secretaries of the Southwest Regional Bureau, 1961–6*

Secretary	Concurrent provincial workplace	Work location during 1950–2
Cheng Gang	Sichuan	Sichuan
Cheng Zihua		Shanxi
Li Dazhang	Sichuan	Sichuan
Li Jingquan	Sichuan	Sichuan
Liao Zhigao	Sichuan	Xikang
Ren Baige	Sichuan	Sichuan
Xu Mengxia	Sichuan	Sichuan
Yan Xiufeng	Sichuan	Sichuan
Yu Jiangzhen		Sichuan
Zhang Jingwu	Tibet	Tibet

For sources see n.51.

35 For example, it was the Chengdu Military Region which organized a Militia Work Conference, 9–20 September 1965, source: Sichuan Radio, 14 October 1965.

36 For example, Sichuan Radio 26 October 1967, SCRB 21 October 1967, editorial 'Totally smash the Li dynasty', part 5 – 'Li Jingquan stubbornly opposed the Party Centre headed by Chairman Mao and turned Sichuan into a watertight independent kingdom'.

37 Sichuan Radio 29 December 1967, Shen Shihong 'Totally settle accounts for Li Jingquan's towering crimes in sabotaging the printing and distibution of Chairman Mao's works'.

38 Guizhou Radio 3 July 1967, Revolutionary Rebels of the Land Fossils Research Institute of the Chinese Academy of Science 'Li Jingquan is the arch-criminal in sabotaging the great proletarian cultural revolution in the southwest', part 1 – 'Li Jingquan stubbornly pushed through the bourgeois reactionary line and opposed Chairman Mao's revolutionary line, frenziedly suppressing the revolutionary masses'.

39 Sichuan Radio 19 and 22 October 1967, Proletarian revolutionaries of the industry and communications political departments of the former Sichuan provincial party committee 'The harm of the "Five-act Sichuan Opera" pushed through by Li Jingquan in industry, communications, and capital construction throughout the southwest was that it took the capitalist road', parts I and II.

40 Guizhou Radio 28 October 1967, Revolutionary Rebels HQ of the Southwest Bureau Offices 'We must settle accounts for Li Jingquan's towering crimes in finance and trade'.

41 Guizhou Radio 20 July 1967, Changying Red Literature and Art Rebellion Group 'Recapture the culture and education battle fronts from the hands of Li Jingquan and his gang'.

42 Sichuan Radio 7 December 1967, Long Chen and Wu Lian 'Thoroughly settle accounts with Li Jingquan for the counter-revolutionary revisionist crimes he committed in the rural areas'.

43 Sichuan Radio 25 September 1967, Proletarian Revolutionaries of the Sichuan Philosophy and Social Sciences Research Institute 'The counter-revolutionary

revisionist Li Jingquan's proposition that "The whole party is of the same mind, strength and kind" was for the purpose of restoring capitalism'.

44 Guizhou Radio 13 July 1967, 'Cut off Li Jingquan's black arms that have been stretched to various places in the Southwest'.

45 Sichuan Radio 31 August 1967, Li Dazhang 'Vehement denunciation of the outrageous anti-party, anti-socialist, and anti-Mao Zedong Thought crimes of the counter-revolutionary revisionist Li Jingquan'.

46 The southwest bureau held plenums to discuss the GPCR in May and June 1966. In addition, it held a plenum on the importance of placing 'Politics in Command' in January 1966, that was addressed by Chen Boda.

47 Guizhou Radio 23 June 1967, Zhang Xiting 'Vehement denunciation of Li Jingquan's outrageous crimes'.

48 See also, Sichuan Radio 23 September 1967, Report of the 20 September Struggle Meeting against Li Jingquan, which confirms that the 'Four clean-ups' in Guizhou was administered by the Southwest Bureau.

49 H. F. Schurmann *Ideology and Organization in Communist China*, p. 183.

50 'The crimes of "the biggest office holder" in the Southwest', by the Proletarian Revolutionaries of the *New Guizhou Daily* broadcast by Guizhou Radio, 4 June 1967.

51 Leaders are defined institutionally as those holding the following positions at provincial and regional levels:

(1) Governor and Vice governor of the provincial people's government.

(2) Commander, Deputy Commander, Political Commissar, and Deputy Political Commissar of the relevant units of the PLA. (Chengdu Military Region for Sichuan; Tibet Military Region; Kunming Military Region for Yunnan and Guizhou; and Guizhou and Yunnan Military Districts for those provinces.)

(3) All Secretaries of the relevant CCP committees.

The identification of the individuals holding those positions has been based on primary sources, notably national and provincial newspapers and journals, provincial radio broadcasts, and *Renmin Shouce* for the appropriate years. Data are presented in D. S. G. Goodman *China's Provincial Leaders, 1949–1985: Vol. 1. Directory* University College Press Cardiff, 1986

Data on career backgrounds has been based on the same sources used to identify individuals as part of the leadership; on my own data culled from the national and provincial media for the period after 1966 (in particular, obituary notices); and on various biographical dictionaries including: *Who's Who in Communist China* Vols. I and II Union Research Institute, Hong Kong, 1969 and 1970; *Hierarchies of the People's Republic of China* Union Research Institute, Hong Kong, 1975; D. W. Klein and A. B. Clark *Biographic Dictionary of Chinese Communism, 1921–1965* Harvard University Press, Cambridge (Mass.), 1971; *Union Research Biographical Series* Union Research Institute, Hong Kong; Huang Chenxia, *Zhonggong junren zhi Dangdai lishi yenjiu suo*, Hong Kong, 1968; *Chinese Communist Who's Who* Institute of International Relations, Taibei, 1970; and *Gendai Chugoku jinmei jiten* Tokyo, 1966.

52 T. J. Matthews 'The Cultural Revolution in Szechwan' in E. Vogel (ed) *The Cultural Revolution in the Provinces* Harvard East Asian Monographs, No. 42, Harvard University Press, Cambridge (Mass.), 1971, p. 94–126.

53 For example, Guizhou Radio 15 September 1968, You Bin 'Refute Li Jingquan's absurd theory that "Without Sichuan, there would be no China"'.
54 For example, Guizhou Radio 6 September 1967, Fei Hongzhuan 'Vehement denunciation of the anti-party, anti-socialist, and anti-Mao Zedong Thought crimes of the counter-revolutionary revisionist Li Jingquan'.
55 R. Baum *Prelude to Revolution* Columbia University Press, London, 1975, pp. 43ff.
56 ibid., pp. 93ff.
57 For example, Guizhou Radio 25 June 1967, Li Li 'Li Jingquan is the deadly enemy of the people of the Southwest'.
58 R. Baum *Prelude to Revolution*, p. 139.
59 For example, Guizhou Radio 23 July 1967, Li Zhengfang's report of Kunming Military Region Conference to denounce Li Jingquan.
60 K. Lieberthal *A Research Guide to Central Party and Government Meetings in China, 1949–1975* International Arts and Science Press, White Plains, New York, 1976, pp. 234–5.
61 ibid., pp. 241–3.
62 R. Baum *Prelude to Revolution*, pp. 101 and 135ff.
63 For example: Sichuan Radio 31 August 1967, Li Dazhang 'Vehement denunciation of the outrageous anti-party, anti-socialist and anti-Mao Zedong Thought crimes of the counter-revolutionary revisionist Li Jingquan'.
64 ibid.
65 R. Baum *Prelude to Revolution*, p. 139.

PROVINCIAL POWER, CENTRAL AUTHORITY

1 D. J. Solinger *Regional Government and Political Integration in Southwest China, 1949–1954* University of California Press, Berkeley, 1977, especially Ch. 8, pp. 241ff.
2 For example: B. Ahn *Chinese Politics and the Cultural Revolution* University of Washington Press, London, 1976, especially p. 23.
3 K. Lieberthal *Research Guide to Central Party and Government Meetings in China, 1949–1975* International Arts and Science Press, White Plains, New York, 1976, pp. 8–9.
4 Several works have highlighted those various characteristics of decision-making. Two of particular interest are: K. Lieberthal *Central Documents and Politburo Politics in China* Michigan Papers in Chinese Studies, No. 33, Ann Arbor, Michigan, 1978; and E. Friedman 'The Politics of Local Models, Social Transformation and State Power Struggles in the People's Republic of China: Tachai and Teng Hsiao-p'ing' in CQ 76, p. 873–90.
5 D. Goodman 'The Shanghai Connection: Shanghai's role in national politics during the 1970s' in C. Howe (ed.) *Shanghai: Revolution and Development in an Asian Metropolis* Cambridge University Press, Cambridge, 1981, p. 125–52.
6 See, for example, Tian Yun 'More authority for enterprises revives the economy' in *Beijing Review* No. 14, 1981, p. 21.
7 Zhao Ziyang 'Principles for All-round Economic Readjustment' in *Eastern Horizon* Vol. 19, No. 5, May 1980, pp. 5–12. Li Jingquan, 'The uninterrupted improvement of relations between the state and the peasants' in XHBYK 20, pp. 52–4.

BIBLIOGRAPHY

I SERIALS

Cai jing kexue (*Financial and Economic Sciences*)
 Chengdu. Monthly.
Chengdu ribao (*Chengdu Daily*)
 Chengdu.
Chengdu wanbao (*Chengdu Evening News*)
 Chengdu.
China Reconstructs
 Peking. Monthly.
Chongqing gongshang (*Chongqing Industry and Commerce*)
 Chongqing. Monthly.
Chongqing ribao (*Chongqing Daily*)
 Chongqing.
Chuannan bao (*South Sichuan News*)
 Luzhou.
Guangming ribao
 Beijing.
Guizhou Jiaoyu (*Guizhou Education*)
 Guiyang. Monthly.
Guizhou ribao, 1957–1960 (*Guizhou Daily*)
 Guiyang.
Hongqi (*Red Flag*)
 Beijing. Monthly.
Hong yan, 1956–1960 (*Red Rock*)
 Chongqing. Monthly.
Jingji Yanjiu (*Economic Research*)
 Beijing. Monthly.
Nanchong ribao (*Nanchong Daily*)
 Nanchong.
New China News Agency
 Beijing. Daily reports in English.
Peking Review (from 1958)
 Beijing. Weekly.
People's China (to 1958)
 Peking. Weekly.
Renmin ribao (*People's Daily*)
 Beijing.

244

Bibliography

Renmin Shouce (*The People's Handbook*)
  Beijing. Annual.
Shangyou, 1958–1960 (*Upstream*)
  Chengdu. Monthly.
Sichuan daxue xuebao: shehui kexue (*Journal of Sichuan University: Social Sciences*)
  Chengdu. Bi-monthly.
Sichuan gongren ribao (*Sichuan Workers' Daily*)
  Chengdu.
Sichuan nongmin ribao (*Sichuan Peasants' Daily*)
  Chengdu.
Sichuan ribao, 1952–64 (*Sichuan Daily*)
  Chengdu.
Sichuan qingnian bao (*Sichuan Youth*)
  Chengdu.
Sichuan qunzhong (*Sichuan Masses*)
  Chengdu.
Sichuan wenxue (from 1960) (*Sichuan Literature*)
  Chengdu.
Tongji gongzuo tongxun (*Statistical Work Bulletin*)
  Beijing.
Tuanjie, 1958–60 (*Unity*)
  Guiyang. Monthly.
Xinan wenyi, 1952–6 (*Southwest Art and Literature*)
  Chongqing. Monthly.
Xinhua (ban) yuekan (*New China (semi-) monthly*)
  Beijing.
Xinhua ribao (*New China Daily*)
  Chongqing.
Xinhua xinwen (*New China News Agency*)
  Beijing. Daily press reports.
Xinqian ribao, 1950–6 (*New Guizhou Daily*)
  Guiyang.
Xin Zigong bao (New Zigong Daily)
  Zigong.
Yibin nongmin (*The Yibin Peasant*)
  Yibin.
Zhengzhi xuexi (*Political Studies*)
  Beijing, Chongqing, Shanghai, Shenyang.

2 TRANSLATION AND RADIO BROADCAST MONITORING SERVICES AND SERIALS

Current Background
  US Hong Kong Consulate-General.
Extracts from China Mainland Magazines
  US Hong Kong Consulate General.
Joint Publications Research Services
  Washington D.C.

Bibliography

Federal Broadcasting Information Service (Section on China)
    Washington D.C., USA
News from Chinese Provincial Radio Stations
    UK Foreign Office, Regional Office, Hong Kong'
Summary of World Broadcasts (Far East Section)
    BBC, Reading, England.
Survey of China Mainland Magazines
    US Hong Kong Consulate-General.
Survey of China Mainland Magazines, Supplement
    US Hong Kong Consulate-General.
Survey of the China Mainland Press
    US Hong Kong Consulate-General.
Survey of the China Mainland Press, Supplement
    US Hong Kong Consulate-General.
Transcripts of PRC provincial broadcasts monitored by China News Agency
    (Taiwan)
    Taiwan, Republic of China.

3 ARTICLES

Boorman, H. L. 'Teng Hsiao-p'ing: a political profile' in *The China Quarterly* No. 21.
Chang Jui-nien 'On the Paochi-Chengtu Railway' in *People's China* No. 18, 1956, 16
    September 1956.
Chang, P. 'Decentralization of Power' in *Problems of Communism* Vol. 21, No. 4, 1972.
Chang, P. 'Provincial Party Leaders' Strategies for Survival during the Cultural
    Revolution' in R. Scalapino (ed.) *Elites in the People's Republic of China* University of
    Washington Press, London, 1972.
Chang, P. 'Research Notes on the Changing Loci of Decision Making in the CCP' in
    The China Quarterly No. 44.
Chang Yiu-sung '13 years in Chungking' in *China Reconstructs* No. 3, 1952.
Cheng Te-k'un 'An Early History of Szechwan' in *The Journal of West China Border
    Research Society* Vol. 16, 1945.
Ch'in Ti 'The Government System in Mainland China in 1967' in *Communist China
    1967* Union Research Institute, Hong Kong, 1968.
Crick, B 'The Elementary Types of Government' in *Government and Opposition* Vol. 3,
    No. 1, 1968.
Crook, F. W. 'The Commune System in the People's Republic of China' in *China: A
    Reassessment of the Economy* Report to Joint Economic Committee, 94th US
    Congress, 1st session, US Government Printing Office, Washington, D.C., 1975.
Dan Wei 'Commune Run Industries: Hongguang Commune' in *Cai jing kexue*
    (Financial and Economic Sciences) No. 3, 1959.
Donnithorne, A. 'Central Economic Control in China' in R. Adams (ed.) *Contemporary
    China* Peter Owen, London, 1969.
Donnithorne, A. 'Centralization and Decentralization in China's Fiscal Management'
    in *The China Quarterly* No. 66.
Donnithorne, A. 'China's Cellular Economy: Trends since the Cultural Revolution' in
    The China Quarterly No. 52.

Bibliography

Dreyer, J. T. 'Autonomy in the Northwest' in *Current Scene* (Hong Kong) Vol. 12, No. 8, September 1974.

Eberhard. W. 'Chinese Regional Stereotypes' in *Asian Survey* Vol. v, No. 12, 1965.

Echols, J. M. 'Politics, Budgets and Regional Equality in Communist and Capitalist Systems' in *Comparative Political Studies* Vol. 8, No. 3.

Falkenheim, V. C. 'Continuing Central Predominance' in *Problems of Communism* Vol. 21, No. 4, 1972.

Falkenheim, V. C. 'Provincial Leadership in Fukien, 1949–66, in R. Scalapino (ed.) *Elites in the People's Republic of China* University of Washington Press, London, 1972.

Falkenheim, V. C. 'Decentralization Revisited: A Maoist Perspective' in *Current Scene* (Hong Kong) Vol. 16, No. 1, 1978.

Fei Xiaotong 'Minority Groups in Guizhou Province' in *Zhongguo yuekan* (China Monthly) December, 1951.

Field, R. M. 'Chinese Provincial Population Data' in *The China Quarterly* No. 44.

Field, R., Lardy, N. and Emerson, P. 'Industrial Output by Province in China, 1949–1973' in *The China Quarterly* No. 63.

Fincher, J. 'Political Provincialism and the National Revolution' in M. Wright (ed.) *China in Revolution: The First Phase 1900–1913* Yale University Press, London, 1968.

Furniss, N. 'The Practical Significance of Decentralization' in *Journal of Politics* Vol. 36, 1964.

Goodman, D. S. G. 'The Provincial First Party Secretary in the People's Republic of China 1949–1978: A Profile' in *The British Journal of Political Science* Vol. 10, No. 1, 1980.

Gordon, L. 'Economic Regionalism Reconsidered' in *World Politics* Vol. 13, No. 2, 1961.

Gottman, J. 'The Political Partitioning of our World: an attempt at analysis' in *World Politics* Vol. 4, 1952.

Hartshorne, R. 'The Functional Approach in Political Geography' in *Annals of the Association of American Geographers* Vol. 40, 1950.

'Basic Summary of Accurate Statistics on the Establishment of Communes in Sichuan' in *Jihua yu tongji* (Planning and Statistics) No. 2, 1960.

Klein, D. 'The State Council and the Cultural Revolution' in *The China Quarterly* No. 35.

Klein, D. and Hager, L. 'The Ninth Central Committee' in *The China Quarterly* No. 45.

Ko Jun-sheng 'Some Experiences in Developing Local Industry in Nanchung' in *600 Million Build Industry* Foreign Languages Press, 1958.

Kwang, C. W. 'The Budgetary System of the People's Republic of China: a preliminary survey' in *Public Finance* No. 4, 1963.

Lang, N. R. 'The Dialectics of Decentralization: economic reform and regional inequality in Yugoslavia' in *World Politics* Vol. 27, No. 3, 1975.

Lardy, N. 'Centralization and Decentralization in China's Fiscal Management' in *The China Quarterly* No. 61.

Levenson, J. 'The Province, the Nation, and the World: the problem of Chinese identity' in A. Feuerwerker, R. Murphy, M. Wright (eds) *Approaches to Modern History* California, 1967.

Lewis, J. W. 'The Leadership Doctrine of the Chinese Communist Party: the lesson of the People's Commune' in *Asian Survey* Vol. III, October 1963.

Bibliography

Li Ching-chuan 'The People's Communes are the Inevitable Outcome of China's Social Development' in *Ten Glorious Years* Foreign Languages Press, Peking, 1970.

Li Shih-fei 'The Party's Middlemen' in *Current Scene* (Hong Kong) Vol. III, 15 August 1965.

Li Xijie 'People's Communes – the best form for the transition of our country from Socialism to Communism' in *Sichuan Daxue Xuebao: Shehui kexue* (Journal of Sichuan University: Social Sciences) No. 3, 1959.

Lin Chao 'The Qinling and DaBaShan as a Barrier to Communications between Sichuan and the Northwestern Provinces' in *Dili xuebao* (Geographical Studies) Vol. XIV, December 1947.

MacFarquhar, R. 'Communist China's Intra-Party Dispute' in *Pacific Affairs* Vol. XXXI, No. 4, December 1958.

MacFarquhar, R. 'Problems of Liberalization and the Succession at the 8th Party Congress' in *The China Quarterly* No. 56.

McColl, R. W. 'Development of Supra-Provincial Administrative Regions in Communist China, 1949–1960' in *Pacific Viewpoint* Vol. VI, No. 1, 1963.

Michael, F. 'Regionalism in Nineteenth Century China' in University of Washington, *Modern Chinese History Project* Far Eastern and Russian Institute, Reprint No. 12.

Moody, P. 'Policy and Power: The Career of T'ao Chu, 1956–66' in *The China Quarterly* No. 54.

Okensberg, M. 'Paths to Leadership in Communist China' in *Current Scene* (Hong Kong) Vol. III, No. 24, 1 August 1965.

Oksenberg, M. 'Local Government and Politics in China, 1955–8' in A. W. Cordier (ed.) *Columbia Essays in International Affairs* Columbia University Press, New York, 1967, Vol. II.

Oksenberg, M. and Yeung, S. 'Hua Kuo-feng's pre-Cultural Revolution Hunan Years, 1949–1966: The making of a political generalist' in *The China Quarterly* No. 69.

Perkins, D. H. 'Centralization and de-Centralization in Mainland China's Agriculture, 1949–1962' in *Quarterly Journal of Economics* Vol. LXXVII, May, 1964.

Portes, R. D. 'The Strategy and Tactics of Economic Decentralization' in *Soviet Studies* Vol. XXIII, No. 4, 1972.

Schram, S. R. 'The Cultural Revolution in Historical Perspective' in S. R. Schram (ed.) *Authority, Participation, and Cultural Change in China* Cambridge University Press, Cambridge, 1973.

Schram, S. R. 'Some Recent Studies of Revolutionary Movements in China in the Early Twentieth Century' in *The Bulletin, School of Oriental and African Studies*, Vol. 35, 1972.

Sichuan Finance College 'The Virtues of Production Based on the Three-level Ownership System: LongMen commune, Wusheng xian' in *Jiongji yanjiu* (Economic Research) No. 1, 1961.

Skinner, G. W. 'Aftermath of Communist Liberation in the Chengtu Plain' in *Pacific Affairs*, Vol. 24, No. 1, March 1951.

Spencer, J. E. 'Kueichou: An internal Chinese colony' in *Pacific Affairs* Vol. 13, No. 2, 1940.

Steward, P. D. 'Attitudes of Regional Soviet Political Leaders: Towards Understand-

Bibliography

ing the Potential for Change' in M. G. Hermann (ed.) *A Psychological Examination of Political Leaders* The Free Press, New York, 1977.

R. T., 'One Night in Chungking' in *Blackwood's Magazine* May, 1934.

Teiwes, F. C. 'Chinese Politics 1949–1965: A Changing Mao' in *Current Scene* (Hong Kong) Vol. XII, Nos. 1 and 2, 1974.

Teiwes, F. C. 'Provincial Politics in China, Themes and Variations' in J. M. Lindbeck (ed.) *China: Management of a Revolutionary Society* University of Washington Press, Seattle, 1971.

Teiwes, F. C. 'The Purge of Provincial Leaders, 1957–1958' in *The China Quarterly* No. 27, July 1966.

Tang Tsou 'Prolegomenon to the Study of Informal Group in CCP Politics' in *The China Quarterly* No. 65.

Vogel, E. 'From Revolutionary to semi-bureaucrat: the regularization of cadres' in *The China Quarterly* No. 29.

Vogel, E. 'From Friendship to Comradeship: The Change in Personal Relationships in China' in *The China Quarterly* No. 21.

Vogel, E. 'Land Reform in Kwangtung 1951–1953: Central Control and Localism' in *The China Quarterly* No. 38.

Walker, K. R. 'Collectivization in Retrospect: The "Socialist High Tide" of Autumn 1955–Spring 1956' in *The China Quarterly* No. 26.

Walker, K. 'Organization of Agricultural Production' in Eckstein, Galenson, and Liu (eds) *Economic Trends in Communist China* Aldine Press, Chicago, 1968.

Wan, K. 'Industrial Development in Szechwan' in *Chinese Economic Journal* Vol. XV, December 1934.

Whang, P. K. 'Szechwan: The Hotbed of Civil Wars' in *China Weekly Review* 22 October 1932.

Wiens, H. 'The "Shu Tao" or Road to Szechwan' in *Geographical Review* Vol. XXXIX, 1949.

White III, L. T. 'Leadership in Shanghai, 1955–69' in R. Scalapino (ed.) *Elites in the People's Republic of China* University of Washington Press, London, 1972.

Whitson, W. 'The Field Army in Chinese Communist Military Politics' in *The China Quarterly* No. 37.

Wright, V. 'Regionalization under the 5th French Republic: The Triumph of the Functional Approach' in L. J. Sharpe (ed.) *Decentralist Trends in Western Democracies* Sage, London, 1979.

Yan Hongyan 'On Sichuan's Agricultural Development' in *Renmin ribao* (*People's Daily*) 4 July 1957.

Yang Chao 'A New Event: Experiences in Implementing the "3 fixed and one substitution" system of labour in Sichuan' in *Hongqi* (*Red Flag*) No. 2, 1965.

Yi Hsiao-hua 'General Conditions in Communist-controlled Southwest China' in *Communist China, 1960* Union Research Institute, Hong Kong, 1962, Vol. 2.

Yu Hong 'Arrangements of Personnel in the Sub-bureaux of the CCP's Central Committee' in *Zuguo zhoukan* (*The Fatherland Monthly*, Hong Kong) No. 552, 5 August 1963.

Zhang Huchen 'The Great Achievements of Fiscal Administration in Sichuan during the Last Decade' in *Caizheng* (*Financial Administration*) No. 19, 9 October 1959.

Zhang Limin 'Special Features in the Changes of Administrative Areas in China' in *Zhengfa yanjiu* (Political and Legal Research) No. 5, 1956.

Bibliography

Zhang Pengnian 'The Circumstances of the 1911 Revolution in Guizhou' in *Xinhai geming huiyi lu* (Reminiscences of the 1911 Revolution) China Publishers, Beijing, 1962, Vol. 3.

Zhao Xiding 'The provincial political system in the Qing dynasty' in *Lishi yanjiu* (*Historical Research*) No. 3, 1980.

Zhou Lin 'Construction of Guizhou – "The Mountain Land"' in *Zhongguo qingnian* (*China Youth*) No. 1, 1 January 1960.

4 BOOKS

Afanas'yeakiy, Ye.A. *Szechwan* Publishing House of Oriental Literature, Moscow, 1962: translated in *JPRS* 15,308 (17 September 1962).

Aird, J. S. *Population Estimates for the Provinces of the People's Republic of China: 1953 to 1974* Bureau of Economic Analysis, US Department of Commerce, Washington D. C., 1974.

Ahn, B. *Chinese Politics and the Cultural Revolution* University of Washington Press, London, 1976.

Armstrong, J. A. *The Soviet Bureaucratic Elite* Praeger, New York, 1959.

Alley, R. *China's Hinterland in the Leap Forward* New World Press, Peking, 1961.

Barnett, A. D. *Cadres, Bureaucracy and Political Power in Communist China* Columbia University Press, New York, 1967.

Barnett, A. D. *China on the Eve of Communist Takeover* Praeger, New York, 1963.

Barnett, A. D. *Communist China: The Early Years, 1949–55* Pall Mall Press, London, 1964.

Barnett, A. D. *Local Government in Szechwan* Institute of Current World Affairs, New York, 1948.

Barth, F. *Ethnic Groups and Boundaries – the Social Organization of Cultural Difference* Universitetsforlaget, Oslo, 1969.

Baum, R. *Prelude to Revolution* Columbia University Press, London, 1975.

Baum, R. and Teiwes, F. C. *Ssu-ch'ing: The Socialist Education Movement of 1962–1966* Centre for Chinese Studies, Berkeley, 1968.

Beauclair, I. de *Tribal Cultures of South West China* Sun Yatsen University, Taipei, 1970.

Bowie, R. R. and Fairbank, J. K. (eds) *Communist China 1955–1959* Harvard University Press, Cambridge (Mass.), 1965.

Brugger, B. *Contemporary China* Croom Helm, London, 1977.

Buck, J. L. *An Agricultural Survey of Szechwan province, China* Institute of Pacific Relations, New York, 1943.

Campbell, A. et al. (ed.) *The American Voter* John Wiley & Sons, New York, 1964.

Chang, P. *Patterns and Processes of Policy-making in Communist China, 1955–1962: Three Case Studies* Ph.D. dissertation, Columbia University, 1969.

Chang, P. *Power and Policy in China*, Pennsylvania State University Press, University Park, Pa., 1978.

Chao, Kang *Agricultural Production in Communist China, 1949–1965* University of Wisconsin Press, London, 1970.

Chao Kuo-chun *Agrarian Policy of the Chinese Communist Party, 1921–59* Asian Publishing House, London, 1960.

Chen, C. and Ridley, C. *Rural People's Communes in Lien-chiang* Hoover Institution, Stanford, 1969.

Bibliography

Chen, Nai-ruenn *Chinese Economic Statistics* Edinburgh University Press, Edinburgh, 1967.

Chi Ch'ao-ting *Key Economic Areas in Chinese History* George Allen & Unwin, London, 1936.

Ch'u T'ung-tsu *Local Government in China under the Ch'ing* Stanford University Press, Stanford, 1969.

Committee on Economy of China *Provincial Agricultural Statistics for Communist China* SSRC, New York, 1969.

Cressey, G. B. *China's Geographic Foundations* McGraw-Hill, New York, 1934.

Cressey, G. B. *Land of the Five Hundred Million* McGraw-Hill, New York, 1955.

Crick, B. *In Defence of Politics* Penguin, Harmondsworth, 1964.

Dikshit, R. D. *The Political Geography of Federalism* Macmillan, Delhi, 1975.

Domes, J. *Socialism in the Chinese Countryside* Hurst, London, 1980.

Donnithorne, A. *The Budget and the Plan in China* Contemporary China Papers No. 3, Australian National University, Canberra, 1972.

Donnithorne, A. *China's Economic System* George Allen & Unwin, London, 1967.

Etzioni, A. *Political Unification* Holt, Rhinehart, Winston, New York, 1965.

Field, R., Lardy, N., Emerson, P. *Provincial Industrial Output in the People's Republic of China: 1949–1975* Foreign Economic Report No. 12, Bureau of Economic Analysis, US Department of Commerce, Washington DC, 1976.

Foreign Language Press *Decision on Agricultural Cooperation* Peking, 1956.

Foreign Languages Press *Eighth National Congress of the Communist Party of China* 3 vols. Peking, 1956.

Foreign Languages Press *People's Communes in China* Peking, 1958.

Foreign Languages Press *Socialist Upsurge in China's Countryside* Peking, 1957.

Friedrich, C. and Brzezinski, Z. *Totalitarian Dictatorship and Autocracy* Harvard University Press, Cambridge (Mass.), 1956.

Goodman, D. S. G. *Research Guide to Chinese Provincial and Regional Newspapers* Contemporary China Institute, Research Notes and Studies No. 2, London, 1976.

Gottmann, J. *The Significance of Territory* University of Virginia Press, Charlottesville, 1973.

Gottman, J. (ed.) *Centre and Periphery: Spatial Variation in Politics* Sage, London, 1980.

He Qiwu *Shinianlai zhi Guizhousheng jianshe* (*Construction in Guizhou Province During the Last Decade*) Nanjing Publishing House, Nanjing, 1947.

Hosie, A. *Three Years in Western China* George Philip & Son, London, 1890.

Hosie, A. *Szechwan; its Products, Industries and Resources* Kelly & Walsh, Shanghai, 1922.

Hsia, T. S. *The Commune in Retreat as Evidenced in Terminology and Semantics* Studies in Chinese Communist Terminology No. 11, Centre for Chinese Studies, Institute of International Studies, University of California, Berkeley, 1964.

Institute for International Relations *Chinese Communist Who's Who* 2 Vols., Taipei, 1970.

Institute for International Relations *Classified Chinese Communist Documents: A Selection* National Chengchi University, Taipei, 1978.

Jackson, W. A. D. *Politics and Geographic Relationships: Readings in the Nature of Political Geography* Prentice-Hall, New Jersey, 1964.

Jacques, E. *A General Theory of Bureaucracy* Heinemann, London, 1976.

Johnson, H. *The Upsurge of China* New World Press, Peking, 1961.

Kapp, R. A. *Szechwanese Provincial Militarism and Central Power in Republican China* Yale University, Ph.D., 1970. University Microfilms, Ann Arbor.

Bibliography

Kapp, R. A. *Szechwan and the Chinese Republic: Provincial Militarism and Central Power, 1911–1938* Yale University Press, New Haven, 1973.

Klein, D. and Clark, A. *Biographic Dictionary of Chinese Communism* 2 Vols., Harvard University Press, Cambridge (Mass.) 1965.

Kuo, L. *Agriculture in the PRC: Structural Change and Technical Transformation* Praeger, London, 1976.

Lardy, N. *Economic Growth and Distribution in China* Cambridge University Press, Cambridge, 1978.

Li Jingquan *Duanlian liyang yu zuofeng (Strengthen attitude and workstyle)* Zhongguo chubanshe, Hong Kong, 1948.

Liao Kai-hung *From Yenan to Peking* Foreign Language Press, Peking, 1954.

Lieberthal, K. *A Research Guide to Central Party and Government Meetings in China, 1949–1975* International Arts and Science Press, White Plains, New York, 1976.

Little, A. J. *Through the Yang-tze Gorges or Trade and Travel in Western China* Sampson Low, Marston, Searle & Rivington, London, 1890.

Lipset, S. M. *Political Man* Heinemann, London, 1960.

Lu Baoqian *Zhongguo shidi xianlun (A general discussion of China's historical geography)* Taibei, 1962.

MacFarquhar, R. *The Origins of the Cultural Revolution*, Volume 1: *Contradictions among the People, 1956–1957* Oxford University Press, London, 1974.

Machin, H. *The Prefect in French Public Administration* Croom Helm, London, 1977.

Mao Tsetung (Mao Zedong) *Selected Works*, Vols. I–V Foreign Languages Press, Peking.

Mao Zedong *Mao Zedong sixiang wansui (Long Live Mao Zedong Thought!)* 4 volumes of Mao's speeches and writing not published officially, 1967 and 1969.

Marsh, R. M. *The Mandarins: The Circulation of Elites in China, 1600–1900* The Free Press, Glencoe, Ill., 1961.

Moody, P. *The Politics of the Eighth Central Committee of the Communist Party of China* The Shoe String Press, Hamden, Connecticut, 1973.

Perleberg, M. *Who's Who in Modern China* Ye Olde Printerie, Hong Kong, 1954.

Richthofen, F. von *Tagebücher aus China* 2 Vols. Dietrich Reiner, Berlin, 1907.

Richthofen, F. von *Baron von Richthofen's Letters, 1870–1872* North China Herald, Shanghai, 1873.

Roxby, P. M. (ed.) *China Proper* Great Britain Naval Intelligence Division, Geographical Handbook Series, London (HMSO), 1944.

Sadek, S. E. M. *The Balance Point Between Local Autonomy and National Control* Mouton, The Hague, 1972.

Schattschneider, E. E. *The Semisovereign People* Holt, Rinehart, Winston, London, 1960.

Schram, S. R. (ed.) *Mao Tse-tung Unrehearsed* Penguin, Middx., 1974.

Schram, S. R. *The Political Thought of Mao Tse-tung* Penguin, Harmondsworth, Middx., 1969 (2nd edition).

Schram, Peter *The Development of Chinese Agriculture, 1950–1959* Chicago University Press, Chicago, 1961.

Schurmann, H. F. *Ideology and Organization in Communist China* University of California Press, Berkeley, 1968 (2nd Edition).

Shabad, T. *China's Changing Map* Praeger, New York, 1972.

Shi Jingtang et al. (ed.) *Zhongguo nongye hezuohua yundong Shiliao (Historical Materials on*

Bibliography

China's Agricultural Co-operativization Movement) 2 Vols. Sanlian Shudian, Beijing, 1959.

Smedley, A. *The Great Road: The Life and Times of Chu Teh* Monthly Review Press, London, 1972.

Solinger, D. J. *Regional Government and Political Integration in Southwest China, 1949–1954* University of California Press, Berkeley, 1977.

Solomon, R. *Mao's Revolution and the Chinese Political Culture* University of California Press, Berkeley, 1971.

Swatz, M. J. (ed.) *Local-Level Politics* University of London Press, London, 1968.

Stanford China Project *South West China* Human Relations Area Files Inc., New Haven, 1956.

Sun Jingzhi et al. *Xinan diqu jingji dili (An Economic Geography of Southwest China)* Kexue chubanshe, Beijing, 1960.

Teiwes, F. C. *Policies and Purges in China* Dawson, Folkestone, 1979.

Teiwes, F. C. *Provincial Party Personnel in Mainland China, 1956–1966* East Asian Institute, Columbia University, New York, 1967.

Tien Hung-mao *Government and Politics in Kuomintang China 1927–1937* Stanford University Press, Stanford, 1972.

Truman, D. *The Government Process* Knopf, New York, 1957.

Union Research Institute *Communist China, 1949–1959* Hong Kong, 1961.

Union Research Institute *Who's Who in Communist China* Hong Kong, 1966.

Union Research Institute *Who's Who in Communist China* 2 Vols. Hong Kong, 1969 and 1970.

Union Research Institute *Documents of the Chinese Communist Party Central Committee, September 1956–April 1969* 2 Vols. Hong Kong, 1971.

United States Consulate-General *Agricultural Attaché Report on Mainland China* Hong Kong, 1967.

Vogel, E. *Canton under Communism* Harper & Row, New York, 1971.

Watt, J. R. *The District Magistrate in Late Imperial China* Columbia University Press, New York, 1972.

Whitney, J. B. R. *China: Area, Administration and Nation Building* University of Chicago, Department of Chicago Research Paper No. 123, Chicago, 1970.

Whitson, W. *The Chinese High Command* Macmillan, London, 1973.

Wiles, P. J. *The Political Economy of Communism* Blackwell, Oxford, 1962.

Wu Yuan-li *The Spatial Economy of China* Praeger, New York, 1967.

Yang Dingsheng *Sichuan lishi (A History of Sichuan)* Zhejiang State University Press, Chengdu, 1942.

Zhang Xiaomei *Guizhou jingji (The Economy of Guizhou)* Southwest Economy Reprint No. 2, Republic of China Economic Research Institute, 1939.

Zhang Xiaomei *Sichuan jingji cankao ziliao (Reference Materials on the Economy of Sichuan)* Republic of China, Economic Research Institute, Chongqing, 1939.

Zhengfu gongzuo baogao huibian 1950 (1950 Collection of Government Work Reports) People's Publishing House, Beijing, 1951.

Zhonggong zhongyang bangongting *Zhongguo gongchandang dibaci quanguo daibiao dahui wenxian (Documents of the 8th National Congress of the CCP)* Beijing, 1957.

Zhonggong zhongyang bangongting *Zhongguo noncun de shehui zhuyi gaochao (The Socialist 'High Tide' in China's Countryside)* 3 Vols. Beijing, 1956.

Zhonghua renmin gongheguo fensheng dituji (A Provincial Atlas of the People's Republic of China) Map Publishing House, Beijing, 1974.

Bibliography

Zhou Fang *Woguo guojia jigou* (*Our Country's State Organization*) China Youth Publishing House, Beijing, 1955.

Zhou Lisan et al. *Sichuan jingji dituji* (*An Economic Atlas of Sichuan*) Nanjing, 1946.

Zuguo de Guizhou (*Guizhou of the Fatherland*) Guizhou People's Publishing House, Guiyang, 1955.

INDEX